VERGIL

A LEGAMUS

TRANSITIONAL READER

THE LEGAMUS READER SERIES

edited by

Kenneth F. Kitchell Jr., University of Massachusetts Amherst,
and Thomas Sienkewicz, Monmouth College

The *LEGAMUS* series was created to address the needs of today's students as they move from "made up" Latin to the Latin of real authors who lived over two thousand years ago. Both established and innovative pedagogical techniques are employed to ease the problems facing students as they begin to read authentic Latin authors. At its core, the series intends to facilitate **reading** before all else, and the many innovations in the series all stem from a single question: "What makes reading this author difficult for students?"

The series is intended for use in intermediate and upper-level Latin courses in both college and high school. Volumes in the series may be used individually as an introduction to a given author or together to form an upper-division reading course.

Published

Vergil: A LEGAMUS Transitional Reader
THOMAS J. SIENKEWICZ & LEAANN A. OSBURN

Catullus: A LEGAMUS Transitional Reader
KENNETH F. KITCHELL JR. & SEAN SMITH

Ovid: A LEGAMUS Transitional Reader
CAROLINE PERKINS & DENISE DAVIS-HENRY

Forthcoming

Horace: A LEGAMUS Transitional Reader
RONNIE ANCONA & DAVID J. MURPHY

Cicero: A LEGAMUS Transitional Reader
JUDITH SEBESTA & MARK HAYNES

VERGIL

A LEGAMUS
TRANSITIONAL READER

THOMAS J. SIENKEWICZ
& LEAANN A. OSBURN

Bolchazy-Carducci Publishers, Inc.
Wauconda, Illinois USA

Series Co-Editors:
Kenneth F. Kitchell and Thomas J. Sienkewicz

General Editor
LeaAnn A. Osburn

Cover Design & Typography:
Adam Philip Velez

Cover Illustration:
Jean Baptiste Joseph Wicar, French in Italy, 1762–1834, Virgil Reading the "Aeneid" to Augustus, Octavia and Livia, 1790–93, oil on canvas, 111.1 x 142.6 cm, Wirt D. Walker Fund, 1963.258
Reproduction, The Art Institute of Chicago.

Map Page Illustration:
William Urban

Laocoon Illustration:
Drawing by Julia Sienkewicz

LEGAMUS Transitional Reader Series
Vergil: A LEGAMUS Transitional Reader

Thomas J. Sienkewicz and LeaAnn A. Osburn

Bolchazy-Carducci Publishers, Inc.
Wauconda, Illinois 60084
www.bolchazy.com

Printed in the United States of America
2008
by United Graphics

ISBN 978-0-86516-578-6

Library of Congress Cataloging-in-Publication Data

Sienkewicz, Thomas J.
  Vergil : a Legamus transitional reader / Thomas J. Sienkewicz & LeaAnn A. Osburn.
    p. cm. -- (Legamus transitional reader series)
  English; selected texts in Latin.
  Includes 11 passages covering 197 lines from Virgil's Aeneis, books 1, 2, and 4.
  ISBN 0-86516-578-5 (pbk.)
  1. Latin language--Readers. 2. Aeneas (Legendary character)--Problems, exercises, etc. 3. Epic poetry,
Latin--Problems, exercises, etc. I. Osburn, LeaAnn A. II. Virgil. Aeneis. Selections. III. Title. IV. Series.

PA2095.S495 2004
478.6'2421--dc22

2004010648

TABLE OF CONTENTS

APPENDIX:

INDEX:

LIST OF ILLUSTRATIONS

FOREWORD

The LEGAMUS Transitional Reader Series

The transition from the "made-up Latin" of today's popular Latin textbooks for first and second year Latin students to the "real" Latin of ancient authors represents one of the major hurdles facing today's Latin students and one of the greatest challenges facing us as teachers. In fact, somewhere during the early stages of a student's first encounter with "real" Latin, the student comes to realize that he or she cannot translate upper division authors with anything resembling fluency. While the frustration of the teacher is great, that of the student is even greater and it is little wonder that in most schools the drop-off in enrollment between Latin II and Latin III is astronomical.

The LEGAMUS Committee, sponsored by Bolchazy-Carducci Publishers, was created to study this problem. From its inception, the committee included both college/university and high/middle school Latin teachers and studied the many problems related to this transition for several years. Members of the committee presented panels and obtained teacher feedback at ACL and CAMWS meetings alike where suggestions from teachers in the audience did much to help us form our plans.

Briefly put, the committee's studies have made clear the following facts. First, to move from the controlled world of an elementary Latin program to the unpredictable world of an actual author is to take a quantum leap that is unparalleled in the students' experience and demands a much wider set of skills than is generally recognized. Students must move from a world of controlled plot line, familiar and recurring characters, repetitive vocabulary, and fairly straightforward word order into a realm where the author does exactly what he wants and does so in elevated language and, often enough, meter. Add expanded vocabulary, rhetorical word order, stylistic quirks of various authors, and the issue of cultural literacy and it is little wonder that modern students often quickly become frustrated in upper division Latin.

Yet, whereas the new generation of elementary textbooks changed radically over the past two to three decades, textbooks which make the transition into reading "real" Latin have lagged behind. They rarely go beyond the now common strategy of having notes and vocabulary on the same page or facing the text (a "trick" as old as the age of manuscripts).

Ironically, this transition was less of a problem before the field changed. It was formerly a universal that after a year of grammar all students would move on to Caesar. Thus, several excellent transitional books were created which gradually and effectively introduced the student to Caesar's vocabulary, style, and syntax. *Fabulae Faciles* is but one example. Today, however, since the upper division curricula are quite varied, a new set of transitional readers is required.

This volume is one in a series of *LEGAMUS* transitional Latin readers designed to facilitate the transition from beginning Latin to reading a major Latin author. Each volume concentrates on the specific problems faced by beginning readers of that particular author. The peculiarities of a Ciceronian sentence, for example, need not be taught in a Vergil transitional reader and teaching the vocabulary of love poetry would be pointless in a Cicero text.

We stress that the series is not intended to produce just another annotated edition of the author. It is not an exhaustive teaching edition of the author. Instead, its purpose is expressly and solely to address those very things which make the transition to reading a given author difficult. Other issues, for example literary interpretation or the niceties of scansion, can wait for the actual course in an author —once the student can actually read that author! The premise is as simple as it is important—identify the specific hurdles a student must clear to be able to read a given author and then teach them skills to address each issue.

Here, then, is an overview of the series.

1. Each volume is designed to be used at the point of transition from elementary texts to advanced texts, i.e., at the point when students move from learning grammar and reading made-up texts to reading authentic Latin.

2. The goal of each volume is to enable students to read the unchanged text of that author in as short a time as possible.

3. Volumes are designed to be flexible and to fit into a variety of curricula at both the high school and college levels. They can thus be used individually as an introduction to a particular author but can also be used together in any combination to serve as the textbooks of a survey course.

Each volume is co-authored by a college teacher and a pre-collegiate teacher. Each volume is short, containing a limited number of readings, each one envisioned as a single night's assignment. Passages gradually increase in length and difficulty throughout the volume and gradually introduce the student to quirks of the author's style, vocabulary, grammatical preferences, diction, and the like.

Each reader uses a set tool kit of techniques designed for teaching the student how to read the given author. These include the following.

1. Pre-reading exercises in English or Latin help the student deal with the issue of culturally based impediments to understanding, addressing what E. D. Hirsch has called "cultural literacy." We would hope that the student can thus begin to read each passage predisposed to understand its contents and thus ready to concentrate solely on the language based hurdles it faces.

2. Frequently, before the student reads an unchanged passage, she or he is presented with a simplified, rearranged, or shortened Latin version of complex passages. Selections of poetry are often given first in a prose summary.

3. The Latin text of complex passages is, at first, often shown in innovative layout and with typography to enable students to see the individual sense units in complex sentences. Such techniques will be used liberally early on, but in every case the rearranged Latin version will be followed directly by the unchanged Latin text of the original. Moreover, the last section of each volume presents unchanged text only. By this time the student, one hopes, has become accustomed to the author's style.

4. There is frequent use of exercises designed to teach the author's favorite vocabulary and syntax.

5. Other exercises teach major stylistic preferences of the author.

6. Of course, traditional notes and vocabulary will accompany each passage and a brief grammar and full vocabulary are at the end of each volume.

To move into the world of "real" Latin really means to move into the world of high literature. Imagine having to read Dickens after two years of high school English! It is the hope of the authors and editors that this series will help ease this difficult transition and bring more students into direct contact with the beauty and inspiration reading these authors can provide.

Kenneth F. Kitchell Jr.
University of Massachusetts Amherst

PREFACE

HOW TO USE THIS READER

This reader is designed to help students make the transition from studying Latin grammar and "reading made-up Latin" to reading an authentic ancient text. More advanced students who are reading Vergil's *Aeneid* for the first time may also find this reader a good introduction to the poet, his vocabulary and his style. Users of this reader are encouraged to interact with Vergil's text in a variety of ways, including grammatical examples and exercises, vocabulary drills, and pre-reading and comprehension questions, as well as translating. The purpose of this foreword is to explain some of the special features of this reader.

Included are eleven passages from the *Aeneid* I, II, and IV, covering 197 lines of the epic. The length of the passages increases gradually from eleven lines to twenty-four. While every group of students works at a different pace and it is difficult to anticipate how long it will take for a class to work through the entire reader, it should be emphasized that this reader is intended to be an introduction or a "taste" of Vergil rather than a full-semester or full-year book. Some teachers might use this reader in the last month of the academic year before Vergil will be read in the fall. Or this reader might be used at the beginning of an academic year or semester devoted to reading Vergil's *Aeneid*. Another model would be to use this reader in conjunction with the other volumes in the *LEGAMUS* series to introduce transitional readers to a variety of Roman authors.

In general we follow the text as it appears in Pharr's *Aeneid*. However, we use a consonantal "i" instead of a "j"; e.g. *iuvabit*, not *juvabit* at I, 203. We also use dashes where Pharr uses parentheses; e.g., —mīrābile dictū—not (mīrābile dictū) at I, 439.

The following paragraphs describe the format of the readings from Books I and II.

BEFORE YOU READ WHAT VERGIL WROTE

The reading passage from the *Aeneid* is introduced by a variety of pre-reading materials, including a short overview and background to the passage. Where necessary, cultural aspects of the reading that may be unfamiliar to the transitional student are introduced here. These explanations are designed to familiarize the users with the subject matter and to prepare them to read the text. They are not intended to provide the detailed textual analysis or scholarly discussion that students will find in more advanced readers. Often, in this introductory material students are asked questions based upon their own opinion and personal experience. These questions are designed to provide some context prior to reading, and a student should be able to respond to these questions even before looking at or translating the text.

This introduction is usually followed by a discussion of grammar or vocabulary related to the reading. Grammatical explanations are short and simple, with examples and practice exercises based upon the reading passage.

HELPING YOU TO READ WHAT VERGIL WROTE

In this section, a passage from the *Aeneid* is presented with a number of reading aids:

a. **Summary** This plot summary is designed to give the general context of the passage.

b. **Questions** These introductory grammar questions are to be answered before working through the passages. These questions direct attention towards basic structural features of the text (e.g., main verbs, subjects, adjective/noun agreement, etc.).

c. **Vocabulary** English meanings for all the Latin words appearing in the passage are found either in a running vocabulary list on the page facing the reading or in a vocabulary pullout in the back of the book. This pull-out (from Pharr's *Aeneid*) includes all words found twenty-four times or more in the first six books of the *Aeneid*. Any word not included on this pull-out is defined in the running vocabulary. This running vocabulary does not necessarily list all possible meanings of a word but focuses on the meanings most useful in understanding the Latin word in the context of the passage. Students do not need a separate dictionary to use this reader.

d. **Notes** The notes appear on the page facing the passage and are designed to aid in basic translation and comprehension. Material which provides enrichment and background, rather than essential information, does not appear in these notes. These notes contain no reference to meter or figures of speech.

e. **Visual Aids** Gapped words understood in Vergil's original Latin are inserted into the text in parentheses in order to assist in translation. Parentheses are also used here to indicate syncopated forms like *audī(v)erat*. Different fonts are used to show noun-adjective agreement and what words refer to one another. These special fonts are used only when the reader may need assistance. By the end of the book, the students read passages from the *Aeneid* without such visual aids. Macrons, however, are always used.

What Vergil Actually Wrote

In this section the same passage from the *Aeneid* is presented without the vocabulary or visual aids used in the first version. Notes on the facing page draw attention to stylistic questions and the difficulties of understanding plain text. These notes also illustrate Vergil's use of figures of speech.

After Reading What Vergil Wrote

Here important grammatical and stylistic features of Vergil's *Aeneid* in general, and of this reading passage in particular (e.g., gapping or understood words, compounding language, etc.), are discussed in more detail. These discussions may be accompanied by grammatical or vocabulary exercises.

The unit concludes with a number of discussion questions on content, plot, analysis, etc. These questions are based upon the actual text students have read; i.e., the questions can be answered without additional knowledge of Vergil or the *Aeneid*. A few analysis (i.e., AP-type) questions appear here. Questions may also be based upon material and topics introduced in the pre-reading section ("Before You Read What Vergil Wrote").

In the last four reading passages, i.e., the ones from Book IV, many of the special transitional aids found in the first part of the book are eliminated and the text is presented only in its traditional format. In this portion of the book there are no introductory grammar questions, no special fonts or gapped words in parentheses, and no plot summaries.

Grammatical Appendix

Following the last reading passage is an appendix that contains a summary of the forms and syntax of Latin grammar. While this material is based upon *Graphic Latin Grammar* (Wauconda, Ill.: Bolchazy-Carducci, 2002), every effort has been made to use words and examples appropriate to the *Aeneid*.

Although meter is not discussed in the body of this reader, the basic rules of quantity and versification are provided in the twelfth section of this appendix for the benefit of students and teachers who wish to consult them. This information (from Pharr's *Aeneid*) is accompanied by the scansion of the first seven lines of the *Aeneid* and some hints on the metrical reading of Latin poetry (also from Pharr).

The last section of this appendix is a list of figures of syntax and rhetoric from Pharr's appendix.

DEDICATION

NOSTRĪS DISCIPULĪS

ACKNOWLEDGEMENTS

The authors would like to thank a number of people who have offered help and suggestions as this reader was being written, including:

Ken Kitchell, Ginny Lindzey, Dwight Castro, Patty Lister and the other members of the LEGAMUS committee for inspiring this project;

Ken Kitchell for his help as co-editor of the LEGAMUS Transitional Reader Series;

Tom Sienkewicz' Fall 2002 Latin Directed Readings class at Monmouth College for early feedback and ideas;

Bill Urban for his map;

Julia Sienkewicz for her artwork;

Laurie Jolicoeur and Rebecca Wick for field testing the reader in their classes and to them and their students for their helpful comments;

Michelle Wu for her suggestions regarding the pre-reading material;

audiences at CANE 2002, ACL 2002 and 2003, CAMWS 2003, and Luther College in Decorah, Iowa, for their helpful comments;

Bev McGuire for her careful word processing;

Alexander G. McKay and Matthew Sparapani for their peer reading and suggestions;

Vicki Wine, Jim Betts, and Marty Pickens for their meticulous proofreading;

Laurie Haight Keenan and Elisa Denja for their help in moving this book through the editorial process;

Mark Ducar Sr. and Anne W. Sienkewicz for their loyal support and patient endurance of long and late night phone calls;

and, especially, Lou and Marie Bolchazy for their faith in this book and for their encouragement in difficult times.

KEY

Actium, -iī, n. A promontory in western Greece near which Augustus defeated Antony and Cleopatra in a naval battle in 31 BC

Āfrica, -ae, f. Africa, the territory around Carthage

Asia, -ae, f. Asia (Minor), the Roman province in western Turkey

Athēnae, -ārum, f. pl. Athens, the capital of Attica in Greece

Campānia, -ae, f. Campania, a region of central Italy south of Rome

Carthāgo, Carthāginis, f. Carthage, the city of Dido

Charybdis, Charybdis, f. Charybdis, a dangerous whirlpool opposite the rock of Scylla in the straits between Italy and Sicily

Crēta, -ae, f. Crete

Cūmae, -ārum, f. pl. Cumae, an ancient city of Campania, where Aeneas meets the Sibyl

Cyclopum Orae, Cyclopum Orārum, f. pl. the shores of the Cyclopes, the one-eyed monsters

Ēpīrus, -ī, f. A country on the west coast of Greece, in present-day Albania, where Aeneas visits Andromache and Helenus

Graecia, -ae, f. Greece

Hellespontus, -ī, m. the Hellespont, the body of water between the Aegean Sea and the Black Sea, also known as the Dardanelles

Ītalia, -ae, f. Italy

Lāvīnium, -iī, n. Lavinium, a town in Latium founded by Aeneas and named after his wife Lavinia

Lȳdia, -ae, f. Lydia, a region in Asia Minor

Mare Aegaeum, Maris Aegaeī, n. the Aegean Sea

Mare Internum, Maris Internī, n. the Internal Sea, i.e., the Mediterranean Sea

Mare Iōnium, Maris Iōniī, n. the Ionian Sea, the sea between Italy and the Balkan coast

Mare Tyrrhēnum, Maris Tyrrhēnī, n. the Etruscan Sea, the sea between Italy and the islands of Corsica and Sardinia

Phrygia, -ae, f. Phrygia, a region in Asia Minor

Rōma, -ae, f. Rome, the main city of Latium, of Italy and of the Roman Empire

Rutulī, -ōrum, m. pl. the Rutilians, a people of ancient Latium ruled by Turnus, Aeneas' antagonist in the *Aeneid*

Scylla, -ae, f. Scylla, the dangerous rock opposite Charybdis in the straits between Italy and Sicily

Sicilia, -ae, f. Sicily, the island south of Italy

Tenedos, -ī, f. Tenedos, an island in the Aegean Sea near Troy

Troia, -ae, f. Troy, a city in Asia Minor; home of Aeneas

Note: Aeneas' voyage is marked by a dotted line.

JOURNEY OF AENEAS

·AN INTRODUCTION TO VERGIL·

VERGIL'S INFLUENCE

J.R.R. Tolkien's *Fellowship of the Ring*, George Lucas' *Star Wars* series, and other 20th-century adventure stories reveal a debt to Vergil in their heroic journeys and cosmic scale. Vergil's influence is also seen in Robert Frost's poem written for the inauguration of John F. Kennedy. In the 14th century the Florentine Dante consciously expressed his debt to Vergil in the creation of his masterpiece the *Divine Comedy* by making Vergil his guide through hell. John Milton's *Paradise Lost* also contains many Vergilian characteristics. Ovid's *Metamorphoses*, Lucan's *Pharsalia*, and other later Roman epics owe much of their language and structure to Vergil's epic. From the time it was written in the first century before Christ until today, Vergil's *Aeneid* has maintained a continuing influence upon other authors and on Western and world cultures.

But Vergil's influence has been felt not only by poets and authors but also by the many people who have read his epic for the past two thousand years. Students who read the *Aeneid* in school today are following in the footsteps of ancient Roman students who also studied the epic. The appeal of Vergil to such readers lies in the good adventure story well-told, the human hero Aeneas who struggles to reach his goal, and the timeless themes of fate, destiny, spurned love, and personal flaws.

As Rose Williams, author of the *Labors of Aeneas*, has written, "Vergil's *Aeneid* forms a priceless part of the cultural heritage of Western civilization. Vergil's flowing, spirited *Aeneid* remains one of the greatest literary works of all time. This multi-dimensional tapestry of Vergil's work has grandeur, tragedy, beauty, and strength. . . Vergil's poetry expresses in powerful and beautiful language the humanity that we share with *Aeneas*."

Many lines of the *Aeneid* have become proverbial. Here are a few examples:

Love
Quis fallere possit amantem? (IV, 296) Who can deceive a lover?
Agnōscō veteris vestīgia flammae. (IV, 23) I recognize the signs of an old flame.

Women
Dux fēmina factī. (I, 364) A woman was the leader of the deed.

The Gods and Rome
Tantaene animīs caelestibus īrae? (I, 11) Do divine minds have such great angers?
Tantae mōlis erat Rōmānam condere gentem. (I, 33) So huge a task was it to found the Roman state.
Ō passī graviōra, dabit deus hīs quoque fīnem (I, 99) O you having suffered more grievous things, god will give an end to these also.

War
Timeō Danaōs et dōna ferentīs. (II, 48) I fear the Greeks even bearing gifts.
Ūna salūs victīs nūllam spērāre salūtem. (II, 354) The one refuge for the conquered is to hope for no refuge.

Human Suffering and Endurance
Forsan et haec ōlim meminisse iuvābit. (I, 202) Perhaps it will be pleasing to remember even these things some day.
Sunt lacrimae rērum. (I, 462) These are the tears of things.
Possunt, quia posse videntur. (V, 231) They are able because they seem to be able.
Facilis dēscēnsus Avernō. (VI, 126) The descent to hell is easy.
Audentīs Fortūna iuvat. (X, 284) Fortune helps the daring.

The themes expressed in these quotations reflect both the subject matter and the philosophy of the *Aeneid*, in which Vergil confronts his readers with the power of love, the sufferings of war, and the resilience of the human spirit in the face of hardship. How many of these quotations reflect your own experiences?

Since many English translations of the *Aeneid* are available, why read the epic in Latin? To answer this question, let's compare just one line of the *Aeneid* in five translations:

> *Forsan et haec ōlim meminisse iuvābit.* (I, 203)

> Perhaps even these things some day it will be pleasing to remember. (a literal translation of the line)

> One day—who knows? —even these will be grand things to look back on. (Lewis, 1952)

> One day you may look back on these memories as pleasant memories. (Dickinson, 1961)

> Some day these memories, too, will bring a smile. (Copley, 1965)

> Some day, perhaps, remembering even this will be a pleasure. (Fitzgerald, 1981)

One reason to read the *Aeneid* in Latin is that no single translation captures the full meaning of Vergil's original. In this line Vergil emphasizes the uncertainty of what the future may bring by placing *forsan* (perhaps) as the first word in the line. Lewis's and Dickinson's translations place the emphasis instead on "One day" and likewise Copley and Fitzgerald emphasize "Some day." The uncertainty alluded to in "perhaps" is expressed by the more colloquial "who knows?" in Lewis's translation and by the word "may" in Dickinson's line. Copley's translation leaves out this word. Fitzgerald does use the word "perhaps" but places it after "Some day," and thereby reduces its impact.

By making the Latin word *iuvābit* the last word in the line, Vergil also stresses the idea that remembering these troubles will be pleasurable in the future. The idea of this pleasure is lost in Lewis' translation. Dickinson uses the word "pleasant" to convey this idea but stresses instead "memories." Fitzgerald uses the word "pleasure," places it last in the line of poetry, and thus comes closest to Vergil's meaning. Copley, like Vergil, stresses the idea of pleasure in his line but translates *iuvābit* as "bring a smile," which is a much more colloquial phrase, and thus the grandeur of Vergil's line is lost.

There are also other reasons to read the *Aeneid* in Latin. No translation can produce the beauty of the sound and rhythm of Vergil's Latin. The flow of the dactylic hexameter meter can only be hinted at in English. Nuances, allusions, word play, and figures of speech are usually lost in translation. In sum, by reading Vergil's *Aeneid* in Latin, the reader gains a greater depth of understanding what Rome's greatest poet wrote.

VERGIL'S LIFE

Vergil (Publius Vergilius Maro) was born on October 15, 70 BC near the Italian town of Mantua. Thus, like many other Latin authors, he was not Roman but Italian. Many of the details of the poet's life are uncertain. The ancient biographical tradition suggests that his father was rich enough to give his son an excellent education, first in Cremona and Milan and then in Rome. In the capital Vergil probably studied rhetoric and early Roman literature, including the works of the early 2nd-century BC Latin poet Ennius. While in Rome he also met the poet Catullus (c. 97–57 BC). Vergil appeared only once as a lawyer in a legal trial before he abandoned the law and moved to Naples, where he studied philosophy under the Epicurean Siro.

The tumultuous years following the assassination of Julius Caesar in 44 BC were difficult ones for all Romans, and Vergil was no exception. His father probably lost his property in the land confiscated for war veterans in 41 BC (The tradition that this property was later restored to the poet is unlikely.)

Vergil himself refers to the loss of this farm in his first major book of poems, the short pastoral poems called *Eclogues*, published in 37 BC. During this period, Vergil gained the attention of the wealthy Maecenas who became the poet's patron and introduced him to his powerful friend Octavian, later the emperor Augustus. Vergil, in turn, introduced his good friend, the poet Horace (65–8 BC), to Maecenas and Octavian. The trip to Brundisium by Vergil, Horace, and Maecenas, celebrated in Horace's Satire I.5, probably took place in 37 BC.

The *Eclogues* were followed by the longer *Georgics*, usually described as didactic farming poems, published in 30 BC. However, there is little practical advice in the *Georgics*, which are really a celebration of the joys of the rural life. In these poems, dedicated to Maecenas, Vergil tells the sad story of Orpheus and Eurydice.

After completing the *Eclogues*, Vergil may have taken a trip to Greece before beginning work on his masterpiece, the *Aeneid*, on which he worked for the rest of his life. In 19 BC Vergil began a tour of Greece and Asia, but, while in Athens, the poet was persuaded by the emperor Augustus to return to Italy with him. Vergil fell ill on the return voyage and died on September 20, 19 BC in the Italian city of Brundisium. He was buried in Naples in a tomb with the following inscription, which he himself is said to have composed on his deathbed:

> Mantua mē genuit, Calabrī rapuēre, tenet nunc
> Parthenopē; cecinī pascua rūra ducēs.

> Mantua bore me, the Calabrian verses [of Ennius] seized me, and now
> Naples holds me; I sang of shepherds, fields, leaders.

Vergil never married and left instructions that if the *Aeneid* remained unfinished at his death, the epic should be burned. Augustus did not allow the poet's wishes to be carried out.

VERGIL'S TIMES

Although the events described in Vergil's *Aeneid* take place in the distant, mythic times of the Trojan War and its aftermath, Vergil expected his audience to interpret these events through Roman eyes and through contemporary events. The hero of Vergil's epic, the Trojan Aeneas, is destined to found a city in Italy from which the Roman people will descend. The success of Aeneas means the success of Rome. Aeneas' son Ascanius, also known as Ilus or Iulus, is seen as the founder of the famous Julius *gens* ("clan"), which includes Julius Caesar and his adopted son the emperor Augustus. Thus, the Julians could claim descent from the goddess Venus, Aeneas' mother. (See Aeneas' Family Tree on p. xxi)

The events described in the *Aeneid*, then, look ahead to later events in the history of Rome, including the founding of the city by Romulus, the city's prolonged rivalry with Dido's city of Carthage in the Punic Wars (264–146 BC), and events during the Civil Wars that followed the assassination of Julius Caesar in 44 BC, including the naval battle of Actium (31 BC) in which the forces of Octavian defeated Antony and Cleopatra. The Dido depicted in the *Aeneid* is, in fact, not only the queen of Carthage, Rome's arch enemy. She also prefigures the dangerous Egyptian queen Cleopatra, whom Vergil and his contemporaries feared.

VERGIL'S SOURCES

In addition to Roman history and contemporary events, Vergil was influenced by many earlier Latin and Greek authors. The depiction of Medea in Apollonius of Rhodes' third-century BC epic *Argonautica* is probably a source for the Vergilian Dido. The influence of Greek tragedy, especially dramas like Euripides' *Medea*, can also be seen in the *Aeneid*. The tragedies and epic (now lost) of the early 2nd-century BC Latin poet Ennius probably played a similar role in Vergil's poetic development. The poet owes his greatest debt, however, to the Greek epic poet Homer. The first half of the *Aeneid*, which deals with the wanderings of Aeneas from the time he leaves Troy until he arrives in Italy, resembles Homer's *Odyssey* with its focus on the wanderings of Odysseus after the Trojan War. The last half of the *Aeneid*, with accounts of the many battles fought by Aeneas and his men to found a home in Latium, resembles the *Iliad*. Although the *Aeneid* uses Homer's poems as a model, the epic is thoroughly Roman in thought, mood, and message. Such imitation was common in the past. Such copying was not considered plagiarism but a compliment to the model.

Epic

The *Aeneid* is an epic, a long narrative poem centered around a hero. Vergil includes in his epic many of the following characteristics found in earlier classical epics, especially the *Iliad* and the *Odyssey*:

In medias res, i.e., beginning in the middle of the story. Vergil begins the *Aeneid* not at the beginning of the story, i.e., in the Trojan War, but with a storm which drives Aeneas' fleet onto the coast of Africa, near Carthage.

Flashback. If the story begins *in medias res*, then the poet must, at some point, tell the story up to that point. Vergil does this in *Aeneid* II–III, in which Aeneas tells Dido and her court everything that happened to him from the fall of Troy until his arrival in Carthage.

Invocation. A prayer to the Muse, the goddess of inspiration. When the poet prays for poetic inspiration, he usually summarizes the plot of the epic. Invocations can also appear at important points in the plot, such as Aeneas' entry into the Underworld in Book VI.

Catalogues or lists, such as the list of heroes and historical figures Aeneas meets in *Aeneid* VI.

Divine machinery or the involvement of the gods in the plot. The roles of the goddesses Venus and Juno are particularly important in the *Aeneid.*

Epithets or descriptive phrases used with the name of a hero, place, etc.; e.g. *pius Aenēās* ("loyal Aeneas") and *miserrima Dīdō* ("very unhappy Dido").

Similes or comparisons. Some of these are brief while others are longer and take on a life of their own.

Descent into the underworld. In *Aeneid* VI Aeneas descends into the Underworld to see the ghost of his dead father Anchises. His father will show Aeneas the future city of Rome and reveal a moral code sanctioned by the gods.

Dactylic Hexameter. This meter used by Homer and other Greek poets was introduced to Latin by the poet Ennius and became the standard meter for Roman epic poets. The meter is based on six feet (hexameter) consisting of dactyls ($-\cup\cup$) or spondees ($-$ $-$). While meter is not discussed in this transitional reader, it is important to be aware from the beginning that Vergil is using this complex rhythm in his poetry.

Many important cultural practices of the ancient world also appear in the *Aeneid*:

Speech-making. Characters in the *Aeneid* tend to speak longer and more formally than we might expect them to do today.

Elaborate descriptions. Detailed descriptions of people and things. The more important the object, the longer the description, like the extended description of Aeneas' new armor in *Aeneid* VIII.

Xenia or the Law of Hospitality, which encourages Dido to welcome Aeneas and the Trojans into her kingdom.

AENEAS' FAMILY TREE

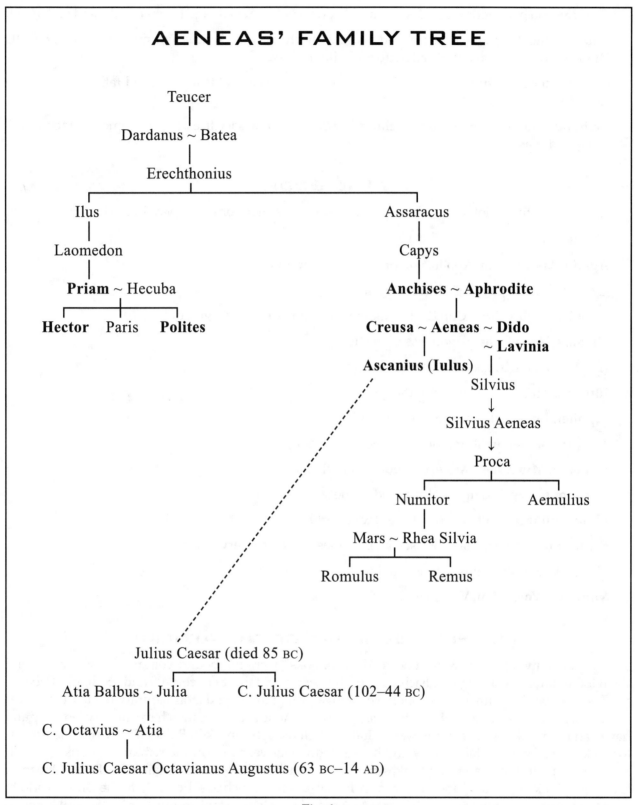

Fig. 1.
Aeneas' Family Tree.

Notes: The names in bold are mentioned in the passages read in this book.
The dashed line indicates the traditional descent of the Julian *gens* from Aeneas' son Iulus.

Feasting and banqueting, such as the meal Dido serves to Aeneas and his men at the end of *Aeneid* I.

Entertainment, e.g., the minstrel and his song. In the *Aeneid*, Aeneas assumes this role as he tells Dido and her court about his adventures in Books II–V.

Games, especially funeral games, such as the ones Aeneas holds for his dead father Anchises in *Aeneid* V.

Religious practices and beliefs, including prayers, animal sacrifices, augury, omens, oracles, auspices, and magic.

The Gods

You can expect the following gods and goddesses to be mentioned or play important roles in the *Aeneid*:

Apollō, Apollinis m. Apollo, god of prophecy and music

Cerēs, Cereris f. Ceres, goddess of grain

Cupīdō, Cupidinis m. Cupid, also known as **Amor, Amōris** m. god of love

Diāna, Diānae f. Diana, goddess of the hunt

Īris, Īr(id)is f. Iris, goddess of the rainbow

Iūnō, Iūnōnis f. Juno, queen of the gods

Iuppiter, Iovis m. Jupiter, king of the gods

Mercurius, Mercur(i)ī m. Mercury, the messenger god

Mīnerva, Mīnervae f. Minerva, goddess of wisdom

Neptūnus, Neptūnī m. Neptune, god of the sea

Plūto, Plūtōnis m. Pluto, god of the Underworld

Proserpina, Proserpinae f. Proserpina, goddess of the Underworld

Venus, Veneris f. Venus, goddess of love

Volcānus, Volcānī m. Vulcan, god of fire

A Plot Summary of the Aeneid

The *Aeneid* is divided into twelve books. These "books" were not bound volumes as we understand them today, but rolls of papyrus. Each book of the *Aeneid* contains between 705 and 952 lines of poetry.

The poet begins with an invocation, i.e., with a prayer to the gods for inspiration. He then moves immediately into the middle of the story (*in medias res*). Aeneas and his men have already left Troy and have had many adventures on the way to Italy. Vergil uses flashback in Books II–III to enable Aeneas to retell the story of the fall of Troy and his subsequent adventures. In the remaining books (IV–XII) Vergil returns to the present and takes the hero from his ill-fated love affair with Dido, Queen of Carthage (Book IV), to the funeral games for his dead father Anchises (Book V), to the Underworld to visit the ghost of Anchises (Book VI), and to Aeneas' efforts to establish himself in his new home in Latium (Books VII–XII).

Here is a brief summary of the three books (Books I, II, and IV) represented in this reader.

BOOK I

At the request of the goddess Juno, Aeolus, the god of the winds, sends a fierce storm which scatters Aeneas' fleet and drives him to an unknown land. Upon landing, Aeneas meets his mother Venus in disguise and learns that he is on the shore of Carthage, ruled by Queen Dido. The queen welcomes Aeneas and his men to the city and agrees to help them repair the damage from the storm. For their own reasons Juno and Venus agree to have Dido fall in love with Aeneas. For this purpose Cupid, disguised as Aeneas' son Ascanius, is sent down to Carthage. Dido's fatal passion for Aeneas begins at a banquet in honor of the Trojans, and the book closes with the queen's request that Aeneas tell the story of the fall of Troy and his own subsequent adventures.

BOOK II

In a flashback Aeneas narrates to Dido and her court the story of the fall of Troy and his escape from the burning city. Aeneas describes how the Greeks feign departure from Troy and leave behind a wooden horse filled with troops. A Greek spy named Sinon persuades the Trojans to take the fatal horse into the city. The Trojan priest Laocoon warns the Trojans not to do this and is horribly killed along with his sons by serpents sent from the sea. The capture and destruction of the city follows. Aeneas witnesses the death of Polites, son of King Priam of Troy, and then the death of the king himself. Then the hero returns home to protect his own family. He flees the city with his father Anchises on his shoulders and his son Ascanius (Iulus) at his side.

BOOK IV

Aeneas and Dido spend weeks enjoying each other's company. Dido, at least, assumes that their relationship is permanent, and Aeneas spends his time assisting in the building of Carthage. Eventually Jupiter sends his son Mercury down to remind Aeneas of his destiny to settle in Italy, and the hero reluctantly begins secret preparations for departure. Dido senses his plans but cannot change Aeneas' mind. After Aeneas leaves Carthage, the queen commits suicide on a funeral pyre piled high with all the mementos of her relationship with Aeneas.

SOME TRANSLATIONS OF THE AENEID

Before you read the *Aeneid* in Latin, it might be helpful to read it in English. Note that the poet's name is sometimes spelled "Virgil" instead of "Vergil." Many good translations are available. Here are some of them:

Copley, Frank O. *Vergil. The Aeneid*. Indianapolis, Ind.: Bobbs-Merrill Company, Inc., 1965.

Dickinson, Patric. *The Aeneid*. New York: New American Library., 1961.

Fitzgerald, Robert. *The Aeneid of Virgil*. New York: Random House., 1981.

Humphries, Rolfe. *The Aeneid of Virgil*. New York: Charles Scribner's Sons., 1951.

Knight, W. F. Jackson. *Virgil. The Aeneid*. Baltimore, Md.: Penguin., 1956.

Lewis, C. Day. *The Aeneid of Virgil*. Garden City, N.Y.: Doubleday., 1952.

Lind, L. R. *Vergil's Aeneid*. Bloomington, Ind.: Indiana University Press., 1968.

Mantinband, James H. *Vergil. The Aeneid*. New York: Frederick Ungar Publishing Co., 1964.

SOME WORKS FOR FURTHER REFERENCE

Anderson, William S. *The Art of the Aeneid*. Englewood Cliffs, N.J.: Prentice-Hall, 1969.

Bloom, Harold, ed. *Virgil's Aeneid*. Edgemont, Pa.: Chelsea House, 1987.

Cairns, Francis. *Virgil's Augustan Epic*. Cambridge: Cambridge University Press, 1989.

Camps, W. A. *An Introduction to Vergil's Aeneid*. Oxford: Oxford University Press, 1969.

Commager, Steele, ed., *Virgil: A Collection of Critical Essays*. Englewood Cliffs, N.J.: Prentice-Hall, 1966).

Griffin, Jasper. *Virgil*. Oxford: Oxford University Press, 1986.

Johnson, W. R. *Darkness Visible: A Study of Vergil's "Aeneid."* Berkeley: University of California Press, 1976.

Keith, A. M. *Engendering Rome: Women in Latin Epic*. Cambridge: Cambridge University Press, 2000.

Martindale, Charles, ed. *Virgil and His Influence*. London: Bristol Classical Press, 1984.

Otis, Brooks. *Virgil. A Study in Civilized Poetry*. Oxford: Oxford University Press, 1963.

Perkell, Christine, ed. *Reading Vergil's Aeneid. An Interpretive Guide*. Norman, Okla.: University of Oklahoma Press, 1999.

Pharr, Clyde. *Vergil's Aeneid. Books I–VI*. Revised Edition. Wauconda, IL.: Bolchazy-Carducci Publishers, 2002.

Putnam, Michael. *The Poetry of the Aeneid*. Cambridge, Mass.: Harvard University Press, 1965.

Quinn, Kenneth. *Virgil's "Aeneid:" A Critical Description*. Ann Arbor: University of Michigan Press, 1968.

Quinn, Stephanie. *Why Vergil? A Collection of Interpretations*. Wauconda, Ill.: Bolchazy-Carducci, 2000.

Williams, Gordon. *Technique and Ideas in the Aeneid*. New Haven: Yale University Press, 1983.

Williams, Rose. *Labors of Aeneas. What a Pain It Was to Found the Roman Race*. Wauconda, Ill.: Bolchazy-Carducci, 2003.

Wiltshire, Susan Ford. *Public and Private in Vergil's Aeneid*. Amherst: University of Massachusetts Press, 1989.

Ziolkowski, Theodore. *Virgil and the Moderns*. Princeton: Princeton University Press, 1993.

BOOK I

VERGIL INTRODUCES HIS THEME: OF ARMS AND A MAN
(*Aeneid* I. 1–11)

BEFORE YOU READ WHAT VERGIL WROTE

Introduction

The opening lines of Vergil's poem introduce the hero and provide a short plot summary of the entire epic. The story is about a hero of wars and wanderings. From the beginning the poet introduces the role of the gods, and especially the goddess Juno, whose hatred for Aeneas lasts through almost the entire *Aeneid*. Vergil explains how Aeneas' sufferings will lead to the founding of Rome and then prays to the Muse, the goddess of inspiration, to help him tell his tale. This prayer by an epic poet for divine guidance is called an invocation. Notice how the Muse inspires Vergil and how Juno affects Aeneas' life.

The ancient Romans believed that destiny (*fātum, -ī*, n. fate, destiny) and the will of the gods significantly affected human events. Thus, Aeneas is driven by fate (*fātō profugus*, I.2) and by the anger of Juno (*Iūnōnis ob īram*, I.4) towards his destiny in Italy.

As you read the *Aeneid*, think about the factors which influence Aeneas' actions and compare them to those which are thought to influence a person's decisions today, including family obligations, peer pressure, and political allegiance, as well as divine will and religious beliefs.

Keep This Grammar in Mind   PARTICIPLES—TENSE AND VOICE

Participles are verbal adjectives, i.e., they are verbs used to describe nouns or pronouns. Participles in both English and Latin have tense and voice. The letter combinations marked in bold in the chart below will help you recognize the tense and voice in Latin.

The passage you are going to read contains the following participles:

> *laesus* (from *laedō*, to wound)   *passus* (from *patior*, to suffer)
> *iactātus* (from *iactō*, to toss)   *dolēns* (from *doleō*, to grieve)

What are the tense and voice of each of these participles? Translate each into English.

	Active	**Passive**
Present	*iactantem* tossing	lacking
Perfect	lacking	*iactātum* (having been) tossed
Future	*iactātūrum* about to (going to) toss	*iactandum* tossing, must be tossed

Latin participles also show gender, number and case. Look at these examples:

> *Rēx vīdit virum iactantem saxa in mare.*   The king saw the man **tossing** rocks into the sea.
>   *Iactantem* is masculine singular accusative modifying *virum*.

1

*Rēgīna vīdit nāvem **iactātam** in marī.*   A queen saw the ship **tossed** on the sea.
    Iactātam is feminine singular accusative modifying *nāvem*.

*Virī **iactātūrī** saxa in mare rēgem vīdērunt.*   The men **about to toss** rocks into the sea saw the king.
    Iactātūrī is masculine nominative plural modifying *virī*.

Now It's Your Turn   PARTICIPLES

Translate each of the following participles (marked in bold) and indicate the tense, voice, gender, number, and case.

1. nāvēs **iactantēs**   3. virīs **laesīs**   5. rēgēs **passī**
2. rēgīnae **dolentis**   4. deā **laesūrā** virum   6. Aenēās **iactātus**

HELPING YOU TO READ WHAT VERGIL WROTE

Questions

Before reading the Latin text on the next page, answer these questions about the passage. The answers will help you to translate the Latin.

Line 1: *Canō* has two direct objects. What are they?
Line 1: What is the antecedent of *quī* and what is the verb in this relative clause?
Line 3: How is the participle *iactātus* translated and to whom does it refer?
Line 4: Use the special fonts to find the word which **memorem** modifies.

Vocabulary

1. **canō, canere, cecinī, cantum** to sing of, sing about

2. **profugus, -a, -um** exiled, an exile

3. **iactō, iactāre** to toss
   altum, -ī, n. the deep (sea)
   et . . . et both . . . and

4. **ob** + acc. on account of
   saevus, -a, -um cruel
   memor, memoris mindful, unforgetting

Notes

1. **canō** The direct objects of *canō* become the objects of the English preposition, "about" or "of."
   arma "Arms, the tools of war" stand for the war itself.
   Troiae Translate with *ōrīs*, "the shores of Troy."
   virum The name of this *virum* is Aeneas.
   fātō Ablative of means; translate "by fate."

2. **Lāvīn(i)a** The Lavinian shores refer to Italy's shores. *–que* connects *Lāvīna lītora* with *Ītaliam*.

3. **ille** This demonstrative pronoun can be translated "that man" with the word "man" understood or can be translated "he."
   multum A neuter accusative adjective sometimes, as here, is used in Latin as an adverb. Translate with *iactātus* "much."
   terrīs Vergil uses the plural to emphasize the many different places where Aeneas suffered.

4. **vī** Ablative of means; translate, "By the force of."
   superum Translate this contracted adjective with *deōrum* understood "of the gods above."

Summary

Vergil tells of a war and a hero who was fated to escape from Troy and go to Italy. This man endured many hardships during his journey to find a new home for his people and their gods. From these followers and these gods the Roman people will be descended. Before beginning the details of the story, Vergil asks the Muse to tell him why Juno is so angry with the Trojans.

Making Sense of It

In this adaptation from the *Aeneid* the words in parentheses have been added to assist in translation and do not appear in the original. Different fonts are used to link words that agree grammatically or refer to one another, but only when the relationship between these words is not self-evident by position or word ending. You will find the meanings of the words you do not know either in the vocabulary pull-out at the back of the book or in the vocabulary list at the left. Keep these directions in mind since they will not be repeated in future chapters.

1 Arma virumque canō, Troiae quī prīmus ab ōrīs

2 (ad) Ītaliam fātō profugus *Lāvīn(i)a*que vēnit

3 *lītora*—multum ille (vir) et (in) terrīs iactātus et (in) altō

4 vī super(ōr)um (deōrum), **saevae memorem Iūnōnis ob īram**,

Fig. 2.
The Goddess Juno.

Questions

Before reading the Latin text on the next page, answer these questions about the passage. The answers will help you to translate the Latin. These directions will not be repeated again in this book.

Lines 6–7: What three things are descended from the gods Aeneas brought from Troy to Italy?
Line 8: To whom does *mihī* refer?
Line 9: For what verb is *rēgīna* the subject? Hint: The answer is in line 11.
Line 9: What declension and case is *cāsūs*?
Line 10: What is the name of the *virum*?

Vocabulary

5. **patior, patī, passum** to endure, suffer
    quoque also

6. **īnferō, īnferre, īntulī, īllātum** to bring (into)
    condō, condere, condidī, conditum to found, establish
    Latium, -(i)ī, n. Latium, the area around Rome

7. **Latīnus, -a, -um** Latin, of Latium
    orior, orīrī, ortum to arise
    Albānus, -a, -um Alban
    Rōma, -ae, f. Rome

8. **Mūsa, -ae,** f. Muse, goddess of the arts
    memorō, memorāre to recount, relate
    causa, -ae f. reason
    laedō, laedere, laesī, laesum to hurt, offend

9. **doleō, dolēre, doluī, dolitum** to grieve (over), be angry (at)
    tot adv. so many

10. **īnsignis, īnsigne** distinguished
    pietās, pietātis, f. loyalty, sense of duty
    adeō, adīre, adīvī, aditum to approach

11. **impellō, impellere, impulī, impulsum** to drive, force
    caelestis, caeleste divine, heavenly

Notes

5. **multa** Translate this neuter plural accusative substantive as "many things."
    passus Translate "having suffered."

6. **dum conderet . . . īnferretque** Translate this subjunctive clause as "until he could found . . . and bring in."
    deōs The household gods whose statues Aeneas brought from Troy to Italy.
    Latiō Dative of direction; translate "to Latium."
    unde Translate "from which."

7. **Albānī** Rome is located in the Alban Hills.
    moenia altae Rōmae Translate "the high walls of Rome."
    orta sunt Translate "are descended."

8. **quō nūmine laesō** Ablative of means; translate "by which deity having been wounded." This indirect question and the following one explain why Juno is angry.

9. **quidve . . . dolēns** *Quid* is the direct object of *dolēns*. "Or grieving over what."
    volvere Translate "to undergo."
    cāsūs The direct object of *volvere*.

10. **pietāte** Ablative of respect; translate, "in duty."
    virum Direct object of *impulerit* in line 11.

11. **impulerit** Perfect active subjunctive in an indirect question. Translate in the past tense "forced."
    Tantaene . . . (sunt)? Translate "Are there such great . . . ?"

Making Sense of It CONTINUED

5   multa quoque et (in) bellō (ille vir) passus, dum conderet urbem

6   īnferretque deōs Latiō—*genus* unde *Latīnum*

7   ***Albānī***que ***patrēs*** atque altae moenia Rōmae (orta sunt).

8   (Ō) Mūsa, mihī causās memorā, quō **nūmine laesō** *having been*

9   quidve **dolēns rēgīna** de(ōr)um tot volvere cāsūs

10   *īnsignem* pietāte *virum*, (et) tot adīre labōrēs

11   *perf. subj* impulerit. Tantaene (in) **animīs caelestibus** īrae (sunt)?

Stopping for Some Practice   USING ENGLISH DERIVATIVES

Each of the following English words is derived from a Latin word that appears in this first reading. Use the letters in bold to help you identify the Latin word. What is the meaning of the Latin word? As you do this, think about how the English derivative helps you remember the Latin meaning.

Example:	English derivative **celest**ial	Latin Word *caelestis*	Meaning of the Latin word divine, heavenly

1. **caus**al   6. **dolor**ous   11. **amus**e

2. oc**cas**ion   7. **les**ion   12. **vir**ile

3. **memor**able   8. **de**ification   13. **labor**ious

4. re**volv**e   9. **insign**ia   14. **ira**te

5. **anim**ate   10. **numin**ous   15. **prim**ate

Notes

Notes and vocabulary supplied earlier in this chapter will not be repeated here. Keep this in mind since these directions will not be given later in this reader.

2. **Ītaliam** Vergil omits prepositions frequently in the *Aeneid*, especially with places. Since *Ītaliam* is accusative, *ad* is the omitted word.

    Lāvīnaque *Lāvīna* is the alternate spelling of *Lāvīnia*.

3. **ille** Note that *vir* is understood. Translate *ille* as either "that man" or "he."

    terrīs . . . altō The preposition *in* is understood with both of these words.

    iactātus This perfect passive participle modifies *ille*.

4. **superum** The contracted form of *superōrum*. Translate "of the gods above."

    saevae . . . īram The word order is important here. Note how *saevae* modifies *Iūnōnis* while *memorem* modifies *īram* to create the following pattern:

saevae	memorem	Iūnōnis	īram
A	**B**	**A**	**B**

    This placement of words in an A B A B pattern is a figure of speech called **synchesis** or **interlocked word order**.

5. **bellō** Supply the preposition "in."

    passus The perfect passive participle of a deponent verb is translated actively, i.e., "having suffered."

6–7. **genus . . . Rōmae** A word such as *sunt* (or *orta sunt*) has been omitted.

7. **altae moenia Rōmae** Logically Rome's walls are high, but grammatically *altae* modifies *Rōmae*.

8. **Mūsa, mihī** Note the repetition of the same consonant sound at the beginning of these two consecutive words. This figure of speech is called **alliteration**.

9. **deum** The contracted form of *deōrum*. Translate "of the gods."

9–10. **tot . . . tot** Such repetition of the same word is a figure of speech called **anaphora**.

10. **tot volvere . . . tot adīre** The conjunction *et* has been omitted between these two infinitive phrases. Such an omission of conjunctions is called **asyndeton**.

11. **īrae** This plural noun should be translated in the singular. Supply *sunt* in translating this line.

What Vergil Actually Wrote

As It Was

Now read the passage arranged as Vergil actually wrote it.

1 Arma virumque canō, Trōiae quī prīmus ab ōrīs

2 Ītaliam fātō profugus Lāvīnaque vēnit

3 lītora—multum ille et terrīs iactātus et altō

4 vī superum, saevae memorem Iūnōnis ob īram,

5 multa quoque et bellō passus, dum conderet urbem

6 īnferretque deōs Latiō—genus unde Latīnum

7 Albānīque patrēs atque altae moenia Rōmae.

8 Mūsa, mihī causās memorā, quō nūmine laesō

9 quidve dolēns rēgīna deum tot volvere cāsūs

10 īnsignem pietāte virum, tot adīre labōrēs

11 impulerit. Tantaene animīs caelestibus īrae?

A Note About Figures of Speech

Vergil uses verbal and grammatical techniques that enhance his poetic language. These figures of speech use the sound, form, meaning, and order of words for special effect.

anaphora The repetition of words causes an emphasis to be placed on these words.

alliteration The repetition of the same sound may be used to create emphasis or to mimic some sound.

asyndeton The lack of conjunctions may be used to indicate some rush or immediacy.

synchesis Also known as interlocked word order, this figure of speech may indicate that certain items or thoughts are closely connected.

Now look back in this passage to find an example of each of these figures of speech. Such figures can be found throughout the *Aeneid*. Be prepared to see more types and examples as you read more selections from the poem.

AFTER READING WHAT VERGIL WROTE

Thinking about How the Author Writes   GAPPING OR UNDERSTOOD WORDS

Gapping, or the omission of understood words, is a common feature of language. Examples in English include the following, where the phrases often gapped are put in parentheses:

Where is the book? Here (it is).
Did you see the film? Yes, I did (see it).
Many (people) agree with me.

Such gapping occurs frequently in Vergil and is a special challenge for translation. For example, in the phrase

6   *genus unde Latīnum*
7 *Albānīque patrēs atque altae moenia Rōmae (orta sunt).*

Vergil leaves understood the verb *orta sunt* of which *genus Latīnum, patrēs,* and *moenia* are the subjects. These gapped words (like *ortī sunt* or *orta sunt*) are provided in parentheses the first time the Latin text is provided in each chapter of this book, but be prepared to understand such gapped words on your own as you read Vergil's *Aeneid*.

Another type of gapping occurs when an adjective is used like a noun. Substantives, i.e., adjectives used as nouns, are very common in Latin. When an adjective is a substantive, a noun is omitted in Latin. The most commonly omitted nouns are man, woman, and thing and their respective plurals. In order to know what noun has been omitted, the case, number, and gender of the adjective must be determined. In line 5 of the passage you have just read, the phrase *multa . . . passus* contains the substantive *multa*. In order to understand *multa*, you need to recognize that it is neuter plural accusative. Then it can be translated "many things." Substantives can occur in all cases, numbers, and genders. Here are a few examples of substantives in the nominative case:

bonus	a good man	bona	a good woman	bonum	a good thing
bonī	good men	bonae	good women	bona	good things

Stopping for Some Practice   SUBSTANTIVES

Practice translating these substantives into English. Watch out for singular vs. plural and masculine vs. feminine vs. neuter. Remember that some endings can be more than one case or gender.

1. bonō	6. potentēs	11. pulchrī	16. optimī
2. bonae	7. mala	12. pulchrae	17. prīma
3. bonōrum	8. altae	13. pulchra	18. superī
4. bonōs	9. fortēs	14. celerēs	19. superīs
5. bonās	10. fortibus	15. celeria	20. pius

Thinking about What You Read

1. Which of the following factors does Vergil suggest in this passage influenced Aeneas' actions: family obligations, peer pressure, political allegiance, divine will or religious beliefs? What Latin words suggest your answer?

2. How many reasons can you suggest why Vergil refers to his hero at the beginning of his poem only as *virum* (1) and does not mention his name?

3. What type of skills and personality traits will Aeneas need in order to withstand troubles *et terrīs et altō* (3)? Will they be different from the ones he will use to *conderet urbem* (5)?

4. Why is Juno's mindful wrath (*memorem Iūnōnis ob īram*, 4) so important in this passage?

5. Why does Aeneas bring his household gods with him (*īnferret deōs*, 6) and what does this mean to the Romans? What sort of things would you take, if, like Aeneas, you were leaving your home in a hurry and moving to a new country? What do immigrant families bring with them when they come to the United States?

6. When Vergil calls Aeneas *īnsignem pietāte* (10), what do you think he means? What English word is derived from *pietāte*? What does this English word mean? To what kinds of actions might the Latin word *pietās* have been applied in ancient times?

7. To whom does Vergil address the question *Tantaene animīs caelestibus īrae* (11)? How might he/she answer this question? How would you answer it?

Keep This Vocabulary in Mind   PEOPLE AND PLACES

Many of these people and places will be mentioned in the *Aeneid*. Although these Latin words look somewhat similar, it is important to be able to distinguish one from another.

Latin Word	English Translation	Explanation
Latium, -ī, n.	Latium	The region of Italy where the Latin people lived.
lingua Latīna, -ae, f.	the Latin language or Latin	The language spoken in Latium.
Latīnus, -ī, m.	Latinus	The name of Latium's king who became Aeneas' father-in-law later in the epic.
Latīnus, -a, -um	Latin	The adjective used to describe Latinus' people and places near Latium.
Rōma, -ae, f.	Rome	The city which was later founded in Latium near Lavinium.
Rōmānus, -a, -um	Roman	The adjective used to describe the people of Rome and places near Rome.
Lāvīnium, -ī, n.	Lavinium	The city which Aeneas founded in Italy after he defeated the Rutulians later in the epic.
Lāvīnia, -ae, f.	Lavinia	The daughter of Latinus whom Aeneas later married and after whom he named the town of Lavinium.
Lāvīn(i)us,-a, -um	Lavinian	The adjective used to describe the people of Lavinium and places near Lavinium.

AFTER A STORM
(*Aeneid* I. 195–209)

BEFORE YOU READ WHAT VERGIL WROTE

Introduction

After explaining why Juno hates the Trojans, Vergil describes how the goddess convinces the wind god Aeolus to create a terrible storm that scatters the Trojan fleet. Aeneas and his followers are left on the coast of North Africa. The Trojans are wet, tired, hungry, and worried about their missing companions. Aeneas and his best friend Achates kill seven deer to provide food for the men and bring out some wine which Acestes, the King of Sicily, had given to them previously.

In this passage Vergil is describing one of those difficult times when people look to their leader for strength. However, a leader, like any other person, may have his or her own fears and worries. Which of the following emotions do you think a leader (whether ancient or modern) would show and which do you think would be kept inside: hope, fear, worry, concern, caring, despair, confidence, grief? As you read this passage, watch closely how Aeneas behaves and which emotions he displays and which he keeps hidden.

Keep This Vocabulary in Mind   Synonyms

Vergil uses some of the following groups of synonyms in lines I.1–11 (which you have already read) and some groups in the passage you are about to read. Read this list of synonyms, noting which words are from lines I.1–11 and which ones, by elimination, must be from lines I.195–209.

ōra, -ae, f. shore

lītus, lītoris, n. shore

scopulus, -ī, m. rock, cliff

saxum, -ī, n. rock

cāsus, -ūs, m. misfortune

malum, -ī, n. evil

cor, cordis, n. heart, feelings

pectus, pectoris, n. breast, heart

veniō, venīre, vēnī, ventum to come

accēdō, accēdere, accessī, accessum to approach

referō, referre, retulī, relātum to recall, relate, say

memorō, memorāre to recall, recount, relate

maereō, maerēre to grieve, mourn (for)

doleō, dolēre, doluī, dolitum to grieve, suffer

deus, -ī m. god or **dea, -ae,** f. goddess

nūmen, nūminis, n. divine power, god

superus, -a, -um above, the god above

caelestis, caeleste heavenly, the heavenly god

Keep This Grammar in Mind   ALTERNATE ENDINGS AND SYNCOPATED WORDS

Latin words sometimes have alternative or syncopated (i.e., contracted) endings, especially in poetry. The most important of these endings in Vergil are:

1. **Accusative plural, third declension:** *īs* can be used instead of *-ēs* in the accusative plural of third declension nouns, adjectives, and participles. For example, *sonantīs scopulōs*.

2. **Perfect active indicative, third person plural:** *-ēre* can be used instead of *-ērunt* in the perfect active indicative, third person plural. For example, *tenuēre* for *tenuērunt*. Be careful not to confuse such syncopated perfect endings with the endings of present infinitives in the second conjugation, i.e., *tenuēre* ("they held") and *tenēre* ("to hold").

Latin nouns sometimes feature these alternative or syncopated forms in poetry:

3. **First declension:** *-um* for *-ārum* in the genitive plural

4. **Second declension:** *-um* for *-ōrum* in the genitive plural. For example, *superum* for *superōrum*

5. **Third declension i-stems:**

    A. *-im* for *-em* in accusative singular with words like *Tiberim, puppim, turrim*. (But Vergil also uses the *-em* ending on other words like *nāvem*.)

    B. *-ī* for *-e* in ablative singular with words like *ignī* and *amnī*

    C. *-um* instead of *-ium* in the genitive plural of third declension i-stem nouns and present active participles such as *volucrum, vātum,* and *venientum*.

Latin verbs also have the following syncopated forms in poetry:

6. **All verbs formed from the third principle part:** The syllables *-vi-* and *-ve-* in the perfect tenses can be omitted. For example, *audīerat* for *audīverat* and *amāsse* for *amāvisse*.

7. **All second singular passive verb forms that end in –ris.** The passive ending *-ris* is syncopated by using the ending *-re* instead. For example, *amābāre* for *amābāris* "you were loved."

Watch for examples of syncopation and alternate endings in this reading. In "Making Sense of It" the unsyncopated forms of such words will be indicated by parentheses; e.g., *onerā(ve)rat* (line 195).

Stopping for Some Practice   ALTERNATE AND SYNCOPATED ENDINGS

Translate each of the following nouns and participles and give the regular spelling of the word in the case and number indicated.

1. ardentīs (acc. pl. of ardēns) burning

2. venientum (gen. pl. of veniēns) of the coming

3. sitim (acc. sing. of sitis) thirst

4. ignī (abl. sing. of ignis) by the fire

5. Tiberim (acc. sing. of Tiber) Tiber

6. amnī (abl. sing. of amnis) by the stream

7. venientīs (acc. pl. of veniēns) coming

8. puppim (acc. sing. of puppis) stern

9. turrim (acc. sing. of turris) tower

10. deum (gen. pl. of deus) of the gods

11. sequentum (gen. pl. of sequēns) of the following

12. virum (gen. pl. of vir) of the men

For each of the following syncopated forms, give the unsyncopated form and translate the word into English.

Syncopated Form	Unsyncopated Form	Translation
tenuēre	**tenuērunt**	**they have held**
1. retulēre	retulerunt	they have brought back
2. audīerās	audiveras	you had heard
3. iactāsse	iactavisse	to have thrown
4. patiēre	patieris	you will suffer
5. cecinēre	cecinerunt	they have sung
6. memorasti	memoravisti	you have recounted
7. laedebare	laedebaris	you were wounded
8. accessēre	accesserunt	they have come near
9. condēre	conderis	you were built
10. dedēre	dederunt	they have given
11. memorasset	memoravisset	he had recalled
12. doluēre	doluerunt	they have grieved
13. audieritis	audiveritis	you will be heard

Fig. 3.
The Monster Scylla.

HELPING YOU TO READ WHAT VERGIL WROTE

Questions

Line 195: What is the antecedent of *quae*? Who is giving what to whom?
Line 197: How is the present active participle *maerentia* translated into English?
Line 199: How is the substantive *graviōra* translated?

Vocabulary

195. **vīnum, -ī,** n. wine
     deinde adv. then, next
     cadus, -ī, m. jar, urn
     onerō, onerāre to load, burden

196. **Trīnacrius, -a, -um** Sicilian, Trinacrian
     hērōs, hērōis, m. hero
     abeō, abīre, abiī (abīvī), abitum to depart

197. **dīvidō, dīvidere, dīvīsī, dīvīsum** to divide
     maereō, maerēre to mourn, grieve (for)
     mulceō, -ēre, mulsī, mulsum to soothe

198. **enim** for, indeed, surely
     ignārus, -a, -um ignorant of, inexperienced in
     malum, -ī, n. evil, misfortune, trouble

199. **patior, patī, passum** to suffer, endure
     gravis, grave heavy, grievous, serious
     quoque adv. also

200. **Scyllaeus, -a, -um** of Scylla, a ravenous sea
       monster
     rabiēs, rabiēī, f. rage, fury
     penitus adv. within, deep(ly), wholly
     sonō, -āre, sonuī, sonitum to (re)sound

201. **accēdō, -ere, accessī, accessum** to approach
     scopulus, -ī, m. rock, cliff, crag
     Cyclōpius, -a, -um of the Cyclopes

202. **experior, -īrī, expertum** to experience
     revocō, revocāre to recall, restore
     maestus, -a, -um sad, mournful, gloomy
     timor, timōris, m. fear, dread, anxiety

203. **fors(it)an** adv. perhaps, possibly
     ōlim adv. at some time, someday
     meminī, meminisse to remember, recall
     iuvō, iuvāre, iūvī, iūtum to help, please

Notes

195. **vīna** King Acestes gave this wine to Aeneas in
     Sicily (see Book V). Note the poetic plural.
     Translate *vīna* in the singular.

196. **quae** Direct object of *onerā(ve)rat* and *dederat*;
     "which he had loaded and given."
     abeuntibus Translate *abeuntibus* with *virīs
     Troiānīs*, as "to the Trojan men going away."

197. **(hīs) dictīs** Ablative of means; "with these
     words."

198. **ignārī malōrum** The genitive *malōrum* goes
     with *ignārī*.

199. **passī** Translate "having endured."
     graviōra Accusative neuter plural direct object
     of *passī*.

200. **vōs** The pronoun is the subject of *accestis* (201),
     added for emphasis.
     sonantīs A participle with the alternate
     accusative ending. Modifies *scopulōs*.
     et Along with the *et* in line 201, translate
     "both . . . and."

201. **accestis** Contracted form of *accessistis* "You
     have approached."
     saxa Neuter accusative object of *expertī*.

202. **animōs** In the plural, *animus* means "courage."

203. **mittite** This imperative means "dismiss."
     et Translate here "even."
     iuvābit The infinitive *meminisse* is the
     subject of this impersonal verb; "to have
     remembered these things will please us."

Summary

Bringing out some wine, Aeneas tries to encourage his dispirited men to see the brighter side of this experience. He reminds them that they have suffered worse misfortunes in the past, like their encounters with Scylla and the Cyclops. He expects that a god will end these present misfortunes eventually. They are heading for Italy where all will be calm and a new Troy will arise. While Aeneas is trying to bring hope to his men, inside he himself is quite worried.

Making Sense of It

195   Vīna **bonus** quae deinde (in) cadīs onerā(ve)rat **Acestēs**

> He divided the wines which good Acestes had loaded into jars

196   (in) **lītore Trīnacriō** dederatque (virīs Troiānīs) abeuntibus hērōs

> on the Sicilian shores and the hero had given to the Trojan men going away on the Sicilian shores

197   dīvidit, et (hīs) dictīs maerentia pectora (Aenēas) mulcet:

> and with these words he (Aeneas) soothes the mourning hearts of Aeneas..

198   "Ō sociī (neque enim ignārī sumus ante malōrum),

199   Ō (vōs) passī graviōra, dabit deus hīs (rēbus) quoque fīnem.

200   Vōs et Scyllaeam rabiem penitusque **sonantīs**

> resounding rocks

201   acces(sis)tis **scopulōs**, vōs et Cyclōpia saxa

202   expertī (estis): revocāte animōs **maestum**que **timōrem**

203   mittite; forsan et haec ōlim meminisse (nōs) iuvābit.

Fig. 4.
A Storm at Sea.

Helping You to Read What Vergil Wrote

Questions

Line 204: What declension and case is *cāsūs?*
Line 206: Find the subject of the verb *ostendunt* (206). Hint: This subject is in line 205.
Line 208: How should the neuter plural substantive *tālia* be translated?

Vocabulary

204. **varius, -a, -um** varied, different
     tot adv. so many
     discrīmen, discrīminis, m. crisis, danger

205. **Latium, -ī,** n. Latium
     quiētus, -a, -um calm, peaceful

206. **ostendō, ostendere, ostendī, ostentum** to
     show, promise
     illīc adv. there
     fās, n. (indecl.) divine will, right
     resurgō, resurgere, resurrēxī, resurrēctum to
     rise again

207. **dūrō, dūrāre** to harden, endure
     secundus, -a, -um following, favorable

208. **aeger, -gra, -grum** sick, weary

209. **spēs, -eī,** f. hope, expectation
     vultus, -ūs, m. countenance, face
     simulō, simulāre to imitate, pretend
     premō, premere, pressī, pressum to (re)press,
     control
     cor, cordis, n. heart, spirit, feelings
     dolor, dolōris, m. grief, pain, suffering

Notes

204. **cāsūs** Object of *per* "through misfortunes."
     discrīmina Accusative plural neuter and object
     of *per.*

205. **tendimus** Translate with *cursum* "we aim our
     course."
     sēdēs From the noun *sēdēs,* not the verb *sedeō.*
     fāta Neuter plural nominative.

206. **fās (est)** "It is right." This construction is
     followed by an infinitive.
     rēgna resurgere Troiae Translate "that the
     kingdom of Troy rise again."

207. **vōsmet** The suffix *-met* on the end of *vōs*
     gives the accusative pronoun "you" more
     emphasis. Translate with *servāte* "Save
     yourselves."
     rēbus secundīs Dative of purpose; translate
     "for favorable things."

208. **tālia** The direct object of *refert.*
     vōce Ablative of means; translate "with his
     voice."
     aeger This nominative singular adjective
     modifies *Aenēās,* the understood subject of
     simulat (209).
     cūrīs ingentibus Ablative of cause with *aeger;*
     "sick with great cares."

Making Sense of It CONTINUED

204 Per **variōs cāsūs,** per tot discrīmina rērum

205 tendimus (cursum) in Latium, **sēdēs** ubi fāta (nobīs) **quiētās**

206 ostendunt; illīc fās (est) rēgna resurgere Troiae.

207 Dūrāte, et vōsmet **rēbus** servāte **secundīs."**

208 Tālia vōce refert cūrīsque **ingentibus** (Aenēās) aeger

209 spem (in) vultū simulat, (et) premit **altum** (in) corde **dolōrem.**

in heart   grief   res,

Keep This Vocabulary in Mind   VOCABULARY MATCHING

A. Directions: See how well you can recognize some important words in this reading by matching the Latin word in Column A with its English meaning in Column B.

Column A	Column B
1. spēs	A. countenance, face
2. dūrō	B. to mourn, grieve
3. secundus	C. sick, weary
4. maereō	D. to harden
5. ostendō	E. favorable
6. mulceō	F. heart, spirit, feelings
7. aeger	G. hope, expectation
8. vultus	H. to soothe
9. fās	I. divine will, right
10. cor	J. to show

B. Directions: Now distinguish between some look-alike Latin words by matching the Latin word in Column A with its meaning in Column B.

Column A	Column B
1. cūrīs	A. we hold, we have
2. curris	B. kingdoms
3. cāsūs	C. we stretch, we aim
4. causās	D. with cares, concerns
5. tendimus	E. reasons
6. tenēmus	F. queen
7. rēgīna	G. misfortunes
8. rēgna	H. you run

Notes

195. **cadīs** Vergil often expresses an ablative of place where without the preposition *in*; "in jars."

onerārat Translate this syncopated pluperfect verb "he had loaded."

196. **Trīnacriō** from **Trīnacrius, -a, -um** Trinacrian or Sicilian. Trinacria is an ancient name for Sicily. The prefix "tri-" in *Trīnacriō* refers to the triangular shape of the island.

lītore Again, the preposition *in* has been omitted in an ablative of place where.

abeuntibus This participle in the dative plural is also a substantive. The English noun "men" or the pronoun "them" must be understood. Translate "to them leaving."

hērōs A Greek word which retains its Greek nominative singular ending (as does *Dēlos*). While *hērōs* is closer to the verb *dīvidit*, most editors take this word as the subject of *dederat*.

197. **dīvidit** Translate *dīvidit* "he divided" but understand that "he" is Aeneas.

198–199. **Ō sociī . . . Ō passī** Note the **anaphora**.

199. **passī** *Vōs* is the understood vocative pronoun that *passī* modifies.

hīs Translate this substantive "these things."

dabit deus Note the **alliteration**.

200. **Scyllaeam** Although Aeneas is referring to the caves of Scylla, *Scyllaeam* is an adjective that modifies *rabiem*, which is linked with *scopulōs* by the connector *-que*. Vergil writes "the Scyllaean madness and her deeply sounding caves." This can also be translated as "the sounding caves of mad Scylla."

201. **Cyclōpia saxa** Literally "Cyclopian rocks" to parallel *Scyllaeam rabiem* (200).

202. **expertī** Understand *estis*. *Experior* is deponent. "You have experienced."

203. **iuvābit** Although *meminisse* is the subject of *iuvābit*, in English a gerund can be substituted for the infinitive in such a phrase: "Remembering will please us." *Iuvābit* can also be translated impersonally as "It will please us to have remembered."

204. **per** Note the repetition of *per* (**anaphora**).

206. **fas.** *Est* is omitted here, as is common in Vergil's poem.

rēgna Accusative subject of the infinitive *resurgere*. An important theme of the *Aeneid* is that a new Troy in Italy will become Rome long after Aeneas is dead.

208. **aeger** This adjective modifies the understood "he" that is the subject of *simulat*.

vōce Saying that Aeneas spoke "with his voice" is obvious and superfluous. This is called **pleonasm**.

209 **vultū** and **corde** Vergil again omits the preposition *in*. Both phrases are ablatives of place where. Vergil is describing how a person can use his inner resources to suppress his own feelings.

altum dolōrem Literally "deep grief;" translate "grief deep in his heart."

209. **spem . . . simulat, premit . . . dolōrem** In the first phrase the direct object (*spem*) precedes the verb (*simulat*) while in the second phrase the verb (*premit*) comes before the direct object (*dolōrem*). This ABBA pattern is called **chiasmus**. Also note the lack of the connector *et* between *simulat* and *premit* (**asyndeton**). This expression is also an example of **antithesis**, a group of contrasting words or phrases.

WHAT VERGIL ACTUALLY WROTE

As It Was

195 Vīna bonus quae deinde cadīs onerārat Acestēs

196 lītore Trīnacriō dederatque abeuntibus hērōs

197 dīvidit, et dictīs maerentia pectora mulcet:

198 "Ō sociī (neque enim ignārī sumus ante malōrum),

199 Ō passī graviōra, dabit deus hīs quoque fīnem.

200 Vōs et Scyllaeam rabiem penitusque sonantīs

201 accestis scopulōs, vōs et Cyclōpia saxa

202 expertī: revocāte animōs maestumque timōrem

203 mittite; forsan et haec ōlim meminisse iuvābit.

204 Per variōs cāsūs, per tot discrīmina rērum

205 tendimus in Latium, sēdēs ubi fāta quiētās

206 ostendunt; illīc fās regna resurgere Troiae.

207 Dūrāte, et vōsmet rēbus servāte secundīs."

208 Tālia vōce refert cūrīsque ingentibus aeger

209 spem vultū simulat, premit altum corde dolōrem.

AFTER READING WHAT VERGIL WROTE

Thinking about How the Author Writes   COMPOUNDING LANGUAGE

Much of Vergil's poetic power is based on the effective use of compound phrases, especially ones with similar or contrasting ideas, synonyms or antonyms.

Here are just a few examples from the passage you have just read.

per variōs cāsūs (204)	and	*per tot discrīmina rērum* (204)
dūrāte (207)	and	*vōsmet servāte* (207)
variōs cāsūs (204)	and	*sēdēs quiētās* (205)
spem vultū simulat (209)	and	*premit altum corde dolōrem* (209)

Usually these compounds are joined by conjunctions like *et* or *-que*, but sometimes the connectors are intentionally omitted (**asyndeton**). Can you find the words that connect these phrases? Which ones do not have connectors? Which phrases express similar ideas? Which ones are contrasting?

Thinking about What You Read

1. Which emotions does Aeneas reveal to his men in this passage? Which does he keep hidden? What Latin words suggest your answer?

2. When Aeneas tells his men that *deus* (199) might bring an end to their sorrows, *deus* can be translated into English as "a god," "some god," "the god," or simply "God." Which translation do you think best fits the context and why?

3. When and how do you think Aeneas and his men may be able to find it pleasing (*iuvābit*, 203) to remember these troubles? In your own life have you had any difficulties which now are pleasing to remember?

4. Why does Aeneas describe his future home as *quiētās* (205)? Some might consider this dull. Why would such a place be appealing to Aeneas and his men?

5. What sort of favorable events do you think Aeneas might be referring to with the words *rēbus secundīs* (207)?

6. How does the meaning of the line change when you understand *corde* (209) as an ablative of place where or an ablative of means? Which do you prefer and why?

7. Why do you think Vergil uses chiasmus in line 209? In what ways might this figure of speech enhance the meaning?

AENEAS MEETS HIS MOTHER

(*Aeneid* I. 318–334)

BEFORE YOU READ WHAT VERGIL WROTE

Introduction

After a night of worry, Aeneas goes off with his companion Achates to inspect the strange land in which the Trojans find themselves. They meet Aeneas' mother, the goddess Venus, disguised as a huntress. Venus pretends that she has been out hunting with her sisters and asks the Trojans if they have seen any sign of them. Aeneas suspects that he is in the presence of a goddess. He asks her who she is and where they are.

Such interaction between a god and a human being is not unusual in the ancient world. Roman deities are anthropomorphic, i.e., they have human shape. So Venus is here disguised as a huntress. The ancient gods can exhibit human faults as Venus does here when she lies to Aeneas and tells him that she is hunting with her sisters. At the same time the ancient gods demonstrate more positive human characteristics like the affection Venus shows for her son Aeneas.

Despite their mother-son relationship, Aeneas and Venus remain separated by the barrier that divides all humans from the gods. Human beings die. The gods do not. In what ways does Vergil make readers of this passage aware of this barrier between mortals and immortals?

Keep This Grammar in Mind   REFLEXIVE/MIDDLE VOICE

The voice of a verb indicates whether the subject is acting (active voice) or being acted upon (passive voice). Greek has a third voice (middle) used to indicate that the subject is acting upon itself. English and Latin usually express the middle voice by the use of reflexive pronouns.

ACTIVE	PASSIVE	MIDDLE/REFLEXIVE
They gather.	They are gathered.	They gather themselves.
Colligunt.	*Colliguntur.*	*Colligunt sē.*

Vergil, however, sometimes uses a passive verb form as a middle/reflexive. Passive verbs do not normally take a direct object. A Latin verb in the passive voice **with** a direct object is usually being used as a reflexive/middle voice verb. At line 320 in this reading, Vergil uses the expression *collēcta est* as a reflexive/middle with *sinūs* as direct object.

Sinūs collēcta (est) fluentīs.   She gathered (for herself) the flowing folds (of her garments)

Now compare the voices in these Latin sentences:

ACTIVE	*sinūs collēgit fluentēs.*	She gathered the flowing folds.
REFLEXIVE	*sinūs collēgit sibi fluentēs.*	She gathered for herself the flowing folds.
PASSIVE	*sinūs fluentēs collēctī sunt.*	The flowing folds were gathered.
MIDDLE	*sinūs collēcta (est) fluentēs.*	She gathered for herself the flowing folds.

HELPING YOU TO READ WHAT VERGIL WROTE

Questions

Lines 318–319: Of what verbs is *vēnātrīx* the subject?
Line 320: What case is the participle *fluentīs*? N.B. It has an alternate ending.
Line 322: How is the participle *errantem* translated?
Line 324: What noun does the participle *spūmāntis* modify?

Vocabulary

318. **mōs, mōris,** m. custom, manner
     arcus, -ūs, m. bow
     habilis, habile easily handled, handy
     suspendō, suspendere, suspendī, suspēnsum
       to suspend, hang

319. **vēnātrīx, vēnātrīcis,** f. huntress
     coma, -ae, f. hair
     diffundō, diffundere, diffūdī, diffūsum to
       scatter

320. **nūdus, -a, -um** nude, bare
     genū, -ūs, n. knee
     sinus, -ūs, m. fold, hollow, bay
     fluō, fluere, flūxī, flūxum to flow
     nōdus, -ī, m. knot
     colligō, colligere, collēgī, collēctum to gather,
       collect

321. **prior, -ius** first
     heus interj. Hey! Hello!
     inquam -is, -it to say
     iuvenis, iuvenis, m. (f.) youth
     mōnstrō, mōnstrāre to show, point out

322. **soror, sorōris,** f. sister

323. **succingō, succingere, succīnxī, succīnctum** to
       gird (up)
     pharetra, -ae, f. quiver
     teg(i)men, teg(i)minis, n. skin
     lȳnx, lyncis, m. (f.) lynx, wild cat
     maculōsus, -a, -um spotted

324. **spūmō, spūmāre** to foam, froth
     aper, aprī, m. wild boar
     premō, premere, pressī, pressum to (re)press,
       control, pursue

Notes

318. **dē mōre** Translate "according to custom."

319. **dederat** From *dō, dare*. The meaning that best
       fits this context is "to allow."
     diffundere An infinitive used to express
       purpose. Translate with *dederat comam* as
       "she had allowed her hair to scatter . . . ."

320. **nūda** Modifying Venus, whose lower legs are
       bare.
     genū Accusative of respect; "In respect to her
       knee." Translate *nūda genū* "bare up to her
       knee."
     nōdō Ablative of means; "with a knot."
     sinūs *Sinūs* is the direct object of *collēcta (est)*,
       which is in the reflexive/middle voice.

321. **inquit** "She says." This word is used in direct
       discourse and is always placed inside the
       phrase being spoken.

322. **forte** This word is from *fors, fortis* f. chance, not
       from *fortis, forte* brave. Translate "by chance."
     quam = *aliquam*. In a *sī* clause, *aliquam* becomes
       quam; translate "any."

323. **succīnctam** "Girded." This refers to the quivers
       and lynx skins tied around the waist.
     pharetrā et tegmine Ablative of means; "with
       quivers and skins."

324. **spūmāntis** Present active participle.
     prementem Translate here with *cursum*
       "following the track."
     clāmōre Translate "with shouting."

Summary

In the middle of the woods Aeneas meets his mother, who is disguised as a huntress. Venus speaks first and asks Aeneas and Achates if they have seen any of her sisters dressed for hunting and chasing a wild boar. Aeneas replies that she does not seem like a human being and asks if she can tell him where he is.

Making Sense of It

318   Namque (in) umerīs dē mōre **habilem** suspenderat **arcum**

319   vēnātrīx dederatque comam diffundere (in) ventīs,

320   **nūda genū** nōdōque **sinūs** collēcta **fluentīs**.

321   Ac prior "Heus," inquit (Venus), "iuvenēs, mōnstrāte, **meārum**

322   vīdistis sī **quam** hīc **errantem** forte **sorōrum**

323   **succīnctam** pharetrā et **maculōsae** tegmine **lyncis**,

324   aut **spūmāntis aprī** cursum clāmōre **prementem**."

Stopping for Some Practice   MORE ON REFLEXIVE/MIDDLE VOICE

In this passage Vergil uses a verb in the reflexive/middle voice to describe Venus' appearance. The same idea could have also been expressed in the active voice:

Reflexive/Middle	*Sinūs collēcta est fluentīs*	She gathered for herself the flowing folds.
Active	*sinūs collēgit fluentēs*	She gathered the flowing folds.

The following phrases are taken from passages you have already read. Here their active verbs have been rewritten in the reflexive/middle voice. See if you can supply an English translation for each reflexive/middle phrase:

Active	*Umerīs suspenderat arcum.*	She had hung a bow on her shoulders.
Reflexive/Middle	*Umerīs suspēnsa erat arcum.*	
Active	*Spem vultū simulāvit.*	He feigned hope with his face.
Reflexive/Middle	*Spem vultū simulātus est.*	
Active	*Pressit corde dolōrem.*	He suppressed grief in his heart.
Reflexive/Middle	*Pressus est corde dolōrem.*	

The subjunctive mood can be used as the main verb in a sentence to express a polite command, a wish, a potentiality, or a question with no clear answer. Usually these different types of independent subjunctives can only be distinguished in context. Many terms, as delineated below, are used to distinguish these different types of subjunctives; as a group, however, they are called independent subjunctives because they are main rather than subordinate verbs. While all but the volitive subjunctive appear in other tenses besides the present, Vergil tends to use these constructions in the present tense and thus only present tense examples are provided here. To express a negative with volitive and optative subjunctives *nē* is used, while the negative *nōn* appears with potential and deliberative subjunctives.

1. **The volitive subjunctive:** The volitive subjunctive (sometimes called hortatory and sometimes jussive) indicates a weak command or encouragement. In the first and third persons, singular and plural, the volitive subjunctive is translated into English with the word "let." In the second person singular and plural, the English word "may" is used.

Simus fēlīcēs.	Let us be favorable.
Doceās eōs.	May you teach them.

2. **The optative subjunctive:** The optative subjunctive is a sentence that expresses a wish. The present subjunctive translates with the word "may."

Sīs fēlīx.	May you be favorable.
Mē doceās.	May you teach me.

3. **The deliberative subjunctive:** The deliberative subjunctive is a question in which something is being considered or deliberated. The present subjunctive is translated into English with phrases like "Am I to . . . ?", "Are you to . . . ?", etc.

Simne fēlīx?	Am I to be favorable?
Docēamne tē?	Am I to teach you?

4. **The potential subjunctive:** The potential subjunctive is a sentence which expresses the opinion of the speaker as an opinion. The present subjunctive translates with "should, would" or in potential questions with "can."

Velim tē fēlīcem esse.	I should like for you to be favorable.
Velim tē docēre.	I would like for you to teach.

Now It's Your Turn INDEPENDENT SUBJUNCTIVES CONTINUED

First read each of the following sentences and decide whether it has a volitive, optative, deliberative, or potential subjunctive. Then translate the sentence into English. Finally put these sentences into chronological order according to the story contained in the *Aeneid*.

1. Videās vēnātrīcem aprī cursum prementem.

2. Achātēs mē comītet.

3. Velim vōs, meōs sociōs, dūrāre.

4. Iuvet haec ōlim meminisse.

5. Forte videātis aliquam sorōrum!

6. Multae hostiae ante ārās tuās cadant.

7. Abeatne Aenēās Troiae ab ōris?

8. Aenēās vīna dīvidat.

9. In Latium tendāmus.

Keep This Vocabulary in Mind DERIVATIVES

You have already seen the following vocabulary words from this reading passage in previous passages of the *Aeneid*. Consider what each Latin word means and then think of an English derivative from each word. If these words are not in the pull-out vocabulary at the back of the book, the line number in parentheses indicates where this word was seen before.

Example:	Latin Word **dea, -ae** f.	English Meaning goddess	English Derivative deify

sonō, sonāre (200)

errō, errāre

vultus, -ūs, m. (209)

vōx, vōcis, f.

labōs (or), labōris m.

Helping You to Read What Vergil Wrote

Questions

Lines 330–332: Use the independent subjunctives *sīs*, *levēs*, and *doceās* to outline what three things Aeneas is asking Venus to do in these lines.

Line 333: How should the participle *āctī* be translated and what does it modify?

Vocabulary

325. Venus, Veneris, f. goddess of love and beauty
fīlius, (i)ī, m. son
contrā adv. opposite, in turn
ordior, ordīrī, orsum to begin

326. soror, sorōris, f. sister

327. memorō, memorāre to (re)call
virgō, virginis, f. girl, maid(en)
vultus, -ūs, m. countenance, face

328. mortālis, mortāle mortal, human
homō, hominis, m. (f.) mortal, human
sonō, sonāre, sonuī, sonitus to (re)sound, roar
certē adv. certainly, surely

329. an (interrogative) or, whether
Phoebus, -ī, m. Apollo, brother of Diana, goddess of the hunt
soror, sorōris, f. sister
nympha, -ae, f. nymph, a minor divinity, represented as a beautiful maiden

330. fēlīx, fēlīcis happy, propitious
levō, levāre to lift, lighten
quīcumque, quaecumque, quodcumque whoever, whatever

331. orbis, orbis, m. circle, orb, world

332. iactō, iactāre to toss, buffet
doceō, -ēre, docuī, doctum to tell
ignārus, -a, -um ignorant, unaware
-que . . . -que both . . . and
homō, hominis, m. (f.) mortal, human

334. hostia, -ae, f. victim, sacrifice
cadō, cadere, cecidī, cāsus to fall, die.

Notes

326. nūlla Translate here "none."
mihī Dative of agent; translate "by me."

327. quam Translate "whom?" or "what?"
memorem The deliberative subjunctive shows that Aeneas is deciding how he should address this stranger. Translate as "am I to call?"
tibi . . . (est) *Tibi* is dative of possession with *est*. Literally "there is to you" but translate "you have."

328. nec (tuus) vōx hominem sonat "Nor does your voice sound human."

329. Phoebī soror The sister of Phoebus, i.e., Diana.
sanguinis Partitive genitive with *ūna*. "One of nymphs' blood."

330. quaecumque Note that a form of *esse* must be understood with this word.
quaecumque (es) Translate "whoever you are."
sīs, levēs. Both of these verbs, and *doceās* (332), are optative subjunctives expressing wishes. Translate "May you . . . ."

331. orbis (terrārum) Literally "of the circle of the lands." Translate "of the world."

332. iactēmur Present passive subjunctive in two indirect questions introduced by *quō* and *quibus in ōrīs*.
doceās Optative subjunctive.

334. tibi Dative of reference with *cadet;* "will fall for you."
multa . . . hostia Translate this singular phrase in the plural, "many victims."
nostrā . . . dextrā (manū) Ablative of means. Translate **nostrā** "my."

Making Sense of It CONTINUED

325 Sīc Venus (dīxit). Et Veneris contrā sīc fīlius orsus (est):

326 "Nūlla *tuārum* audīta (est) mihī neque vīsa (est) **sorōrum**,

327 Ō, quam tē memorem, virgō? Namque haud tibi **vultus**

328 **mortālis** (est), nec (tuus) vōx hominem sonat; Ō dea certē,

329 —an Phoebī soror (es)? An nymphārum sanguinis ūna (es)?—

330 sīs fēlīx **nostrum**que levēs, quaecumque (es), **labōrem**

331 et quō sub caelō tandem (iactēmur), **quibus** orbis (terrārum) in **ōrīs**

332 iactēmur (mē) doceās; (nōs) ignārī hominumque locōrumque

333 errāmus ventō hūc *vastīs* et *flūctibus* āctī:

334 **multa** tibi ante ārās **nostrā** cadet **hostia dextrā** (manū)."

Fig. 5.
Head of Venus.

WHAT VERGIL ACTUALLY WROTE

Notes

318. umerīs As often in Vergil's poetry, the preposition *in* has been left out.

319. ventīs Again, the preposition *in* has been omitted.

321. prior Translate "first." Vergil uses the comparative instead of *prīmus*, because he means that Venus spoke before Aeneas could speak. Note that the subject (Venus) of *inquit* is understood from the context.

322. sorōrum There are no sisters out hunting. This story is part of Venus' disguise.

323. pharetrā et maculōsae tegmine lyncis Notice the ABAB word order (**synchesis**).

324. cursum clāmōre The repetition of "c" sounds in this phrase suggests the noise of the hunt. Repetition of the same sound in successive words is called **alliteration**.

325. Sīc Venus. There is no verb in this sentence. A verb such as *dīxit* is understood.
fīlius Aeneas is, of course, Venus' son, but he does not know that his mother is speaking to him. *Fīlius* is used from the perspective of the narrator or author of the story.
orsus Understand *est*.

326. tuārum audīta vīsa sorōrum Note the **chiasmus** (ABBA pattern of words).

330. fēlīx When addressed to a god by a human, this word means "propitious, favorable." Aeneas is asking the goddess to look kindly on him when he says here "please, be favorable."
quaecumque Note that a form of *esse* must be understood with this word.

332. (mē) Understand this pronoun to be the direct object of *doceās*.
ignārī This adjective modifies the understood subject of *errāmus*, "we." Translate "we, ignorant of . . . , wander."

334. nostrā This "our" can be understood in two ways. Either Aeneas here refers to himself in the plural and speaks the way kings speak (i.e., in "the royal plural") or Aeneas is speaking on behalf of his men as well as himself.

As It Was

318   Namque umerīs dē mōre habilem suspenderat arcum

319   vēnātrīx dederatque comam diffundere ventīs,

320   nūda genū nōdōque sinūs collēcta fluentīs.

321   Ac prior "Heus," inquit, "iuvenēs, mōnstrāte, meārum

322   vīdistis sī quam hīc errantem forte sorōrum

323   succīnctam pharetrā et maculōsae tegmine lyncis,

324   aut spūmantis aprī cursum clāmōre prementem."

325   Sīc Venus. Et Veneris contrā sīc fīlius orsus:

326   "Nūlla tuārum audīta mihī neque vīsa sorōrum,

327   Ō, quam tē memorem, virgō? Namque haud tibi vultus

328   mortālis, nec vōx hominem sonat; Ō dea certē,

329   —an Phoebī soror? An nymphārum sanguinis ūna?—

330   sīs fēlīx nostrumque levēs, quaecumque, labōrem

331   et quō sub caelō tandem, quibus orbis in ōrīs

332   iactēmur doceās; ignārī hominumque locōrumque

333   errāmus ventō hūc vastīs et flūctibus āctī:

334   multa tibi ante ārās nostrā cadet hostia dextrā."

AFTER READING WHAT VERGIL WROTE

| Thinking about How the Author Writes | | INDIRECT REFERENCES |

Vergil often refers to characters by descriptive phrases or epithets rather than by name. Vergil assumes that his reader will understand such references. In the examples below, note how often these phrases are geographical or genealogical:

Vergil's Words	English Translation	Place or Person
lītora Lāvīnia (I. 2–3)	Lavinian shores	Italy
arcēs Tyriās (I. 20)	Tyrian citadel	Carthage
pater omnipōtens (I. 60)	almighty Father	Jupiter
lūx alma (I. 306)	nurturing light	dawn or sun
Phoebēā lampade (IV. 6)	the Phoeban lamp	the sun
Tȳdīdē (I. 97)	son of Tydeus	Diomedes
Cytherēa (I. 257)	the Cytherian	Venus
Maiā genitum (I. 297)	born of Maia	Mercury

| Thinking about What You Read |

1. In describing Aeneas' encounter with his mother, how does Vergil emphasize the barrier between mortals and immortals?

2. What two examples of indirect references are found in this passage?

3. Why do you think Venus appears to Aeneas in disguise (318–320)? Why do you think that Venus speaks before her son does? Why does she lie to him?

4. What might be the difference between the voice of a god and the voice of a human being (*nec vōx hominem sonat*, 328)? How could the difference be shown in a modern movie?

5. Both Venus and Aeneas ask favors of each other. Compare the way they express their requests grammatically. How and why are these requests different in form?

6. For what *labōrem* (330) do you think Aeneas is asking the goddess' help?

7. All of the details in Vergil's description of Venus disguised as a huntress are contrary to the way Roman women would dress and behave. Use this passage to describe how a Roman woman would **not** dress and behave.

Aeneas Looks at Carthage

(*Aeneid* I. 421–440)

Before You Read What Vergil Wrote

Introduction

After informing Aeneas and Achates that they are on the shore of Africa and that their missing ships are safe, Venus hides them in a cloud so that they can travel into the city of Carthage safely. From a hilltop, the Trojans look down at the growing city. Vergil compares the Carthaginians building their city to a hive of bees. Aeneas admires the rising walls and expresses his envy of the Carthaginians, who have already mastered the difficulties of finding the land and resources to found a new city.

In what ways is Aeneas' envy of the Carthaginians a positive character trait? In what ways is such envy more negative? As you read this passage, think about how Vergil uses this emotion to develop the character of Aeneas. How does it affect your impression of him as a hero and a leader?

Keep This Vocabulary in Mind   On Building a City

In this passage, you will read about the Carthaginians building their city. Here is some vocabulary associated with an ancient city that Vergil is most likely to use. See how many of these words you can find in the reading.

āra, -ae, f. altar	**porta, -ae,** f. gate, door, opening
arx, arcis, f. citadel, fort; height, hill	**portus, -ūs,** m. port, harbor, haven
campus, -ī, m. plain, field, level surface	**scaena, -ae,** f. stage, background
columna, -ae, f. column, pillar	**strātum, -ī,** n. pavement, bed
domus, -ūs, f. house(hold), home, race,	**tēctum, -ī,** n. roof; house, home, abode
fundāmentum, -ī, n. foundation	**templum, -ī,** n. temple, shrine
līmen, līminis, n. threshold, doorway	**theātrum, -ī,** n. theatre
moenia, moenium, n. walls; city; structure	**urbs, urbis,** f. city, town
mūrus, -ī, m. (city) wall, rampart	**via, -ae,** f. way, road, journey, street

How many of the building features listed above can you find in the following picture?

Fig. 6.
An Ancient City.

31

Keep This Grammar in Mind

Supines: The Latin supine is a fourth declension noun formed from the perfect passive participle, i.e., the fourth principal part of a Latin verb. Only the accusative and ablative singular of the supine is used. The supine is translated as an infinitive in English.

Examples:

parātum or *parātū*	to prepare	*ductum* or *ductū*	to lead
habitum or *habitū*	to have, to hold	*dictum* or *dictū*	to say
		audītum or *audītū*	to hear

The supine is a verbal noun used in the accusative to express purpose with verbs of motion. The supine is also used in the ablative to express respect with adjectives.

Purpose (Accusative):   *Venīmus vīsum.*   We are coming to see.

We are coming in order to see.

Respect (Ablative): *mīrābile dictū*   a wonderful thing to say ("in respect to saying")

Now It's Your Turn

Translate each of the following phrases and indicate whether the supine expresses purpose or respect.

1. amābīle visū   *a lovable thing to see*

2. veniunt audītum   *they have come to hear*

3. ūtile ductū   *a useful thing to lead*

4. facile dictū   *it easy to say*

5. errāmus vīsum   *we wander to see*

6. nectar dulce gustātū   *a sweet nectar to taste*

Fig. 7.
The Head of Vergil.

Keep This Grammar in Mind

Complementary Infinitives: In both English and Latin certain verbs take infinitives to complement or complete their meanings.

Volō mūrōs dūcere.	I want to extend the walls.
Īnstant saxa subvolvere.	They press on to roll rocks.
Cupit legēs legere.	He wishes to choose laws.
Debēmus portūs effodere.	We ought to dig out the harbor.
Possunt arcēs mōlīrī.	They are able to make the citadel.

Sometimes the Latin infinitive is not translated with "to." For example,

Possunt arcēs mōlīrī.	They can make the citadel.
Debēmus portūs effodere.	We must dig out the harbor.

Vergil likes to string a number of such infinitives together in a single sentence like this:

Īnstant mūrōs ducereque legēs legereque portūs effodereque arcēs mōlīrīque.
They press on to extend the walls, to choose laws, to dig out the harbor and to make the citadel.

Now It's Your Turn

Each of the following sentences contain complementary infinitives. Translate these sentences.

1. Volumus saxa subvolvere.

2. Cupit mūrōs dūcere.

3. Īnstat legēs legere.

4. Possunt portūs effodere.

5. Debēmus arcēs mōlīrī.

6. Possumus urbem vidēre.

Fig. 8.
Vergil.

HELPING YOU TO READ WHAT VERGIL WROTE

Questions

Lines 421–422: Identify the three direct objects of *mīrātur*.
Lines 423–425: Find the five complementary infinitives in these lines.

Vocabulary

421. **mīror, mīrārī, mīrātum** to wonder (at), admire
molēs, molis, f. mass, burden, structure
māgālia, māgālium, n. (pl.) huts, hovels

422. **porta, -ae,** f. gate, door, opening
strepitus, -ūs, m. noise, uproar
strātum, -ī, n. pavement; bed

423. **īnstō, īnstāre, īnstitī, īnsātūrum** (with dat.) to urge on, press on
mūrus, -ī, m. (city) wall, rampart

424. **mōlior, mōlīrī, mōlītum** to make
subvolvō, subvolvere, subvolvī, subvolūtum to roll up

425. **optō, optāre** to choose
conclūdō, conclūdere, conclūsī, conclūsum to (en)close
sulcus, -ī, m. furrow, trench, ditch

426. **iūs, iūris,** n. law, justice, decree
magistrātus, -ūs, m. magistrate
legō, legere, lēgī, lēctum to choose
sānctus, -a, -um sacred, holy, revered
senātus, -ūs, m. senate

427. **effodiō, effodere, effōdī, effossum** to dig out, excavate
theātrum, -ī, n. theatre

428. **fundāmentum, -ī,** n. foundation
locō, locāre to place
columna, -ae, f. column, pillar

429. **rūpēs, rūpis,** f. rock, cliff, crag
excīdō, excīdere, excīdī, excīsus to cut out, destroy
decus, decoris, n. ornament
scaena, -ae, f. stage, background

Notes

423. **īnstant** This word takes a complementary infinitive.
ardentēs This present participle means "burning." Translate here "eagerly."
pars This word is often used in a pair to distinguish two different groups. "One group is doing this; another is doing that."
dūcere mūrōs Literally "to lead walls," here this phrase means "to extend walls."

425. **tēctō** Dative of purpose. Translate with *locum* "a place for a house."
conclūdere The understood object is *locum tēctō* but "it" can be used also.

426. **legunt** Note that in Vergil this word does not mean "to read" but "to collect, gather."
sānctumque Translate "and a revered."

427. **hīc** This is the adverb *hīc* which means "here."
portūs This fourth declension word for "port" is not to be confused with the first declension *porta* ("gate") used in line 422.
aliī Like *pars*, *aliī* can be used in a pair to distinguish two different groups. The two groups are "some" and "others."
alta This adjective can mean "high" or "deep." Here translate *alta* "deep."
theātrīs Dative of purpose; translate "for theatres."

428. **immānīs** The poetic, long -īs ending replaces the prose accusative plural ending of -ēs.

429. **scaenīs** Dative of purpose; "for stages."

Summary

Aeneas and Achates follow the road which Venus pointed out to them. They climb a hill near Carthage and look over the citadel of the city. Aeneas wonders at the size of the city and at the houses. He is amazed at gates that are already built and the noisy streets. The Carthaginians are busily building walls, erecting the citadel, and working on other tasks involved with creating a city. The work of the Carthaginians is like that which busies bees in the summer when they are stowing honey and stretching the cell with nectar. Aeneas, looking at the city, envies those who have already begun the construction of their city. Hidden in the cloud, Aeneas mingles with the men and is not seen at all.

Making Sense of It

421 Mīrātur mōlem Aenēās, māgālia quondam,

422 mīrātur portās strepitumque et strāta viārum.

423 Īnstant **ardentēs Tyriī**: pars dūcere mūrōs (īnstat)

424 mōlīrīque arcem et manibus subvolvere saxa,

425 pars optāre locum tēctō et conclūdere sulcō (īnstat);

426 iūra magistrātūsque legunt sānctumque senātum.

427 Hīc portūs aliī effodiunt; hīc **alta** theātrīs

428 **fundāmenta** locant aliī, **immānīs**que **columnās**

429 (ex) rūpibus excīdunt, **scaenīs** decora alta **futūrīs**.

Fig. 9.
An Ionic Capital.

Questions

Line 431: What is the subject of *exercet*? What is the direct object of this verb? Hint: The object is in line 430.

Vocabulary

430. **quālis, -e** such (as), of what sort
apis, apis, f. bee
aestās, aestātis, f. summer
flōreus, -a, -um flowery
rūs, rūris, n. country (district)

431. **exerceō, -ēre, exercuī, exercitum** to train, occupy
sōl, sōlis, m. sun; day
adultus, -a, -um grown, adult

432. **fētus, -ūs,** m. offspring, swarm
ēdūcō, ēdūcere, ēdūxī, ēductum to lead forth
līquēns, līquentis liquid, flowing
mel, mellis, n. honey

433. **stīpō, stīpāre** to stow
distendō, -ere, -ī, distentum to distend, stretch
dulcis, dulce sweet, dear, fresh
nectar, nectaris, n. nectar
cella, cellae, f. cell, storeroom

434. **onus, oneris,** n. burden, load

435. **fūcus, ī,** m. drone
ignāvus, -a, -um lazy, idle
pecus, pecoris, n. flock, swarm
praesēpe, praesēpis, n. stall, hive
arceō, arcēre, arcuī to keep off

436. **ferv(e)ō, fervēre, fervuī** or **ferbuī** to glow, boil
opus, operis, n. work, deed, toil
redoleō, redolēre, redoluī to smell (of)
thymum, ī, n. thyme
fragrāns, fragrantis fragrant

437. **fortūnātus, -a, -um** fortunate

438. **fastīgium, -iī,** n. summit, top
suspiciō, -ere, suspexī, suspectum to look up (at)

439. **īnferō, īnferre, īntulī, īnlātum** to bear (in, into)
saepiō, saepīre, saepsī, saeptum to enclose
nebula, -ae, f. cloud, mist, fog
mīrābilis, mīrābile wonderful, marvelous

440. **misceō, miscēre, miscuī, mixtum** to mix

Notes

430. **quālis** such as. This word indicates that Vergil is making a comparison.
aestāte novā Ablative of time.

430–431. **apēs . . . exercet . . . labor** "The work occupies the bees."

431. **cum** Here and in line 432, *cum* is the conjunction "when," not the preposition "with."

431–432. **adultōs fētūs** The ending of *adultōs* shows that *fētūs* is accusative plural. Translate in the singular "adult offspring."

434. **(apium) venient(i)um** The parentheses here indicate that *venientum* is the syncopated form *venientium* (genitive plural present active participle) with the word *apium* understood. Translate "of the bees coming (and going)."
agmine factō An ablative absolute; "when a (battle) line (of bees) had been made."

435. **ignāvum fūcōs pecus** Since *pecus* is neuter, it is accusative here in apposition to *fūcōs*, i.e., the *fūcōs* or drones are described as *ignāvum pecus*, "an ignorant herd."

437. **Ō fortūnātī** A substantive in the vocative.
quōrum *Fortūnātī* is the antecedent of *quōrum*. Translate this genitive of possession with *moenia* "whose walls."

439. **īnfert sē** Literally "he bore himself." Translate into English "he went."
saeptus This perfect passive participle modifies Aeneas, the understood subject of *īnfert*.
nebulā Ablative of means; translate "by a cloud."
mīrābile A neuter singular adjective used substantively.
dictū This is an ablative supine.

440. **ūllī** Dative of agent; translate "by anyone."

Making Sense of It CONTINUED

430 Quālis apēs **aestāte novā** per flōrea rūra

nom. pl., abl. *flowery country*
such work occupies the bees during a new summer through the flower country under the sun, when the

431 exercet sub sōle labor, cum gentis **adultōs**

adult offspring lead forth, or wh...

432 ēdūcunt **fētūs**, aut cum līquentia mella

they stow flowing honey, and str... the storerooms with the sweet ho...

433 stīpant et **dulcī** distendunt **nectare** cellās,

or they accept the load of bees coming and going

434 aut onera accipiunt (apium) venient(i)um, aut **agmine factō**

or when a line (of bees) has been made an ignorant ne... keeps off the hive

435 **ignāvum** fūcōs **pecus** ā praesēpibus arcent;

436 fervet opus redolentque thymō fragrantia mella.

work glows and smells with a thyme of fragrant smell.

437 "Ō fortūnātī, quōrum iam moenia surgunt!"

O fortunate ones whose walls are now arising! Aeneas says and looks up to the top of the city.

438 Aenēās ait et fastīgia suspicit urbis.

439 Īnfert sē saeptus nebulā—Mīrābile (est) dictū!—

He bears having been enclosed by a cloud, a marvelous thing to say

440 per mediōs (Tyriōs), miscetque virīs neque cernitur ūllī.

through the middle of Tyrians, he mixes with men and does is not ... by anyone.

#W

Stopping for Some Practice   COMPOUND WORDS AND THE DATIVE

Some Latin words are formed by adding a prefix like *ad-*, *ante-*, *con-*, *in-*, or *ob-* to the stem. These are *discov...* called compound words. Sometimes the two parts are simply combined:

adversus	from ad + versus	opposite
īnstō	from in + stō	to urge on
obstō	from ob + stō	to hinder, oppose
obvius	from ob + via	in the way
subvolvō	from sub + volvō	to roll up

Sometimes the combination of consonants results in a blending of sounds called **assimilation**:

accēdō	from ad + cedō	to approach, reach
immineō	from in + mineō	to overhang, menace
conclūdō	from cum + claudō	to (en)close

Sometimes not only the consonants change but also the vowel in the verb stem changes:

accipiō	from ad + capiō	to receive, accept, learn, hear
colligō	from con + legō	to gather, collect
corripiō	from con + rapiō	to snatch (up), hasten on

Many of these Latin compound verbs take a dative object. This dative is often expressed with a preposition in English, but sometimes the English verb takes a simple direct object.

Collis imminet urbī   The hill projects over the city. (Here "city" is the object of "over.")
                            The hill overhangs the city. (Here "city" is the object of the verb.)

Rex populō īnstat.   The king urges on the people. (Here "people" is the object of "on.")
                            The king urges the people. (Here "people" is the object of the verb.)

Populus obstat rēgī.   The people stand in the way of the king. (Here "king" is the object of "of.")
                            The people oppose the king. (Here "king" is the object of the verb.)

Directions: Each of the following sentences contains compound words which take a dative. Find the compound and the dative. Then translate the sentence.

1. Collis imminet portuī.   6. Alta columna theātrō imminent.
2. Urbs imminet portae.   7. Venus Troiānīs īnstat.
3. Ducēs sodālibus īnstant.   8. Deī hominibus īnstant.
4. Aenēās matrī accēdit.   9. Rēx populō obstat.
5. Māter obvia fīliō stat.   10. Quae mōra tardīs noctibus obstant?

WHAT VERGIL ACTUALLY WROTE

Notes

421-422. Notice how both of these lines begin with the same word (*mīrātur*). Such repetition is called **anaphora.** Note also the alliteration of *mīrātur mōlem*.

423. pars Understand *īnstat* with this word and with *pars* in line 425.

425. tēctō Note that this word literally means "roof," but Vergil wants you to understand the whole house. This use of a part for the whole is called **synecdoche.**

426. sānctumque senātum Note the **alliteration.**

427. portūs Note the poetic plural.

429. rūpibus Vergil understands *ex* from *excīdunt* with this word.
scaenīs decora alta futūrīs Note the **chiasmus.**

430. Quālis Vergil does not say to what the bees are being compared, but the comparative adjective *quālis* indicates that Vergil is making a **simile,** i.e., an expressed comparison. A comparison like this one in which more than one thing is being compared, is called an **extended simile.**

437. Ō fortūnātī The individuals Vergil is addressing are not present or cannot hear him. Such use of direct address is called **apostrophe.**

437–438. Vergil has reversed the logical order of events in these two lines. Aeneas would look at the summit of the city and then speak rather than vice versa. Such a reversal is called **hysteron proteron.**

439. Mīrābile dictū This is a parenthetical remark addressed by Vergil to his audience.

As It Was

421 Mīrātur mōlem Aenēās, māgālia quondam,

422 mīrātur portās strepitumque et strāta viārum.

423 Īnstant ardentēs Tyriī: pars dūcere mūrōs

424 mōlīrīque arcem et manibus subvolvere saxa,

425 pars optāre locum tēctō et conclūdere sulcō;

426 iūra magistrātūsque legunt sānctumque senātum.

427 Hīc portūs aliī effodiunt; hīc alta theātrīs

428 fundāmenta locant aliī, immānīsque columnās

429 rūpibus excīdunt, scaenīs decora alta futūrīs.

430 Quālis apēs aestāte novā per flōrea rūra

431 exercet sub sōle labor, cum gentis adultōs

432 ēdūcunt fētūs, aut cum līquentia mella

433 stīpant et dulcī distendunt nectare cellās,

434 aut onera accipiunt venientum, aut agmine factō

435 ignāvum fūcōs pecus ā praesēpibus arcent;

436 fervet opus redolentque thymō fragrantia mella.

437 "Ō fortūnātī, quōrum iam moenia surgunt!"

438 Aenēās ait et fastīgia suspicit urbis.

439 Īnfert sē saeptus nebulā—Mīrābile dictū!—

440 per mediōs, miscetque virīs neque cernitur ūllī.

AFTER READING WHAT VERGIL WROTE

Thinking about How the Author Writes   TIME EXPRESSIONS

Time is very important in the *Aeneid* in which the past is closely connected with the future. Vergil makes careful reference to past, present, and future in this passage, not only by the use of different tenses, but also by a number of adverbial words and phrases which express time.

These are the temporal words or phrases Vergil used in this selection:

Present:	*intereā*	"meanwhile"
	iam	"now"
Past:	*quondam*	"once"
Future:	*scaenīs futurīs*	"for future scenes"

Find these words and phrases in the reading and explain to what events they refer.

Now do the same with these words and phrases you have already seen in earlier passages from the *Aeneid*:

prīmus (I. 1)	past	*ōlim* (I. 20 and I. 203)	future
ante (I. 198)	past	*nunc* (I. 221)	present

Latin also uses case (with or without a preposition) to distinguish different types of time expressions.

Examples:

1. The accusative is used to show extent or duration of time.
    Examples: *ter centum annōs rēgnābitur.* (I.272)
    He will reign for three hundred years.
                   or
    He will reign three hundred years.

    per noctem (I. 305)   through the night

2. The ablative case is used to show time when or within which.
    Example: *aestāte novā* (I. 430)   in the new summer or
                                                at the beginning of summer

Vergil often replaces simple adverbial words and phrases with more elaborate subordinate clauses to express time. Paying attention to these temporal words is another way to make the reading of the *Aeneid* easier.

Examples:

ut prīmum lūx alma data est (I. 306)   "when dear light was first given" or "at dawn"

ubi mātrem agnōvit (I. 405-406)   "when he recognized his mother"

Thinking about What You Read

1. How does Vergil use envy to develop the character of Aeneas in this passage? How does his expression of this emotion affect your impression of Aeneas as hero and leader?

2. Write an English sentence in which the word "roof" is used for "house." Can you think of other examples of synecdoche in English?

3. Why do you think that Vergil describes the Carthaginians as *ardentēs* in line 423?

4. Comment on the phrase *māgālia quondam* (421). Why does Vergil mention that these buildings were once no more than huts? What does he want his reader to imagine the buildings look like now?

5. What effect does Vergil's use of alliteration and anaphora have in lines 421–422?

6. What words or phrases from the text suggest that Aeneas is considering his own future city as he looks at the growing walls of Carthage?

7. How does Vergil's use of the simile of the bees affect the reader's understanding of this passage?

Fig. 10.
Bees Busy at a Beehive.

Fig. 11.
The Head of Laocoon
by Julia Sienkewicz

BOOK II

SERPENTS FROM THE SEA
(*Aeneid* II. 201–222)

BEFORE YOU READ WHAT VERGIL WROTE

Introduction

Aeneas has been invited to a banquet at Dido's palace in Carthage. Near the end of the banquet Dido asks Aeneas to tell her and her court about the fall of Troy. Aeneas explains how the Greeks left a huge wooden horse filled with their soldiers on the plain in front of the gates of Troy. The rest of the Greeks had already sailed away to the nearby island of Tenedos in order to convince the Trojans that they had returned to Greece. Most of the Trojans wanted to bring the wooden horse inside the city walls, but the priest Laocoon tried to convince them that this would not be a good idea. Laocoon also hurled a spear at the side of the wooden horse, and a hollow sound was heard. This should have convinced the Trojans that it was not safe to bring the horse inside. But Sinon, a Greek left behind on the plain at Troy, persuaded the Trojans that the wooden horse was an offering to the goddess Minerva, an omen that would bring good luck to the Trojans. At this point, another terrifying omen appeared: two snakes came from the sea. Sinon said that they were a punishment for Laocoon having struck the horse with his spear. The snakes from Tenedos attacked first the sons of Laocoon and then their father. The monsters strangled the bodies in their spiraling coils. Laocoon tried in vain to fight the snakes and died like a sacrificial beast. The two snakes then sought shelter at the shrine of Minerva.

The ancient Romans placed great importance on omens as warnings or good luck. Priests, such as Laocoon, were often entrusted with interpreting these omens. In this passage, the Trojans are faced with two different interpretations of the wooden horse—one from Laocoon and one from Sinon. Laocoon realizes that the horse is a bad omen for the Trojans. Sinon and the gods see the horse as a good omen for the Greeks. Vergil assumes that his readers understand that it was fated for Troy to fall and that these snakes were sent by the gods to persuade the Trojans to take the horse into the city. Remember that Aeneas, an eyewitness to these events, is telling the story from a Trojan point of view.

Fig. 12.
The Trojans Take the Horse into the City.

Keep This Vocabulary in Mind   WORDS FOR SNAKES AND SACRIFICES

In this passage, Laocoon is performing a sacrifice, and then snakes attack him. Some of the vocabulary of snakes and sacrifices from this passage appear below.

Words for Snakes

anguis, anguis, m. (f.) snake, serpent
dracō, dracōnis, m. dragon, serpent
serpēns, serpentis, m. (f.) serpent, snake

Describing Snakes

immēnsus, -a, -um immense, immeasurable
squāmeus, -a, -um scaly
venēnum, -ī, n. poison, venom, drug

The Snakes' Coils

nōdus, -ī, m. knot; fold, coil
orbis, orbis, m. circle, fold, coil; earth
spīra, -ae, f. fold, coil, spire
volūmen, volūminis, n. fold, coil, roll

Other Body Parts of the Snakes

cervīx, cervīcis, f. neck
collum, -ī, n. neck
iuba, -ae, f. mane, crest
lingua, -ae, f. tongue, language
morsus, -ūs, m. bite, biting, jaws, fangs
pectus, pectoris, n. chest
tergum, -ī, n. back, body, rear

Snake Movements

amplector, amplectī, amplexum to embrace, fold
arrigō, arrigere, arrēxī, arrēctum to raise, rear
implicō, implicāre, implicāvī or **implicuī, implicātum** or **implicitum** to entwine
lambō, lambere, lambī to lick, lap
sinuō, sinuāre to fold, curve, twist, wind
vibrō, vibrāre to quiver, vibrate, dart

The Sound of the Snakes

sībilus, -a, -um hissing, whirring

Sacrifices

āra, -ae, f. altar
dēlūbrum, ī, n. shrine
hostia, -ae, f. victim, sacrifice (usually an animal)
mactō, mactāre to sacrifice, slaughter; honor
sacer, sacra, sacrum sacred, holy, consecrated; accursed; (n. subst.) sacrifice, holy implement (object); mystery
sacerdōs, sacerdōtis, m. (f.) priest(ess)
secūris, secūris, f. ax (used to slay a sacrificial animal)
templum, -ī, n. temple, shrine
vitta, -ae, f. fillet, garland, band (worn by the priest and by the sacrificial victim)

Now It's Your Turn SNAKES AND SACRIFICES CONTINUED

Match the Latin word in Column A to its meaning in Column B

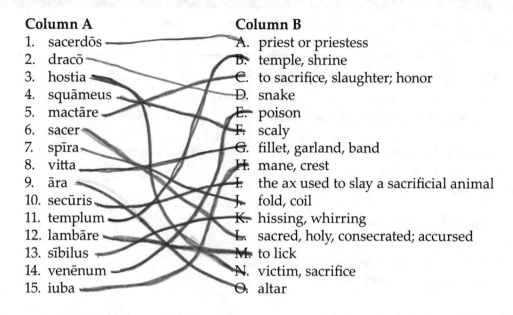

Column A
1. sacerdōs
2. dracō
3. hostia
4. squāmeus
5. mactāre
6. sacer
7. spīra
8. vitta
9. āra
10. secūris
11. templum
12. lambāre
13. sībilus
14. venēnum
15. iuba

Column B
A. priest or priestess
B. temple, shrine
C. to sacrifice, slaughter; honor
D. snake
E. poison
F. scaly
G. fillet, garland, band
H. mane, crest
I. the ax used to slay a sacrificial animal
J. fold, coil
K. hissing, whirring
L. sacred, holy, consecrated; accursed
M. to lick
N. victim, sacrifice
O. altar

Fig. 13.
Snakes from the Sea.

Helping You to Read What Vergil Wrote

Questions

Line 202: Use the fonts to find the adjective which modifies *ārās*.
Line 207–208: Find the two verbs of which *pars* is the subject.

Vocabulary

201. **sors, sortis,** f. lot, fate, destiny
 sacerdōs, sacerdōtis, m. (f.) priest(ess)

202. **taurus, -ī,** m. bull, bullock, ox
 mactō, mactāre to sacrifice
 sollemnis, sollemne annual, solemn

203. **ecce** interj. See! Look! Behold!
 autem conj. moreover, but, however
 altum, -ī, n. the deep (sea); heaven
 tranquillus, -a, -um tranquil, calm

204. **anguis, anguis,** m. (f.) snake, serpent
 immēnsus, -a, -um immense
 orbis, orbis, m. circle, fold, coil
 insula, -ae, f. island
 horrēscō, -ere, horruī to shudder, tremble

205. **incumbō, incumbere, -uī, -itum** (dat.) to lean
 upon
 pariter adv. equally, side by side

206. **arrigō, -ere, arrēxī, arrēctum** to raise
 iuba, -ae, f. mane, crest

207. **sanguineus, -a, -um** bloody
 superō, superāre to surmount
 cēterus, -a, -um rest, remaining
 uterque, utraque, utrumque each
 anguis, anguis, m. (f.) snake, serpent
 pontus, -ī, m. sea, waves

208. **pōne** adv. behind, after
 legō, legere, lēgī, lēctum to skim
 sinuō, sinuāre to fold, twist, wind
 immēnsus, -a, -um immense
 tergum, -ī, n. back, body, rear
 volūmen, volūminis, n. fold, coil, roll

209. **sonitus, -ūs,** m. sound, roar, noise
 spūmō, spūmāre to foam, froth, spray
 salum –ī, n. (the salt) sea, brine

Notes

201. **ductus** Translate here "chosen."
 sorte Ablative of means.

202. **ad** Translate here "at."

204. **immensīs orbibus** Ablative of quality;
 translate "with huge coils."
 referēns In this context *referō* means "tell."
 haec Translate "these things."

205. **pelagō** Dative with the compound verb
 incumbō.

206. **arrēcta** With *sunt* translate "were raised."

207. **pars cētera** "The remaining part" refers to the
 rear part of the snakes' bodies.

208. **pōne** Translate this adverb as "behind." This
 word is not part of *pōnō, pōnere*.
 legit Translate "skims." *Legit* is from *legō, legere*
 which usually means "choose" or "read."
 volūmine Ablative of respect; translate "in a
 coil."

209. **spūmante salō** Translate this ablative absolute
 "with the salt sea spraying."

Summary

Then Aeneas says that an even greater omen appeared to the miserable Trojans. Laocoon, chosen by lot to be priest of Neptune, was busy sacrificing a bull when, suddenly, two serpents with huge coils appeared coming from the island of Tenedos, just a short distance from the plain in front of Troy. They headed side by side for land. Their chests and bloody crests were seen above the waters. The remaining parts of their bodies and their backs in coils skimmed over the sea behind their heads. They were hissing as they reached land, and the Trojans, terrified by the sight, scattered. With their eyes blazing with fire and their tongues flickering, the snakes headed for Laocoon. First the snakes entwined and killed Laocoon's two small sons. Then they wrapped their coils around Laocoon himself twice. Laocoon tried in vain to tear the snakes' coils off his body, but he failed and raised horrific cries to the sky.

Making Sense of It

201 **Lāocoōn, ductus** Neptūnō sorte **sacerdōs,**
Laocoon, chosen priest by the fate of Neptune,

202 **sollemnīs taurum ingentem** mactābat ad **ārās.**
was sacrificing a huge bull to the solemn altars.

203 Ecce autem **geminī** (venientēs) ā Tenedō (insulā) tranquilla per alta
Behold, but twins (comma) from Tenedos (island) coming back through the tranquil

204 —horrēscō (haec) referēns—immēnsīs orbibus **anguēs**
deep—I tremble recounting—twin snakes with immense coils

205 incumbunt pelagō pariterque ad lītora tendunt;
They leaned on the sea and equally and streched to the sea.

206 **pectora** quōrum (serpentium) inter flūctūs **arrēcta** (sunt) iubaeque
The hearts (of them) having been raised among the bloody crests were

207 **sanguineae** superant undās; pars cētera pontum
seen above the waters;   the remaining parts

208 pōne legit sinuatque **immēnsa** volūmine **terga.**
and their backs in immense coils, skimmed over the waves, behin[d]

209 Fit sonitus spūmante salō;
The sound was made with the sea foam spraying

framing = sibila .... ora
chiasmus = sibila liquis vibrantibus ora
onomatopoeia = spumante
synchesis = parva duorum corpora natorum
alliteration = miseros morsu

• because they were heading straight for Laocoon not anyone else
• No he did not know of the sculpture

Questions

Line 210: Find the two ablatives which explain how the snakes' eyes are burning.
Line 215: What is the subject of *dēpascitur*? Hint: The subject is in line 214.

Vocabulary

210. sufficiō, -ere, -fēcī, -fectum to supply, suffuse
lingua, -ae, f. tongue, language

211. sībilus, -a, -um hissing, whirring
lambō, lambere, lambī to lick, lap
vibrō, vibrāre to quiver, vibrate

212. diffugiō, -ere, diffūgī to flee apart
vīsus, -ūs, m. sight, view, vision
exsanguis, exsangue bloodless, lifeless, pale
serpēns, serpentis, m. (f.) serpent, snake
certus, -a, -um sure, fixed, certain
anguis, anguis, m (f.) snake

213. parvus, -a, um small, little
duo, -ae, -o two

214. serpēns, serpentis, m. (f.) serpent, snake
uterque, utraque, utrumque each, both
amplector, amplectī, amplexum to embrace, fold

215. implicō, -āre, -āvī or **implicuī, implicātum** or **itum** to entwine
artus, -ūs, m. joint, limb, body
morsus, -ūs, m. bite, biting, jaws
dēpascor, dēpascī, dēpāstum to feed on, devour

Notes

210. arva tenēbant Translate literally "they held the fields." This means "they arrived upon the fields."
suffectī This middle/reflexive perfect participle should be translated here as "having suffused or having filled." *Oculōs* is the direct object of *suffectī*.
ardentīs This is the poetic accusative plural form of the present active participle.
sanguine et ignī Ablative of means. *Ignī* is a poetic ablative singular that in prose is *igne*.

211. ōra This is the neuter accusative plural of *ōs, ōris,* n. and means "mouths."

212. vīsū Ablative of cause; "at the sight."
agmine certō Ablative of means; translate "in a sure line."

213. Lāocoönta This noun has the Greek accusative singular ending –*a*. Do not confuse it with the the Latin –*a* of the accusative plural neuter as in *corpora* in line 214.
prīmum An accusative adjective, as in Greek, can function as an adverb. Translate "first."

214. amplexus Perfect passive participles of deponent verbs translate actively. Thus *amplexus* means "having enfolded."

215. artūs Accusative plural masculine.
morsū Ablative of means, fourth declension.

Making Sense of It CONTINUED

209   iamque (**serpentēs**) arva tenēbant

an now (the serpents) arrived upon the shores

210 ardentīsque oculōs **suffectī** sanguine et ignī

and having suffused burning eyes with blood & fire

211 **sībila** lambēbant **linguīs vibrantibus ōra**.

they were licking (their) hissing mouths w/ vibrating tongues

212 (**Nos**) diffugimus vīsū (anguium) **exsanguēs**. Illī (serpentēs)

     agmine certō

We lifeless scattered at the sight. Those (serpents) in a sure

213 Lāocoönta petunt; et prīmum parva **duōrum**

line sought Laocoon; and first the snakes entwined and folded

214 corpora **nātōrum** *serpēns amplexus uterque*

each of the two small sons bodies and devoured the miserable bodies

215 implicat et **miserōs** morsū dēpascitur **artūs**;

with biting jaws.

ABBA
‖
chiasmus

Fig. 14.
The Death of Laocoon and His Sons.

Questions

Line 216–217: Identify the subject of *ligant*.

Lines 216–222: Find two perfect passive participles used as reflexive/middles in this passage.

Vocabulary	Notes

Vocabulary

216. **post** adv. afterward; (prep. + acc.) behind
auxilium, -ī, n. help, aid, assistance

217. **corripiō, -ere, corripuī, correptus** to seize, snatch up
spīra, -ae, f. fold, coil, spire
ligō, ligāre to bind, tie, fasten

218. **bis** adv. twice
collum, -ī, n. neck
squāmeus, -a, -um scaly

219. **tergum, -ī,** n. back, body, rear
cervīx, cervīcis, f. neck
superō, superāre to surmount, overcome, survive

220. **dīvellō, dīvellere, dīvellī** or **dīvulsī, dīvulsum** or **dīvolsum** to tear apart
nōdus, -ī, m. knot; fold, coil

221. **perfundō, perfundere, perfūdī, perfūsum** to soak, drench
saniēs, saniēī, f. blood, gore
vitta, -ae, f. fillet, garland, band
venēnum, -ī, n. poison, venom, drug

222. **horrendus, -a, -um** horrible

Notes

216. **post** An adverb, not a preposition. Translate "afterwards."
auxiliō Dative of purpose. Literally, "for aid." Translate "with aid" or "to help."
subeuntem ac ferentem Both present active participles modify *Lāocoönta ipsum*.
subeuntem From *subeō*. "Approaching."

217. **serpentēs** Nominative plural, subject.
spīrīs Ablative plural; translate "with their coils."

218–219. **circum ... datī** A reflexive /middle use of the Latin passive. Translate actively with *terga collō* "having placed their backs around his neck."

218. **collō** Dative with the compound verb *circum ... datī*.

219. **illum** Refers to Laocoon.
capite et cervīcibus altīs Ablative of means. *Capite* is from *caput, capitis*, not from the verb *capiō*. Although *capite* is singular, translate it in the plural.
terga Neuter accusative, direct object of *datī ... circum*.

220. **manibus** Ablative of means; translate "with his hands."

221. **perfūsus** Translate "having soaked."
vittās Accusative, direct object of *perfūsus*.
saniē ātrōque venēnō Ablative of means. The ribbons (*vittās*) worn by Laocoon as a priest are drenched "with blood and dark venom."

Making Sense of It CONTINUED

216 post (Lāocoönta) ipsum auxiliō subeuntem ac tēla ferentem .
after approaching and bearing a spear with aid (serpent's)

217 (serpentēs) corripiunt **spīrīs**que ligant *ingentibus*; et iam
seized (Laocoon) and bind (him) with huge coils; and now twice

218 bis medium (corporis) amplexī, bis collō **squāmea** circum
with the middle (of the body) having been embraced, twice having placed their

219 **terga** datī (illum) superant capite et **cervīcibus altīs**.
scaly backs around his neck they conquered by the heads and high necks.

220 **Ille** simul manibus tendit dīvellere nōdōs
that one at the same time holds with his hands to tear apart the

221 **perfūsus** saniē vittās ātrōque venēnō,
knot about to soak the fillet in black venom and blood,

222 (et) **clāmōrēs** simul **horrendōs** ad sīdera tollit.
and horrendous shouts we upheaved at the same time to heaven

Stopping for Review   COMPREHENSION QUESTIONS

Find the Latin word or phrase that answers each of the following questions in the passage you have just read. Then translate this word or phrase into English.

1. What was Laocoon doing as the snakes appeared?

2. Where were the snakes coming from?

3. What did Aeneas do as he was telling the story about the snakes?

4. What parts of the snakes were raised above the waves?

5. What part of the snakes was in a huge coil and with what did the snakes' eyes burn?

6. What did the snakes do with their tongues?

7. Who fled the sight of the snakes?

8. Whom were the snakes seeking and whom did they attack first?

9. What was Laocoon holding when the snakes attacked him?

10. How many times did the snakes coil around Laocoon's body?

11. What parts of the snakes' bodies stood over Laocoon?

12. What was Laocoon drenched in?

13. What does Laocoon do with his hands?

14. What does he raise to the sky?

WHAT VERGIL ACTUALLY WROTE

Notes

202. **sollemnīs . . . ārās** Notice how Vergil introduces the modifier *sollemnīs* at the beginning of the line but *ārās* does not appear until the end of the line. Such an early appearance of a modifier is called **prolepsis** or **anticipation**.

204. **referēns** Vergil leaves understood the direct object for *referēns* (*haec* "these things"). Thus translate *referēns* as "telling these things."

206. **quōrum** The antecedent of this relative pronoun is *anguēs* (204). The relative pronoun is here used as a personal or demonstrative pronoun. So here translate *quōrum* as "their."

207. **sanguineae superant** Notice that these two succeeding words each begin with the same consonant. This is called **alliteration**.

209. **spūmante salō** The "s" sound in *spūmante* mimics the word's meaning, i.e., the "spraying" sound of the salt water. This is called **onomatopeia**.

211. **sībila . . . linguīs vibrantibus ōra.** Since *sībila* modifies *ōra* and *linguīs* is modified by *vibrantibus*, these four words are an example of a **chiasmus**. Notice that the *linguīs vibrantibus* are inside the *sībila ōra*, thus creating a picture with words.

212. **Illī** From the context this pronoun refers to the snakes. Translate as "they."

213–214. **parva duōrum corpora nātōrum** Notice that *parva* modifies *corpora* and *duōrum* modifies *nātōrum*. This is the A B A B pattern of words which is called **synchesis** or interlocked word order. Note also that these words entwine themselves around one another just as the snakes entwine themselves around Laocoon's sons.

215. **miserōs morsū** Notice the **alliteration** of these words.

216. **ipsum** Modifies the unnamed Laocoon. Translate *ipsum* as "Laocoon himself." The accusative singular *ipsum* is not the object of *post,* which is an adverb here, but the direct object of both *corripiunt* and *ligant* in line 217.

218. **bis** Note the **anaphora** of *bis . . . bis* in this line.
     medium An adjective used as a substantive. Understand "of his body" and translate as "middle part of his body."
     circum *Circum* is separated from the rest of its word *datī* which is in line 219. This is called **tmesis**.

219. **capite et cervīcibus altīs** Note how Vergil uses *caput* in the singular and *cervīx* in the plural, even though he is referring to both snakes. Translate the "poetic singular" *capite* in the plural.

222. **ad sīdera** This is an example of **hyperbole**, exaggeration for effect. The sound of the shouts is made to seem so loud that they could be heard in the stars.

As It Was

201   Lāocoōn, ductus Neptūnō sorte sacerdōs,

202   sollemnīs taurum ingentem mactābat ad ārās.

203   Ecce autem geminī ā Tenedō tranquilla per alta

204   —horrēscō referēns—immēnsīs orbibus anguēs

205   incumbunt pelagō pariterque ad lītora tendunt;

206   pectora quōrum inter flūctūs arrēcta iubaeque

207   sanguineae superant undās; pars cētera pontum

208   pōne legit sinuatque immēnsa volūmine terga.

209   Fit sonitus spūmante salō; iamque arva tenēbant

210   ardentīsque oculōs suffectī sanguine et ignī

211   sībila lambēbant linguīs vibrantibus ōra.

212   Diffugimus vīsū exsanguēs. Illī agmine certō

213   Lāocoönta petunt; et prīmum parva duōrum

214   corpora nātōrum serpēns amplexus uterque

215   implicat et miserōs morsū dēpascitur artūs;

216   post ipsum auxiliō subeuntem ac tēla ferentem

217   corripiunt spīrīsque ligant ingentibus; et iam

218   bis medium amplexī, bis collō squāmea circum

219   terga datī superant capite et cervīcibus altīs.

220   Ille simul manibus tendit dīvellere nōdōs

221   perfūsus saniē vittās ātrōque venēnō,

222   clāmōrēs simul horrendōs ad sīdera tollit.

AFTER READING WHAT VERGIL WROTE

Thinking about How the Author Writes	VERGIL'S USE OF SOUND

This is a particularly good passage in which to appreciate the importance of the sound of words in Vergil's poetry, which was meant to be heard rather than read silently. Vergil himself recited portions of the *Aeneid* publicly. Members of his audience included the emperor Augustus and his family. Wicar's painting on the cover of this reader depicts just such a recitation. Note how one member of the emperor's family has fainted as a result of Vergil's dramatic reading.

Notice how Vergil uses sound to enhance his description of the snakes' approach. He does this especially with **alliteration** and **onomatopoeia**:

199   *Hīc aliud maius miserīs multōque tremendum.* Here the repetition of *m* sound emphasizes the enormity (*maius*) of the omen of the snakes.

207   *sanguineae superant.* This alliteration suggests the hissing sound of the snakes, a sound which Vergil repeats for the snakes with *sinuat* (208), *suffectī sanguine* (210), *sībila* (211), *spīrīs* (217), *squāmea* (218), *saniē* (221), *simul* (222), and *sīdera* (222). These are only some examples of words with the "s" sound in this passage.

209   *sonitus spūmante salō* Here the "s" sound is not only alliteration, but *spūmante* is onomatopoetic because it represents the sound that spraying waves make.

211   *lambēbant linguīs* The repetition of the "l" creates the sound of the licking tongues of the serpents.

215   *miserōs morsū* The repetition of the "m" sound emphasizes how miserable (*miserōs*) they are.

Here are some examples of similar sound play in English:

      the **b**uzzing of the **b**usy **b**ees
      the **h**i**ss**ing of the **sl**ithering **s**nakes
      the **b**anging of the **b**ig **b**rass **b**ell

Can you think of any more examples in English?

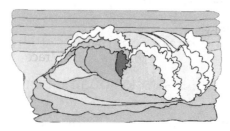

Fig. 15.
Spūmante Salō.

Stopping for Some Review

FIGURES OF SPEECH AGAIN

Define each of the following figures of speech in your own words.

Anaphora	Synecdoche
Alliteration	Simile
Asyndeton	Extended Simile
Synchesis	Apostrophe
Chiasmus	Hysteron Proteron
Antithesis	Pleonasm

Each of the following quotations has been taken from a passage of the *Aeneid* that you have already read. Identify the figure of speech in each line. Then explain the content and context of each quotation.

1. Ō fortūnātī, quōrum iam moenia surgunt!

2. Per variōs cāsūs, per tot discrīmina rērum

3. Tantaene animīs caelestibus īrae?

4. pars optāre locum tēctō et conclūdere sulcō

5. Tālia vōce refert cūrīsque ingentibus aeger

6. aut spūmantis aprī cursum clāmōre prementem

7. īnsignem pietāte virum, tot adīre labōrēs

8. Aenēās ait et fastīgia suspicit urbis

9. Quālis apēs aestāte novā per flōrea rūra

Stopping for Some Review

MORE LATIN SYNONYMS

Match the Latin synonyms from Column A and Column B.

Column A	Column B
1. anguis	A. flūctus
2. saniēs	B. orbis
3. dēlūbrum	C. ōra
4. spīra	D. dracō
5. implicō	E. pontus
6. cervīx	F. vultus
7. pelagus	G. templum
8. unda	H. sanguis
9. ōs	I. collum
10. lītus	J. amplector

Thinking about What You Read

1. In what ways does Vergil depict the appearance of a snake as an important omen or sign from the gods?

2. Why do the two snakes come from Tenedos (*ā Tenedō*, 203) and what significance does this have to the reader's understanding of this passage?

3. How do you think the serpents "lean on the sea" (*incumbunt pelagō*, 205)? What picture is Vergil trying to paint in his reader's mind?

4. To whom do you think that Aeneas is referring when he says "we fled" (*diffugimus*, 212)?

5. The Latin word *agmine* (212) means "army" or "line." How do both meanings of this word fit the context in which *agmine* is used in this passage?

6. How does Vergil's use of interlocked word order in lines 213–214 and tmesis in lines 218-219 aid the picture he is trying to portray in this passage?

7. Why do you think Vergil describes Laocoon's *artūs* as *miserōs* (215), his sons' *corpora* as *parva* (213–214), and the *venēnō* as *ātrō* (221)?

8. Why do you think that the snakes killed Laocoon's sons as well as Laocoon himself? Why do you think that the snakes killed Laocoon's sons first?

9. How is the death of Laocoon like the slaughter of a sacrificial animal? Why do you think the gods send the snakes to kill him?

BEFORE YOU READ WHAT VERGIL WROTE

Introduction

Aeneas is describing to Dido and her court the disasters which befell the Trojans after the wooden horse was brought into Troy and the Greeks captured the city. Vergil uses the relationship between fathers and sons to focus this narrative on *pietās*, on respect for one's parent, country, and gods. Pyrrhus, the son of Achilles, kills Polites, the son of Priam. Priam and his wife Hecuba witness the execution of their son. Priam accuses Pyrrhus of not being as worthy a warrior as his father Achilles. In order to understand this scene fully, Vergil's readers are expected to know that at the end of Homer's *Iliad* Priam had gone to the tent of Achilles to ransom the body of his dead son Hector, whom Achilles had killed in battle. Out of respect for his own father Peleus, Achilles allows Priam to ransom his son. In contrast, Achilles' son Pyrrhus shows no mercy and murders Polites before the eyes of his father Priam.

Keep This Grammar in Mind   VERGIL'S USE OF NUMBER

Vergil does not hesitate to use plurals where the singular makes more sense (and vice versa). This is sometimes called a "poetic plural." For example, in the passage you are about to read, King Priam makes reference to *mea rēgna* ("my kingdoms," II. 543). Although grammatically plural, this phrase could be translated into English as either a singular or a plural. At II. 539 Priam refers to his *patriōs . . . vultūs*. This plural is better translated into English as the singular "fatherly sight."

In the following phrase, the bold word is grammatically **plural** but is better translated into English as a **singular**.

> *Tantaene animīs caelestibus **īrae**?* (I. 11)

In the following phrases the bold word is grammatically **singular** but is better translated into English as a **plural**:

> ***capite** et cervīcibus altīs* (II. 219)

Sometimes Vergil uses the same word in either **the singular or the plural**. For example, both of the substantives below refer to the "deep sea" or "the depths":

> *terrīs ... et **altō*** (I. 3)   *tranquilla per **alta*** (II. 203)

Sometimes a single person is called "we." This is called the "regal plural" or "the royal we."

> *multa tibi ante ārās **nostrā** cadet hostia **dextrā*** (I.334) "by our (i.e., my) hand"

HELPING YOU TO READ WHAT VERGIL WROTE

Questions

Line 533: What is the subject of *tenētur*?
Line 536: What word does the feminine nominative singular *qua* modify?

Vocabulary

526. **ecce** interj. See! Look! Behold!
autem conj. but, however, moreover
Polītēs, -ae, m. son of Priam
ēlābor, ēlābī, ēlapsum to escape
caedēs, caedis, f. slaughter, murder
Pyrrhus, -ī, m. also known as Neoptolemus

527. **hostis, hostis,** m. (f.) enemy, foe

528. **porticus, -ūs,** f. colonnade, portico
vacuus, -a, -um empty, vacant, free
ātrium, -ī, n. great hall, atrium
lūstrō, lūstrāre to traverse, cross

529. **saucius, -a, -um** wounded, hurt
īnfēstus, -a, -um hostile, threatening
vulnus, vulneris, n. wound

530. **īnsequor, īnsequī, īnsecūtum** to follow, pursue
hasta, -ae, f. spear, lance, dart
premō, premere, pressī, pressum to (re)press, pierce

531. **ēvādō, ēvādere, ēvāsī, ēvāsum** to come forth

532. **concidō, -ere, concidī** to fall (in a heap)

533. **quamquam** conj. although

534. **tamen** conj. nevertheless, but
abstineō, abstinēre, abstinuī, abstentum, to refrain, restrain
parcō, parcere, pepercī or **parsī, parsum** (dat.) to spare

535. **exclāmō, -āre** to cry (out), shout
ausum, -ī, n. daring deed, daring
scelus, sceleris, n. crime, sin

536. **pietās, pietātis,** f. loyalty, duty
cūrō, cūrāre to regard, care (for)

Notes

526. **ēlapsus** Translate this perfect passive participle of the deponent verb *ēlābor* actively, "having escaped."

527. **hostīs** Alternative, poetic accusative plural.

528. **porticibus** Ablative of route; translate "along the long porticos."

529. **saucius** Describes Polites, who is wounded.
vulnere Ablative of means. Here *vulnus* is not the wound itself but the blow which will inflict the wound.

530. **(illum) tenet** Pyrrhus is holding Polites.
hastā Ablative of means.

531. **Ut** Since the verb in this *ut* clause, *ēvāsit*, is indicative, instead of subjunctive, translate *ut* with the word "when."

532. **fūdit** Translate "poured out."

533. **hīc** The macron shows this is the adverb "here," not the demonstrative pronoun/adjective "this."
in mediā morte Translate in English "in the middle of death."

534. **vōcī īraeque** Datives with *parcō*.

535. **At** This word means "but." Do not confuse *ac* (and) or *ad* (to) with *at*.
tibi Translate with *dī persolvant grātēs* (536–537).

536. **sī qua** After *si* any form of *aliquis* ("any") drops the *ali*.
est Translate as "there is."
cūret Note the subjunctive in a relative clause of characteristic.

Summary

Polites, one of Priam's sons, flees through the long portico and, wounded, crosses the empty atrium. Pyrrhus, eager for the kill, follows him. Again and again Pyrrhus holds Polites with his hand and pierces him with his sword. When at last Polites escapes, in front of his parents, he collapses and dies. Then, although about to die, Priam cries out in anger to Pyrrhus that, if there was any justice in heaven, the gods would make him pay for making the father witness the death of his son before his very eyes. Priam also announces that Achilles, the father of Pyrrhus, had not acted thus but had respected the honor of a suppliant and had sent Priam home with the body of his dead son Hector.

Making Sense of It

526 Ecce autem **ēlāpsus** Pyrrhī dē caede **Polītēs**,

Look however Polites having escaped from the murder of Pyrrhus, one of the

527 **ūnus** nātōrum Priamī, per tēla, (et) per hostīs

sons of Priam, flees through the weapons and through the enemies along

528 porticibus longīs fugit et vacua ātria lūstrat

the long portico and crosses the empty hall wounded.

529 **saucius**. Illum **ardēns īnfēstō vulnere Pyrrhus** *(that one)*

That burning Pyrrhus threatening follows with a hostile wound

530 īnsequitur, iam iamque manū (illum) tenet et premit hastā (illum).

now at last that were holds and pierces that man spear with the

531 Ut tandem ante oculōs ēvāsit et ōra parentum,

(Polites) finally came forth before the eyes and mouths of the parents, (Polites

532 (Polītēs) concidit ac **multō** vītam cum **sanguine** fūdit.

fell and poured out with much blood his life.

533 Hīc Priamus, quamquam in **mediā** iam **morte** tenētur,

Here Priam, although he was held in the middle of death

534 nōn tamen abstinuit nec vōcī īraeque pepercit:

nevertheless he did not refrain to spare neither his voice nor anger:

535 'At tibi prō scelere,' exclāmat, 'prō **tālibus ausīs**

'but you before crime', he exclaimed,' before such a daring deed of the gods

536 dī, sī **qua** est (in) caelō **pietās** quae tālia cūret,

if anyone's duty is in the sky

Fig. 16.
Portico.

Questions

Line 537: Look in line 536 for the subject of *persolvant* and *reddant*.
Line 541–543: Find the four verbs for which *ille . . . Achillēs* (540) is the subject .

Vocabulary

537. **persolvō, persolvere, persolvī, persolūtum** to pay fully
   grātēs, grātium, f. (pl.) thanks, reward
   dignus, -a, -um worthy, suitable
   praemium, -(i)ī, n. reward, prize
   reddō, reddere, reddidī, redditum to return, render

538. **dēbitus, -a, -um** due, owed
   cōram adv. face to face
   lētum, -ī, n. death, destruction, ruin

539. **vultus, -ūs,** m. face, countenance
   fūnus, fūneris, n. death, funeral
   foedō, foedāre to defile, disfigure

540. **Achillēs, Achillis (-ī, eī),** m. Greek leader
   serō, serere, sēvī, satum to sow, beget
   mentior, mentīrī, mentītum to lie

541. **hostis, hostis,** m. (f.) enemy, foe
   iūs, iūris, n. law, right, justice
   fidēs, fideī, f. faith, fidelity, reliance

542. **supplex, supplicis,** m. (f.) suppliant
   ērubēscō, ērubēscere, ērubuī to reverence, blush (before)
   exsanguis, exsangue bloodless, lifeless
   Hectoreus, -a, -um of Hector
   sepulcrum, -ī, n. tomb, burial

543. **remittō, -ere, remīsī, remissum** to send back

544. **senior, seniōris,** m. old (aged) man
   imbellis, imbelle unwarlike, harmless
   sine prep. + abl. without
   ictus, -ūs, m. stroke, blow, wound

545. **coniciō, -ere, coniēcī, coniectum** to hurl
   prōtinus adv. immediately
   aes, aeris, n. bronze
   raucus, -a, -um hoarse, clanging
   repellō, -ere, reppulī, repulsum to drive back

546. **umbō, umbōnis,** m. boss, knob
   clipeus, -ī, m. shield, buckler
   nēquīquam adv. in vain, uselessly
   pendeō, pendēre, pependī to hang

Notes

537. **persolvant** and **reddant** Both verbs are optative subjunctives used to express wishes. Translate with the English helping verb "may."

538. **mē cernere** This infinitive with a subject accusative is the object of *fēcisti*, i.e., it explains what Pyrrhus made Priam do.

539. **patriōs vultūs** The adjective *patriōs* shows that *vultūs* is accusative plural, not nominative singular, as does the macron on *vultūs*. Note Vergil's use of a poetic plural and translate "a father's face."
   natī The son Priam is referring to is Polites.

540. **(ex) quō** Take this phrase with the participle *satum* and translate "from whom . . . begotten."
   mentīris This verb introduces an infinitive (*satum esse*) with subject accusative (*tē*) in indirect discourse.

541. **in** Translate "toward" rather than "in."

542–543. **sepulcrō reddidit** Literally "he handed over for the grave." I..e., Achilles gave Hector's body back to Priam to be buried.

543. **mea rēgna** Note the poetic plural.

545. **quod** The relative pronoun "which."
   raucō . . . aere Ablative of means.

Making Sense of It CONTINUED

537   persolvant **grātēs dignās** et praemia reddant

538   dēbita (tibi), quī nātī cōram **mē** cernere lētum

539   fēcistī et **patriōs** foedā(vi)stī fūnere **vultūs** (natī).

540   At nōn **ille** (vir), satum (esse) (ex) quō tē mentīris, **Achillēs**

But that Achilles was not such toward the enemy, Priam, from whom

541   **tālis** in **hoste** fuit **Priamō**; sed iūra fidemque

you lie that you were begotten; but he reverences help and faith

542   supplicis ērubuit **corpus**que **exsangue** sepulcrō

of the suppliant and hands the lifeless body over to the grave.

543   reddidit **Hectoreum** mēque in mea rēgna remīsit.'

544   Sīc fātus (est) senior **tēlum**que **imbelle** sine ictū

Thus the fate is an old man and he hurls

545   coniēcit, **raucō** quod prōtinus **aere** repulsum (est),

546   et (dē) **summō** clipeī nēquīquam **umbōne** pependit.

in vain

Fig. 17.
Achilles Agrees to Return Hector's Corpse to Priam.

Stopping for Some Practice   SOME QUESTIONS FOR REVIEW

Read the following statements adapted from this passage and then put the statements in chronological order from what happened first to what happened last.

3 Pyrrhus manū Polītem tenet.

2 Polītēs longīs porticibus fugit.

6 Priamus imbelle tēlum conicit.

1 Corpus Hectoreum ad Priamum reddit Achillēs.

4 Polītēs cum sanguine vītam fundit.

5 Priamus dīcit deōs praemia dēbita Pyrrhō redditūrōs esse.

WHAT VERGIL ACTUALLY WROTE

Notes

527. **per tēla, per hostīs** For dramatic purposes, Vergil omits the connector between these two prepositional phrases. The omission of a conjunction like "and" is called **asyndeton**. Note that the repetition of the word *per* is also an example of **anaphora**.

529. **saucius** Notice the emphatic position of this word at the end of the sentence and at the beginning of a line.
īnfēstō While *īnfēstō* agrees with *vulnere*, in sense it fits better as a **transferred epithet** with *Pyrrhus*. Translate "hostile Pyrrhus." The placement of words that Vergil chose to use in this line, however, *ardēns īnfēstō vulnere Pyrrhus*, forms a **chiasmus**.

530. The **anaphora** of *iam iamque* is immediately followed by the **chiasmus** in *manū tenet et premit hastā*.

534. **vōcī īraeque** These two nouns, joined by the conjunction "et," can be translated with the noun/adjective phrase "angry voice." This type of expression is called **hendiadys**.

538. **quī** The antecedent is *tibi* in line 535.

539. **foedāstī fūnere** Note the **alliteration** of these two words.

Fig. 18.
Atrium.

526 Ecce autem ēlāpsus Pyrrhī dē caede Polītēs,

527 ūnus nātōrum Priamī, per tēla, per hostīs

528 porticibus longīs fugit et vacua ātria lūstrat]

529 saucius. Illum ardēns īnfēstō vulnere Pyrrhus

530 īnsequitur, iam iamque manū tenet et premit(hastā.)

531 Ut tandem ante oculōs ēvāsit et ōra parentum,

532 concidit ac multō vītam cum sanguine fūdit.

533 Hīc Priamus, quamquam in mediā iam morte tenētur,

534 nōn tamen abstinuit nec vōcī īraeque pepercit:

535 'At tibi prō scelere,' exclāmat, 'prō tālibus ausīs

536 dī, sī qua est caelō pietās quae tālia cūret,

537 persolvant grātēs dignās et praemia reddant

538 dēbita, quī nātī cōram mē cernere lētum

539 fēcistī et patriōs foedāstī fūnere vultūs.

540 At nōn ille, satum quō tē mentīris, Achillēs

541 tālis in hoste fuit Priamō; sed iūra fidemque

542 supplicis ērubuit corpusque exsangue sepulcrō

543 reddidit Hectoreum mēque in mea rēgna remīsit.'

544 Sīc fātus senior tēlumque imbelle sine ictū

545 coniēcit, raucō quod prōtinus aere repulsum,

546 et summō clipeī nēquīquam umbōne pependit.

AFTER READING WHAT VERGIL WROTE

Thinking about How the Author Writes   LITERARY AND CULTURAL CONTEXTS

Vergil assumes that his reader is familiar with many people, places, customs, and events to which he makes only passing reference. For example, when Priam tells Pyrrhus in this passage that Achilles had not been so cruel to him when he returned Hector's body to him, Priam is making reference to the story of the ransom of Hector's body in Book 24 of Homer's *Iliad*.

For Vergil's Roman readers, the story of the ransom of Hector's body is closely tied with the ancient law of respect for suppliants to which Priam also refers in the phrase *iūra fidemque supplicis* (II. 541–542). It was customary that persons in dire need, wearing appropriate symbols like wreaths, could approach more powerful individuals, even their enemies, to request help without fear of harm. Such suppliants were considered to be under the protection of the gods, and someone who harmed a suppliant could expect divine retribution. In the passage you have just read, Priam praised Achilles for respecting this law of suppliants and not harming his enemy Priam when he came to ransom his son's body. Pyrrhus' cruelty toward Priam in this scene is intensified by Achilles' respect for the old king in the *Iliad*.

While modern readers can readily understand the horror of slaying a son before the eyes of his father, Vergil adds to the horror for an ancient reader by emphasizing that Pyrrhus drags the king *ad altāria* ("to the altar," II. 550) before slaying him. So Pyrrhus not only disregards the law of suppliants but also commits the sacrilege of killing at an altar.

As you read more of the *Aeneid*, be prepared to deal with many other examples of such literary and cultural references. For example, you have already seen how Vergil refers to the Punic Wars between Rome and Carthage in Book I. In Book III he makes many parallels between the journey of Aeneas and the voyage of Odysseus in Homer's *Odyssey*.

Thinking about What You Read

1. In what ways does Vergil develop the theme of *pietās*, i.e., a son's respect for his father, in this passage?

2. This passage begins in the present tense (*fugit et vacua ātria lūstrat*, 528). When does Vergil move to the perfect tense? Why do you think he switches between the two?
    Line 531, to show that someone was retelling the story instead of it happening.

3. Why does Vergil describe the atrium as *vacua* in line 528?
    Because no one is in the palace because everyone is fighting

4. How does the word order of the phrase *illum ardēns īnfēstō vulnere Pyrrhus īnsequitur* (529–530) parallel the meaning of the phrase?   *īnsequitur = following or last*
    burning is strong = beginning   *The meat of the sentence = in the middle*

5. What adjectives does Vergil use in this passage to create sympathy for Priam and antipathy for Pyrrhus?
    defiled, harmless, lie, worthy

6. If you were Pyrrhus, how would you respond to Priam's words and actions?
    I would be amazed.

THE DEATH OF PRIAM
(*Aeneid* II. 547–566)

BEFORE YOU READ WHAT VERGIL WROTE

Introduction

Aeneas continues telling the story of the fall of Troy to Dido and her court. He relates how Pyrrhus drags Priam to the altar and slaughters the king in the blood of his son Polites. The sight of Priam's body makes Aeneas become concerned about the safety of his family, and he turns to see that his men have abandoned him or lie dead.

In the previous passage Priam contrasted Pyrrhus' cruel treatment of the king with the respectful way Pyrrhus' father Achilles behaved toward Priam when the Trojan king came to ransom the body of his dead son Hector. Here Vergil compares Pyrrhus' behavior with the respect and concern Aeneas displays for his father Anchises. The importance of the father-son relationship is emphasized even in the way characters are named in the *Aeneid*. Vergil often refers to a character by his patronym, i.e, by calling him the son of his father. So Achilles is sometimes *Pēlīdēs* ("son of Peleus") and Aeneas is *Anchīsiadēs* ("son of Anchises").

Keep This Vocabulary in Mind   NAMES AND PATRONYMS

In the previous reading, Vergil referred to Achilles' son only as Pyrrhus. It is not unusual, however, for Vergil to refer to characters by more than one name. In fact, Vergil has several ways of naming a person. Sometimes he uses a patronym. Other times there is a second name for the person. In this passage Pyrrhus is called by his other name Neoptolemus. Vergil can also use an adjective form of a name. So *Aenēius* means "of Aeneas'" or "related to Aeneas." Here are some examples from the *Aeneid*:

NAME	OTHER	ADJECTIVE	PATRONYM	SON
Anchīsēs			Anchīsiadēs	Aenēās
Aenēās		Aenēius	Aeneadēs	Ascānius
Ascānius	Iūlus			
Achillēs		Achillēus	Achillīdēs	Pyrrhus
Pyrrhus	Neoptolemus			
Atreus			Atrīdēs	Agamemnōn/Menelāus
Hector		Hectoreus		
Pēleus			Pēlīdēs	Achillēs
Priamus		Priamēius	Priamidēs	Hector/Helenus/Polites

65

HELPING YOU TO READ WHAT VERGIL WROTE

Questions

Line 551: What is the subject of *trāxit*?
Lines 555–56: What two words are the direct objects of *videntem*?

Vocabulary

547. Pyrrhus, -ī, m. Neoptolemus, son of Achilles
ergo therefore

548. Pēlīdēs, -ae, m. descendant of Peleus, Achilles
factum, -ī, n. deed, exploit

549. dēgeneris, dēgenere, degenerate, ignoble
Neoptolemus, -ī, m. Pyrrhus, son of Achilles

550. morior, morī, mortuum to die
tremō, tremere, tremuī to tremble

551. lāpsō, lāpsāre to slip, stumble, fall

552. coma, -ae, f. hair, locks, tresses
implicō, implicāre, implicāvī or **implicuī, implicātum** or **implicitum** to entwine
laevus, -a, -um f. left (hand)
coruscus, -a, -um flashing, bright

553. ēnsis, ēnsis, m. sword, knife
efferō, efferre, extulī, ēlātum to lift, raise
capulus, -ī, m. hilt, handle, head
tenus prep. (+ abl.) to, up to, as far as
abdō, abdere, abdidī, abditum to hide

554. exitus, -ūs, m. exit, end

555. sors, sortis, f. lot, fate, destiny
incendō, incendere, incendī, incensum to burn, fire
prōlābor, prōlābī, prōlāpsus to slide, fall, perish

556. Pergama, -ōrum, n. pl. (citadel of) Troy
tot adv. so many
populus, populī, m. people
superbus, -a, -um proud, haughty

557. rēgnātor, rēgnātōris, m. ruler, lord
Asia, -ae, f. Asia (Minor), the Roman province in western Turkey

Notes

547. cui Refers to Priam. Translate as a personal pronoun, "to him."
referēs Future indicative. "You will report."
haec Translate this neuter accusative plural substantive as "these things."
nuntius Nominative in apposition to "you" and the subject of *ībis*. Translate "as a messenger."

548. illī Dative indirect object of *nārrāre*; translate "(to) him."

549. mementō This is the rarely seen future imperative form. Translate "remember."
nārrāre Translate "to tell of."

550. morere This passive imperative of a deponent verb translates "die!"
altāria *Altāria*, the high part of the altar where the fire is lit, is plural, but translate in the singular.

551. nātī Genitive singular. Translate "of his son," i.e., Polites, whom Neoptolemus has just killed.
in multō sanguine Literally "in the much blood of his son." Translate "in the copious blood of his son."

552. laevā (manū) Ablative of means.
dextrā (manū) Also ablative of means.

553. laterī Dative of direction; translate "into his side." *Laterī* is from *latus, lateris,* n. "side".
capulō tenus This preposition follows its object.

554. haec . . . fīnis The feminine *haec* indicates that *fīnis* (usually masculine) is here feminine.
hic exitus Subject of *tulit*.
illum . . . videntem Direct object of *tulit* (555). Translate "him to see."

555. incensam . . . prōlāpsa Perfect passive infinitives in indirect statement. Translate "had been burned" and "had fallen."

557. rēgnātōrem In apposition with *illum* (554).
populīs terrīsque Datives of reference with *rēgnātōrem*; "ruler to many peoples and lands."

Summary

In reply to Priam, who has just told Pyrrhus that he is unworthy of his dead father Achilles, Pyrrhus angrily tells the old king to go as a messenger to his dead father in Hades and report on the bad deeds of his son Neoptolemus. Then Pyrrhus drags Priam, who is stumbling in the blood of his dead son Polites, to the altar. Pyrrhus stabs the king's side with his sword. The dead king, who once had been the proud ruler of so many peoples and lands in Asia, lies decapitated on the shore. Aeneas stands horrified at the sight. The image of his own aged father comes to his mind when he sees the old king dying. He also begins to think of his wife Creusa, and his little son Iulus. He looks around and sees that his weary men have deserted him. They have committed suicide by jumping to their deaths or by burning themselves alive in the flames.

Making Sense of It

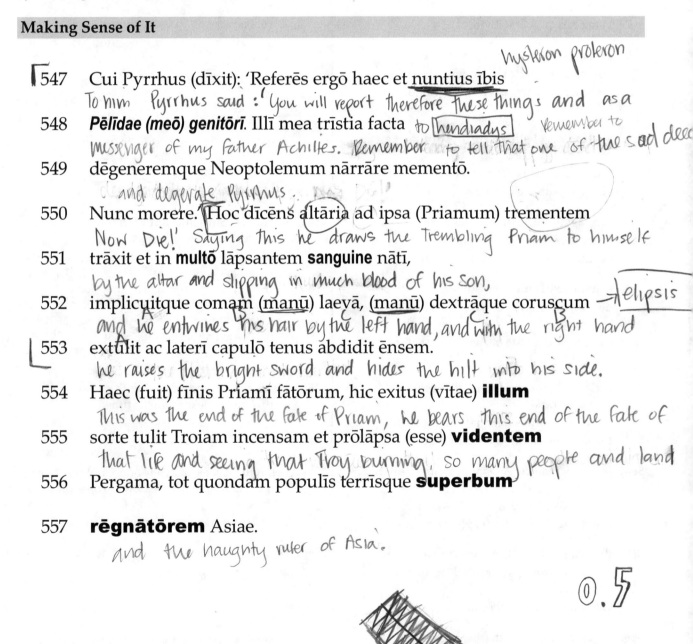

hysteron proteron

547 Cui Pyrrhus (dīxit): 'Referēs ergō haec et nuntius ībis
    To him Pyrrhus said : 'You will report therefore these things and as a

548 **Pēlīdae (meō) genitōrī**. Illī mea trīstia facta to hendiadys   *remember to*
    messenger of my father Achilles. Remember to tell that one of the sad deed

549 dēgeneremque Neoptolemum nārrāre mementō.
    and degerate Pyrrhus.

550 Nunc morere. Hoc dīcēns altāria ad ipsa (Priamum) trementem
    Now Die!' Saying this he draws the trembling Priam to himself

551 trāxit et in **multō** lāpsantem **sanguine** nātī,
    by the altar and slipping in much blood of his son,

552 implicuitque comam (manū) laevā, (manū) dextrāque coruscum → elipsis
    and he entwines this hair by the left hand, and with the right hand

553 extulit ac laterī capulō tenus abdidit ēnsem.
    he raises the bright sword and hides the hilt into his side.

554 Haec (fuit) fīnis Priamī fātōrum, hic exitus (vītae) **illum**
    This was the end of the fate of Priam, he bears this end of the fate of

555 sorte tulit Troiam incensam et prōlāpsa (esse) **videntem**
    that life and seeing that Troy burning, so many people and land

556 Pergama, tot quondam populīs terrīsque **superbum**

557 **rēgnātōrem** Asiae.
    and the haughty ruler of Asia.

Questions

Lines 557–66: Find three first person singular verbs. What do they mean?
Line 564: What word does *quae* modify?

Vocabulary

557. **iaceō, iacēre, iacuī, iacitus** to lie (low, outspread)
    truncus, -ī, n. trunk, body, torso

558. **āvellō, āvellere, āvellī** or **āvulsī, āvulsum** to tear from
    sine prep. (+ abl.) without

559. **saevus, -a, -um** cruel, stern, fierce
    horror, horrōris, m. shudder(ing), horror
    circumstō, -stāre, -stetī to surround, stand around

560. **obstipēscō, obstipēscere, obstipuī** to be dazed, stand agape
    imāgō, imāginis, f. image, likeness
    cārus, -a, -um dear, beloved, fond

561. **aequaevus, -a, -um** of equal age
    crūdēlis, crūdēle cruel, bloody, bitter
    vulnus, vulneris, n. wound, deadly blow

562. **exhālō, exhālāre** to breathe out
    dēserō, dēserere, dēseruī, dēsertum to desert, forsake
    Creūsa, -ae, f. wife of Aeneas, lost at the sack of Troy

563. **dīripiō, dīripere, dīripuī, dīreptum** to plunder, ravage
    parvus, -a, -um small
    Iūlus, -ī, m. Ascanius, son of Aeneas

564. **respiciō, respicere, respexī, respectum** to look back
    lūstrō, lūstrāre to survey; traverse
    cōpia, -ae, f. abundance, plenty, forces

565. **dēfessus, -a, -um** tired, weary, worn
    dēserō, dēserere, dēseruī, dēsertum to desert, forsake
    saltus, -ūs, m. leap, bound, dancing

566. **aeger, aegra, aegrum** sick, weary

Notes

557. **(in) lītore iacet** While King Priam dies in the palace inside Troy, Vergil wants the reader to imagine his mutilated body abandoned on the shore.

561. **ut . . . vīdī** Since the verb is in the indicative mood, translate *ut* "when."
    crūdēlī vulnere Ablative of means.

562. **dēserta Creūsa** Creusa is abandoned only in Aeneas' imagination. The same is true for his plundered house (*dīrepta domus*, 563) and dead son (*parvī cāsus Iūlī*, 563).

563. **cāsus** Not to be confused with *casa* or *causa*, this noun means "misfortune."

564. **respiciō** Aeneas is on a rooftop looking down on Priam's palace. He now turns around to look for his men.
    lūstrō Introduces an indirect question.

565. **dēseruēre** Syncopated form for *dēseruērunt*.
    saltū Ablative of means.

566. **mīsēre** Syncopated form of *mīsērunt*. *Dedēre* = *dedērunt*.
    ignibus Dative of indirect object.

Making Sense of It CONTINUED

557   Iacet *ingēns* (in) lītore *truncus*,

The huge trunk lies on the shore

558   *āvulsum*que (ab) umerīs **caput** et sine nōmine corpus.

and the head having been torn from the shoulders and the body without

559   At mē tum prīmum **saevus** circumstetit **horror**.

a name. And first then the cruel horror surrounded me. I was dazed;

560   Obstipuī; subiit **cārī genitōris** imāgō (meam mentem),

I bore the image of my dear father (my mind),

561   ut *rēgem aequaevum* crūdēlī vulnere vīdī

when I saw the king of equal age breathing out life with

562   vītam *exhālantem;* subiit dēserta Creūsa (meam mentem)

a cruel wound; I bore deserted (entered *my mind*)

563   et **dīrepta domus** et parvī cāsus Iūlī (subiērunt).

and the plundered house et. the misfortune of small Ascanius (They bore)

564   Respiciō et quae sit mē circum cōpia lūstrō.

I look back and I survey the force which is around me.

565   Dēseruēre **omnēs dēfessī**, et corpora saltū

They deserted all the tired ones, and they sent the body to the earth

566   ad terram mīsēre aut ignibus aegra (corpora) dedēre.

with dancing or they gave the sick body to the fire.

Fig. 19.
The Death of Priam.

Stopping for Some Practice   MORE QUESTIONS FOR REVIEW

Find the Latin phrases in the reading which best describe each of the following events. Then put these events in the order in which they occur in this passage.

(9) Aeneas looks around for his companions.
Respicio... lustro.

(10) Aeneas' companions commit suicide. *565 & 566*

(1) Pyrrhus tells Priam to go as a messenger to his father. *Referes... Genitori.   547*

(5) Pyrrhus kills Priam. *capulo... ensem   553*

(8) Aeneas thinks of his father Anchises. *561*

(2) Pyrrhus tells Priam to die. *Nunc morere   550*

(4) Pyrrhus drags Priam to the altar. *551*

(6) Priam's body lies on the seashore. *557*
ingens... truncus

(7) A cruel horror surrounds Aeneas. *559*

(3) Pyrrhus seizes Priam by the hair. *552*

WHAT VERGIL ACTUALLY WROTE

Notes

547. referēs . . . ībis Logically Priam will perform these actions in the opposite order. First he will go (*ībis*) and then he will report (*referēs*). This is called **hysteron proteron.**

548. Pēlīdae genitōrī Dative of direction. In prose it would be *ad genitōrem*, an accusative of place to which with the motion verb *ībis*. *Pēlīdae* translates as "the son of Peleus." Notice Vergil's use of a **patronymic** here.

548–549 trīstia facta . . . dēgeneremque Neoptolemum Translate these two accusative phrases as **hendiadys:** "the unhappy deeds of ignoble Neoptolemus."

550. trementem The pronoun *eum*, referring to King Priam, has been omitted before *trementem*. Translate "him trembling."

551 multō lāpsantem sanguine Notice how carefully Vergil has arranged the words here. The one slipping (*lāpsantem*), namely Priam, is in the middle of the copious blood (*multō sanguine*). The arrangement of the words forms a picture of what the reader is to see in his mind.

552. dextrā Syncopated (contracted) from *dexterā*.
laevā dextrāque Supply the word *manū*, which is understood. Ablative of means. Notice the picture which Vergil draws for the reader with the placement of these words: i.e., the word *laevā* (which means "left") is on the left while *dextrā* (meaning "right") is on the right. Along with *comam* and *coruscum*, these four words also form a **chiasmus.**

556. Pergama Although plural, translate singularly as "Pergamum." Pergamum was the name of the citadel (*arx*) inside the city of Troy.

563 dīrepta domus Notice the **alliteration** here.

As It Was

547   Cui Pyrrhus: 'Referēs ergō haec et nuntius ībis

548   Pēlīdae genitōrī. Illī mea trīstia facta

549   dēgeneremque Neoptolemum nārrāre mementō.

550   Nunc morere.' Hoc dīcēns altāria ad ipsa trementem

551   trāxit et in multō lāpsantem sanguine nātī,

552   implicuitque comam laevā, dextrāque coruscum

553   extulit ac laterī capulō tenus abdidit ēnsem.

554   Haec fīnis Priamī fātōrum, hic exitus illum

555   sorte tulit Troiam incēnsam et prōlāpsa videntem

556   Pergama, tot quondam populīs terrīsque superbum

557   rēgnātōrem Asiae. Iacet ingēns lītore truncus,

558   āvulsumque umerīs caput et sine nōmine corpus.

559   At mē tum prīmum saevus circumstetit horror.

560   Obstipuī: subiit cārī genitōris imāgō,

561   ut rēgem aequaevum crūdēlī vulnere vīdī

562   vītam exhālantem; subiit dēserta Creūsa

563   et dīrepta domus et parvī cāsus Iūlī.

564   Respiciō et quae sit mē circum cōpia lūstrō.

565   Dēseruēre omnēs dēfessī, et corpora saltū

566   ad terram mīsēre aut ignibus aegra dedēre.

AFTER READING WHAT VERGIL WROTE

Thinking about What You Read

1. Do you think that Neoptolemus truly considers himself *dēgenerem* (549)? If not, why does he call himself that? How does Vergil describe Neoptolemus' relationship with his father?

2. Describe in your own words exactly how Pyrrhus uses his right hand and his left hand (552) to kill King Priam. Or draw a sketch of this.

3. How does the word *sorte* (555) affect how you understand this passage?

Thinking about How the Author Writes   MORE PEOPLE AND PLACES

In this passage Vergil refers to Aeneas' city as both Troy and Pergamum. As we noted above for people, Vergil also has a repertoire of names he can use to refer to places and to the people associated with these places. Here are some examples:

TROY	TROJAN	DESCENDANT	WOMAN
Trōia	Trōiānus		
	Trōius		
	Trōs		Trō(i)ades
	Dardan(i)us	Dardanīdes	Dardanis
Īlium	Īliacus	Īliadēs	Īlias
	Teucr(i)us		
	Phrygius		
	Phryx		
	Lāomedontēus	Lāomodontiadēs	
	Lāomedontius		
Pergama	Pergameus		

GREECE	GREEK	DESCENDANT	WOMAN
	Achāicus		
	Achīvus		
Argos	Argīvus		
	Argolicus		
	Danaus		
	Dōricus		
Graecia	Graius		

CARTHAGE	CARTHAGINIAN	DESCENDANT	WOMAN
Karthāgō			
Tyrus	Tyrius		
(Phoenīca)	Phoenix		Phoenissa
(Sīdōn)	Sīdōnius		Sīdōnis

ITALY	ITALIAN	DESCENDANT	WOMAN
Ītalia	Ītalus		Ītalis
Latium	Latīnus		
Hesperia	Hesperius		Hesperis
Ausonia	Ausonius		
	Ausonis		
Lāvīnium	Lāvīnus		Lāvinia
	Tuscus		
	Rutulus		

Why do you think there are so many more words for Troy and Trojans than Greece and Greeks in the *Aeneid*? Watch for words related to Carthage in the readings from Book IV.

AENEAS ESCAPES FROM TROY
(*Aeneid* II. 705–729)

BEFORE YOU READ WHAT VERGIL WROTE

Introduction

Aeneas continues telling Dido and her court about the fall of Troy. Prior to this section, two omens convinced Aeneas' father, Anchises, to join his son in fleeing from Troy. Here Aeneas gives instructions to his aged father, his small son, his wife, and his Trojan companions for escaping the burning city of Troy safely. Aeneas then describes his terrifying journey through the burning city.

The choices Aeneas makes in this scene seem puzzling. He puts his aged father on his shoulders and takes his son by his hand as he flees from burning Troy. He asks his wife Creusa to follow close behind. Why do you think that Aeneas shows more attention to his father and his son?

Keep This Grammar in Mind   MORE USES OF THE DATIVE

Earlier you were reminded of Vergil's use of the dative case with compound verbs. Several examples of this dative taken from the passage you are about to read are listed below. The dative of possession and the dative of reference are also found in this passage.

1. Dative with compound verbs:

    *cervīcī impōnere **nostrae*** (707) "place yourself **on my neck**"

    *succēdōque **onerī*** (723) "and I take **on the burden**"

2. Dative of possession. In the two examples below, the datives *ambōbus* and *mihi* are used with the verb "to be" to express possession. The dative of possession can also be translated as the subject of the verb "to have."

ūna salūs *ambōbus* erit. (710)	There will be one safety **to both** (of us).
	Both (of us) will have one safety.
Mihi parvus Iūlus sit comes. (710-711)	Let little Iulus be a companion **to me.**
	Let me have little Iulus as a companion.

3. Dative of reference. The dative of reference explains in reference to whom something happens.

*Est urbe **ēgressīs** tumulus.* (713)	There is a tomb (in reference) to (you) having set out from the city.
comitīque onerīque timentem (729)	fearing (in reference to) for my companion and my burden

HELPING YOU TO READ WHAT VERGIL WROTE

Questions

Line 707: What case is *cāre pater*? Who is this *pater*?
Lines 705–711: Find at least three verbs in the future tense. What do they mean?

Vocabulary

705. clārus, -a, -um clear, bright

706. prope adv. near; (comp.) **proprius** nearer
aestus, -ūs, m. flood, tide, surge; heat
incendium, -(i)ī, n. flame, conflagration

707. ergō therefore, then, consequently
cārus, -a, -um dear, beloved, fond
cervix, cervīcis, f. neck
impōnō, impōnere, imposuī, impositum (dat.)
    to place (on)

708. gravō, gravāre to burden, load
iste, ista, istud that (of yours)

709. quō . . . cumque (quōcumque) conj. wherever,
    wheresoever, to whatever place
cadō, cadere, cecidī, cāsum to fall, happen
commūnis, commūne common, mutual,
    general
perīc(u)lum, -ī, n. danger, peril, risk

710. salūs, salūtis, f. safety, health
ambō, -ae, -ō (pl.) both
parvus, -a, -um small, little
Iūlus, -ī, m. Ascanius, son of Aeneas

711. longē adv. far (away), (from) afar
vestīgium, -(i)ī, n. step, track, trace

Notes

705. ille Refers to Anchises.
clārior Translate the comparative adjective as a
    comparative adverb. "More clearly."

706. aestūs incendia volvunt The accusative plural
    object of *volvunt* is *aestūs* and should be
    translated in the singular. Literally "the fires
    roll the heat." In English we would say, "the
    fires increase the heat."

707. age From *agō, agere* which means "to do." Here
    the word is being used informally in con-
    versation; translate *age* as "come on."
impōnere Although *impōnere* looks like a
    present active infinitive, it is a passive
    imperative being used as a Greek middle;
    translate as "place yourself."
cervīcī nostrae Dative after the compound
    verb *impōnere;* translate "on my neck."

708. subībō From the verb *subeō, subīre* that means
    "to go under." Here translate, "I will carry."

709. quō . . . cumque When a compound word
    is separated, it is called tmesis. Translate
    quocumque "to whatever place."
cadent Translate "will happen, turn out."
ūnum et commūne Translate without "and."
perīclum The contracted form of *perīculum.*

710. ambōbus (nostrum) Literally translate this
    dative of possession as "to both (of us)." The
    better translation is "both (of us) will have."

711. sit Translate this volitive subjunctive
    "let . . . be."
longē Adverb. Translate "at a distance."
servet From *servō, -āre* this verb commonly
    means "save" but here means "follow."
    Translate this volitive subjunctive
    "let . . . follow."

Summary

As Anchises finishes begging Aeneas to save his family from the Greek invaders, the roar of fire is heard and its heat comes closer. Aeneas tells his father to get on his back so that he can carry him out of the city. His little son Iulus and his wife Creusa will come with them. He instructs the household servants to meet him at an old temple of Ceres just outside the city. Aeneas also tells his father to carry statues of the household gods since it would be a sacrilege for Aeneas himself to touch them with his bloody hands. Aeneas then covers his shoulders with a lion skin and puts his father on his back. Iulus holds his father's right hand and Creusa follows behind as they flee through the darkness.

Making Sense of It

705 Dīxerat ille, et iam per moenia *clārior ignis*

He was leading that one, and for it was heard through the city walls

706 audītur, propriusque aestūs incendia volvunt.

more clearly than fire, and nearer the fires increase the heat.

707 'Ergō, age, cāre pater, **cervīcī** (tē) impōnere **nostrae**;

Therefore, come on, dear father, place yourself on my neck.

708 (Ego) ipse (tē) subībō (meīs) umerīs nec mē **labor iste** gravābit;

(I) myself will carry you with my shoulders, and that labor will not burden m

709 quō rēs cumque cadent, ūnum et commūne perīc(u)lum (nōbīs erit),

to whatever place the things will happen, one common danger will be with us

710 (et) **ūna salūs** ambōbus (nostrum) erit. Mihi parvus Iūlus

and one safety for both of us. Let small Iulus be a friend to me

711 sit comes, et longē servet vestīgia (mea) coniūnx.

and let my wife follow the traces at a distance.

Fig. 20.
The Ruins of the City of Troy.

Questions

Line 715: Use the fonts to find the word which *servāta* modifies.
Line 717: Find the two direct objects of *cape*. What do they mean?

Vocabulary

712. **famulus, -ī,** m. servant, attendant
  advertō, advertere, advertī, adversum to pay attention
  vester, vestra, vestrum your(s), your own

713. **ēgredior, ēgredī, ēgressum** to depart
  tumulus, -ī, m. mound, hill
  templum, -ī n. temple, shrine, sanctuary
  vetustus, -a, -um old, ancient, former

714. **dēserō, dēsere, dēseruī, dēsertum** to desert
  Cerēs, Cereris, f. Ceres, the goddess of grain
  iuxtā adv. near (by), close
  cupressus, -ī, f. cypress (tree)

715. **re(l)ligiō, re(l)ligiōnis,** f. religion, sanctity
  annus, -ī, m. year, season

716. **dīversus, -a, -um** different, various

717. **penātēs, penātium,** m. (pl.) household gods

718. **dīgredior, dīgredī, dīgressum** to (de)part, go away
  caedēs, caedis, f. slaughter, blood(shed), murder
  recēns, recentis recent, fresh, new, late

719. **attrectō, -āre** to handle, touch
  nefās, n. (indecl.) guilt, impiety, wrong
  dōnec conj. until, as long as, while
  flūmen, flūminis, n. river, stream, flood
  vīvus, -a, -um living, alive; running

720. **abluō, abluere, abluī, ablūtum** to wash, purify

Notes

712. **animīs . . . vestrīs** Ablative of means; "with your minds."
  haec quae dīcam A neuter accusative plural substantive. Translate "these things that I will say."

713. **ēgressīs** Perfect passive participles of deponent verbs translate actively. This participle is a dative of reference. Translate *(vōbīs) ēgressīs* "to (you) having departed."

714. **cupressus** Names of trees in Latin are often feminine. Thus *antīqua* modifies *cupressus.*

716. **ex dīversō** The singular *dīversō (locō)* instead of the plural *dīversīs (locīs)* is used. Literally "from a different place." Translate "from different directions."

717. **sacra** A neuter plural substantive; translate "sacred objects."
  penātīs The poetic accusative form –īs for –ēs. The penates were small statues of the gods of each household.

718. **mē** This pronoun is accusative after an impersonal verb. Translate "for me."
  dīgressum Perfect passive participles of deponent verbs translate actively. Modifies *mē.*

719. **vīvō** Translate "running."

720. **abluerō** This future perfect tense verb indicates that the action happened before another action in the future. In English, however, we translate such future perfects in the present tense. Translate "I wash."

Making Sense of It CONTINUED

712   Vōs, famulī, (haec) quae dīcam animīs advertite vestrīs.
you, servants, pay attention with your minds to these things I will sa

713   Est (in) urbe (vōbīs) ēgressīs tumulus templumque vetustum
you having departing there is a hill and the temple of the deserted Ceres, and it

714   **dēsertae Cereris,** iuxtāque (est) antīqua cupressus
is near to the ancient cypress tree having been served by religion

715   relligiōne patrum multōs servāta per annōs.
of the fathers through the years.

716   **Hanc** ex dīversō (locō) **sēdem** veniēmus in **ūnam.**
We come out of different places to this one seat.

717   Tū, genitor, cape sacra manū (tuā) **patriōs**que **penātis;**
You, father, sieze the sacred objects and the household gods with your ha

718   Mē bellō ē tantō dīgressum et **caede recentī**
Having departed from such a war and recent slaughter, for me

719   attrectāre (haec sacra) nefās (est), dōnec mē **flūmine vīvō**
handle the guilt, until I purify my self in the running river.

720   abluerō.'

It is wrong to handle these sacred things, having gone away from so great a war and recent slaughter,

Fig. 21.
Aeneas Prepares to Leave Troy.

Vocabulary

721. **lātus, -a, -um** broad, wide, spacious
subiiciō, subiicere, subiēcī, subiectum to place under
collum, -ī, n. neck

722. **vestis, vestis,** f. cloth(ing), garment, robe
fulvus, -a, -um yellow, tawny, blond
īnsternō, īnsternere, īnstrāvī, īnstrātum to lay on, cover, spread
pellis, pellis, f. hide, skin, pelt
leō, leōnis, m. lion

723. **succēdō, succēdere, successī, successum** (dat.) to go under, approach
onus, oneris, n. burden, load, weight
parvus, -a, -um small, little
Iūlus, -i, m. Ascanius, son of Aeneas

724. **implicō, implicāre, implicāvī** or **implicuī, implicātum** or **implicitum** (dat.) to enfold, wind, twine, cling
passus, -ūs, m. step, pace, gait, stride
aequus, -a, -um equal, even, just

725. **pōne** adv. behind, from behind
opācus, -a, -um dark, obscure, gloomy

726. **dūdum** adv. for a long time, long since
iniiciō, iniicere, iniēcī, iniectum to cast on

727. **adversus, -a, -um** opposing, facing
glomerō, -āre to roll together, assemble
Graius, -a, -um Greek

728. **terreō, terrēre, terruī, territum** to terrify, frighten
sonus, -ī, m. sound, noise, roar
excitō, excitāre to arouse, startle, stir (up)

729. **suspēnsus, -a, -um** doubtful, anxious
pariter equally, side by side
onus, oneris, n. burden, load, weight
timeō, timēre, timuī to fear, dread, be anxious

Notes

721. **haec (dicta) fātus** *Fātus* is the perfect passive participle of the deponent verb *for, fari*. Translate actively as "having spoken these words."

722. **veste . . . pelle** Both are ablatives of means.
īnsternor This present passive verb is being used in the Greek middle form. Translate "I cover myself."

723. **succēdōque onerī** *Onerī* is dative after the compound verb *succēdō;* translate "I take on the burden."
dextrae Dative with the compound verb *implicuit* (724). Thus, the phrase *dextrae . . . implicuit* (723–724) literally means "He entwined himself in my right hand" but translate it "he held my right hand."

724. **nōn passibus aequīs** Ablative of means.

725. **pōne** This is the adverb *pōne*. It is not from the common verb *pono, ponere* that means "to put."
per opāca locōrum *Opāca* is a neuter plural substantive; this is literally "through the dark things of the places" but translate "through dark places."

726. **mē** This word is the object of *terrent* (728).
movēbant. In this context the meaning of this word is more emotional than physical, as in the English expression "I was moved by his tears." Translate here as "bothered" or "disturbed."

728. **aurae** Note that this is the first declension noun *aura* ("breeze"), not the third declension noun *auris* ("ear").

729. **comitīque onerīque** Both words are datives of reference. Since *-que* is with each, translate "for both my companion and my burden."

Making Sense of It Continued

721 [Haec (dicta) fātus (meōs) lātōs umerōs subiectaque colla

acc. *acc.*

Having spoken these words I covered my wide shoulders and neck under the yellow

722 veste super (vestem) *fulvī*que īnsternor *pelle* leōnis,

skin

above clothing the ...

723 succēdōque onerī; dextrae sē parvus Iūlus

I take on the burden; Small Iulus holds my right hand and

724 implicuit sequiturque patrem nōn *passibus aequīs*;

and he did not follow the father with equal pace;

725 pōne subit coniūnx.] Ferimur per opāca locōrum,

[the wife bears behind.] We bear through the dark place and me,

726 et mē, quem dūdum nōn ūlla iniecta movēbant

which for a long time not any weapons cast on bothered

727 tēla neque *adversō* glomerātī ex *agmine* Graiī (movēbant),

nor assembling greeks from opposing armies

728 nunc *omnēs* terrent *aurae*, *sonus* excitat *omnis*

now all breezes terrify me, all sounds startle me

729 (mē) suspēnsum et pariter comitīque onerīque timentem.

anxious and equally frighten for my companion.

Homework (margin annotation)

Stopping for Some Practice   GIVING COMMANDS IN LATIN

This passage contains a number of commands. Notice how these commands can be expressed in Latin by using the **imperative**:

age (707)	come on	*advertite* (712)	pay attention
impōnere (707)	place	*cape* (717)	pick up

or the **subjunctive**:

Mihi parvus Iūlus sit comes. (710–711)	Let small Iulus be my companion.
servet vestīgia coniūnx (711)	Let my wife follow my steps

Now It's Your Turn   GIVING COMMANDS CONTINUED

Indicate whether each of the following commands is an imperative or a subjunctive. Then translate the command into English. (Hint: All the verbs listed here appear in the passage you have just read.)

1. agite	6. ō coniūnx, servā vestīgia
2. impōne	7. advertāmus
3. advertat	8. ēgredere
4. capite	9. dēserite
5. sint comitēs	10. īnsterne

WHAT VERGIL ACTUALLY WROTE

Notes

706. aestūs Translate the poetic plural as a singular in English.

707. nostrae Vergil uses the regal plural here. Translate it singularly.

708. subībō Vergil expects his reader to supply *tē*, " you," as the direct object of *subībō*.

709. quō rēs cumque *Quō* is split from the rest of the word *cumque*. This is called **tmesis.** The English equivalent would be "what things ever."

714. dēsertae Cereris The participle *dēsertae* which modifies *Cereris* grammatically refers to *templum* in context. This is called **a transferred epithet.** When translating, it is correct either to leave the adjective with the noun it modifies or to transfer it to the noun with which it makes sense; i.e. "deserted Ceres" or "deserted temple."

720. abluerō A short line like this one is usually thought to be a sign of the unfinished nature of the *Aeneid*. If Vergil had lived longer, he might have eliminated such short lines by reworking the passage.

722. super *Super* is an adverb and should be translated "above."
veste . . . fulvīque pelle. This phrase, consisting of two nouns joined together by a conjunction can be translated as "with a garment of yellow fur." This is an example of **hendiadys.**

723. dextrae The Latin adjectives for "right" and "left" can be used in the feminine with *manus* ("hand") understood to refer to the right (*dextra*) or left hand (*sinistra*).

728. omnēs terrent aurae, sonus excitat omnis Note the **asyndeton** or lack of a conjunction to join these two phrases and the ABCCBA word order that forms a **chiasmus.**

As It Was

705   Dīxerat ille, et iam per moenia clārior ignis

706   audītur, propriusque aestūs incendia volvunt.

707   'Ergō, age, cāre pater, cervīcī impōnere nostrae;

708   ipse subībō umerīs nec mē labor iste gravābit;

709   quō rēs cumque cadent, ūnum et commūne perīclum,

710   ūna salūs ambōbus erit. Mihi parvus Iūlus

711   sit comes, et longē servet vestīgia coniūnx.

712   Vōs, famulī, quae dīcam animīs advertite vestrīs.

713   Est urbe ēgressīs tumulus templumque vetustum

714   dēsertae Cereris, iuxtāque antīqua cupressus

715   relligiōne patrum multōs servāta per annōs.

716   Hanc ex dīversō sēdem veniēmus in ūnam.

717   Tū, genitor, cape sacra manū patriōsque penātīs;

718   Mē bellō ē tantō dīgressum et caede recentī

719   attrectāre nefās, dōnec mē flūmine vivō

720   abluerō.'

721   Haec fātus lātōs umerōs subiectaque colla

722   veste super fulvīque īnsternor pelle leōnis,

723   succēdōque onerī; dextrae sē parvus Iūlus

724   implicuit sequiturque patrem nōn passibus aequīs;

725   pōne subit coniūnx. Ferimur per opāca locōrum,

726   et mē, quem dūdum nōn ūlla iniecta movēbant

727   tēla neque adversō glomerātī ex agmine Graiī,

728   nunc omnēs terrent aurae, sonus excitat omnis

729   suspēnsum et pariter comitīque onerīque timentem.

AFTER READING WHAT VERGIL WROTE

Thinking about How the Author Writes   SYNONYMS AND SYNECDOCHE

In this passage Vergil uses two different words for "father": *pater* and *genitor*. The poet has a repertoire of synonyms which he uses in his poem. To create these synonyms Vergil very often uses a part for the whole, for example *tēctum* ("roof") for *domus* ("house"). Use of the part for the whole is called **synecdoche**. Being familiar with these synonyms will make it easier to read Vergil. Here are a few examples. As you read more of the poem, try building on this list.

father	house	speak	sea
pater	domus	dīcō	mare
parēns	tēctum ("roof")	for	altum ("deep")
genitor	līmen ("threshold")	ait	fretum
	ātrium	inquit	aequor ("level")
	sēdēs	exclāmō	pelagus
		fert	salum ("salt")
			pontus
			unda
			fluctus

god	city	ship	death
deus	urbs	nāvis	mors
nūmen ("divine power")	arx ("citadel")	puppis ("stern")	lētum
caelestēs ("heavenly")	rēgnum	carīna ("keel")	exitus
dīvus	moenia		obitus

Thinking about What You Read

1. In what ways does Aeneas show more attention to his father and his son than his wife in this passage? Why do you think he does this?

2. In this passage Aeneas speaks of both *labor* (708) and *onerī* (723). What do these two words mean in English and to what is Aeneas referring when he uses these two words?

3. Find four words in this passage which indicate the emphasis which religion has in this scene. Why do you think there is such emphasis on religion?

4. What is the name used for Aeneas' son in line 710? Use the family tree on p. xxi to identify the famous Roman who shares this name. How might this be important to Vergil's Roman audience? Why do you think that the name of Aeneas' father and the name of his wife are not mentioned in this passage?

5. How does the word order of *dextrae sē . . . implicuit* (723–724) enrich the meaning of the phrase? How is it different from simply saying "he held my right hand"? Try to recreate the effect of the Latin word order in the English.

BOOK IV

DIDO IN LOVE
(*Aeneid* IV. 65–89)

BEFORE YOU READ WHAT VERGIL WROTE

Introduction

After Aeneas finishes telling Dido about the events at Troy, he moves in Book III to the story of his voyage from Troy to Carthage. The Trojans land first at Thrace, where an omen from the murdered Polydorus convinces them to continue on to the island of Delos. Here Apollo's oracle instructs them to go in search of their original home that Anchises says was on the island of Crete. On Crete pestilence befalls the Trojans, but a vision of the penates tells Aeneas to go to Italy. The Trojans then stop at Actium where they celebrate games in honor of Apollo and at Epirus where Aeneas meets Andromache and the prophet Helenus, who tells Aeneas to visit the Sibyl in Cumae, Italy. The Trojans then sail to Sicily, where they see the Cyclops and where Anchises dies. As they leave Sicily, the storm described at the beginning of Book I occurs and the weary Trojans are blown to the shore of Carthage. Aeneas finishes the story of his voyage here, at the end of Book III, and, in Book IV Vergil turns the narrative to events in Carthage, where Juno and Venus have plotted with Cupid to make Dido fall in love with Aeneas. In this passage, Vergil describes the effect of Dido's passion.

Keep This Grammar in Mind   ABLATIVE ABSOLUTES

Consider these two sentences in which the words in parentheses are the subordinate clause while the other words form the main clause.

> A deer runs wild (when an arrow has been shot). *Cerva vagātur (cum sagitta coniecta sit.)*

Latin can express the same idea without using a subordinate clause by putting the subject and verb from the subordinate clause in the ablative case. An example of this construction, named an ablative absolute, from the passage you are about to read is printed below and a literal translation is supplied.

> *Cerva vagātur (sagittā coniectā).* A deer runs wild (with an arrow having been shot).

Better English translations, however, use a subordinate conjunction like "when," "since," or "although." Which English conjunction to use can only be determined by context and you will see in the three translations below that the context of this sentence does not support the use of "although."

A deer runs wild (when an arrow has been shot).	Supported by Context
A deer runs wild (since an arrow has been shot).	Supported by Context
A deer runs wild (although an arrow has been shot).	Not Supported by Context

Here are three ablative absolute phrases you have already seen in the *Aeneid*. Try translating them three different ways using "when," "since," and "although."

nūmine laesō (I. 8)   *posthabitā Samō* (I. 16)   *agmine factō* (I. 434)

WHAT VERGIL ACTUALLY WROTE

Vocabulary

65. ignārus, -a, -um ignorant, unaware
vōtum, -ī, n. vow, prayer, (votive) offering

66. dēlūbrum, -ī, n. shrine, temple, sanctuary
iuvō, iuvāre, iūvī, iūtum to help, please
edō, -ere (esse), ēdī, ēsus to eat
mollis, molle soft, yielding, tender
medulla, -ae, f. marrow

67. intereā adv. meanwhile, in the meantime
tacitus, -a, -um silent, noiseless, secret
vīvō, vīvere, vīxī, vīctum to live, be alive
vulnus, vulneris, n. wound, deadly blow

68. ūrō, ūrere, ussī, ustum to burn, consume
vagor, vagārī, vagātum to wander, roam

69. quālis, quāle of what sort, (such) as
coniiciō, -iicere, -iēcī, -iectum to hurl, shoot
cerva, -ae, f. deer, doe
sagitta, -ae, f. arrow

70. incautus, -a, -um unaware, unsuspecting
nemus, nemoris, n. (sacred) grove, wood
Crēsius, -a, -um of Crete, Cretan
fīgō, fīgere, fīxī, fīxum to pierce, imprint

71. pāstor, pastōris, m. shepherd
linquō, -ere, līquī, lictus leave, desert
volātilis, volātile flying, winged, swift

72. nescius, -a, -um ignorant, unaware
saltus, -ūs, m. forest, glade, pasture
peragrō, peragrāre to wander through, scour

73. Dictaeus, -a, -um of Dicte, a mountain in Crete;
Cretan
haereō, -ēre, haesī, haesus cling to (dat.)
latus, lateris, n. side
lētālis, lētāle deadly, mortal, lethal, fatal
harundō, harundinis, f. reed, arrow

75. Sīdonius, -a, -um of Sidon (a famous city of
Phoenicia)
ostentō, ostentāre to show (off), display, exhibit,
parade
ops, opis, f. resources, wealth

Notes

65. vātum These seers were religious figures who
could predict the future by reading signs.
vātum ignārae mentēs Vergil suggests that the
minds of these seers are ignorant because
they encouraged Dido in her hopeless love for
Aeneas.
Quid Translate "how."
vōta With *dēlūbra* (66) the subject of *iuvant* (66).
These are the vows Dido makes and the
sanctuaries she visits in search of divine help
for her love.
(eam) furentem Accusative direct object of
iuvant (66).

66. Ēst is from *edo*, not from *sum*.
mollīs The accusative plural ending *-īs*
shows that this adjective cannot modify the
nominative *flamma*.

65–66. Quid vōta . . . quid dēlūbra Note the
anaphora and **asyndeton**.

67. tacitum . . . vulnus A wound cannot talk, so it
cannot be silent. When a characteristic of a
living thing is applied to an impersonal object,
this is called **personification**. The same idea
appears in the English expression "a silent
tumor."

68. Ūritur . . . vagātur Note how Vergil places one
verb at the beginning of the line and another
at the end. Such balance is called **framing**.

69. quālis Introduces an **extended simile** in which
Dido is compared to a wounded doe (*cerva*).

70. quam . . . incautam Both words refer to *cerva*.

71. pāstor This shepherd is modified by *nescius* (72).
agēns tēlīs . . . volātile ferrum Literally "driving
swift iron with weapons." Translate "shooting
a swift arrow with his bow."

72. illa Refers to *cerva* (69).
fugā Ablative of means or manner; "by flight."

74. Nunc Provides a transition from the *cerva* simile
back to Dido, who is the understood subject of
the twelve main verbs through line 85.

75. Sīdoniāsque . . . opēs urbemque parātam Note
the **chiasmus**.

As It Was

65 Heu, vātum ignārae mentēs! Quid vōta furentem,

Alas, the ignorant minds of the seers!   How the prayers help the raging

66 quid dēlūbra iuvant! Ēst mollīs flamma medullās

how the temples! The flame eats the soft marrows

67 intereā et tacitum vīvit sub pectore vulnus.

meanwhile and the silent wound lives below the chest

68 Ūritur īnfēlīx Dīdō tōtāque vagātur [Framina]

Unlucky Dido is burned she wanders   raging through the whole

69 urbe furēns, quālis coniectā cerva sagittā,

city, such as a deer having been shot by an arrow, which a ignorant

70 quam procul incautam nemora inter Crēsia fīxit

shepherd pierced among the Cretan unsuspecting wood shooting a swift

71 pāstor agēns tēlīs līquitque volātile ferrum

arrow with his bow

72 nescius: illa fugā silvās saltūsque peragrat

that deer by flight wanders the forests and woods

73 Dictaeōs; haeret laterī lētālis harundō.

of Dicte; the deadly arrow clings to the side.

74 Nunc media Aenēān sēcum per moenia dūcit

Now she leads Aeneas through the middle of the city with herself and

75 Sīdoniāsque ostentat opēs urbemque parātam,

shows the wealth of Sidon and the city having been prepared,

(margin notes: extended simile / Homework / 4th enjambment)

Keep This Vocabulary in Mind   WORDS FOR FALLING IN LOVE

In this passage you read about Dido's love for Aeneas. Make a list of English expressions describing someone in love. Here are a few examples to get you started:

madly in love   head over heels in love   infatuated   got the hots for someone

Compare your list to the words Vergil uses in this passage to describe Dido in love:

ūritur (68) "she burns"   *dēmēns* (78) "mad"
fūrentem (65) and *furēns* (69) "raging"   *maeret* (82) "she grieves"

Here are some other expressions Vergil uses in the *Aeneid* IV to describe Dido's love:

effera (642) "wild"   *male sana* (8) "scarcely sane"
āmēns (203) "mindless"   *ardet furōrem* (101) "she burns passion"
bacchātur (301) "she rushes wildly"   *saevit* (300) "she storms"
accēnsa (364) "inflamed"

Fig. 22.
A Deer Runs Wild.

Vocabulary

76. **incipiō, -ere, -cēpī, -ceptum** to begin, undertake
effor, effārī, effātum to speak (out), say
resistō, -ere, -stitī (dat.) to stop

77. **convīvium, -(i)ī,** n. feast, banquet

78. **Īliacus, -a, -um** Trojan, Ilian
iterum adv. again, anew, a second time
dēmēns, dēmentis crazy, mad, distracted

79. **exposcō, -ere, expoposcī** to demand, entreat
pendeō, -ēre, pependī to hang, depend
iterum adv. again, anew, a second time
nārrō, nārrāre to narrate, tell, recount

80. **post** prep. + acc. after, behind; adv. afterward
dīgredior, -ī, dīgressum to (de)part, separate
obscūrus, -a, -um dark, obscure, gloomy
vicissim adv. in turn, by turns

81. **lūna, -ae,** f. moon, moonlight
premō, -ere, pressī, pressum to (re)press
suādeō, suādēre, suāsī, suāsum to persuade, advise
cadō, -ere, cecidī, cāsum to fall, sink, set

82. **maereō, maerēre** to mourn, grieve, pine
vacuus, -a, -um empty, free, vacant
strātum, -ī, n. a covering, blanket; bed, couch

83. **incubō, -āre, -uī, -itum** (dat.) to recline (upon)

83. **absēns, absentis** absent, separated, distant

84. **gremium, -ī,** n. bosom, lap, embrace
Ascanius, -ī m. son of Aeneas
imāgō, imāginis, f. likeness, form, phantom

85. **dētineō, -ēre, -uī, -tentum** to retain, hold back
īnfandus, -a, -um unspeakable, unutterable
fallō, -ere, fefellī, falsum to deceive, cheat, mock, beguile

Notes

76. **incipit effārī** *Incipit* takes a complementary infinitive. "She begins to speak."
mediāque in vōce. Literally "in mid-voice." Translate "in mid-phrase" or "in mid-sentence."

77. **eadem . . . convīvia** Dido tries to recreate the same banquet at which she fell in love with Aeneas, perhaps by inviting the same guests and serving the same menu. *Eadem* is from *īdem* "the same."
lābente diē An ablative absolute indicating "when" Dido seeks feasts. "When day(light) is slipping away or ending."
eadem lābente diē convīvia Note the chiasmus.

78. **Īliacōs . . . labōrēs** This is another kind of **framing** in which the line begins with an adjective (*Īliacōs*) modifying the word at the end of the line (*labōrēs*).
iterum Take this adverb, repeated in line 79, with both *exposcit* and *pendet*. Dido "again and again" asks Aeneas to tell her the story of the fall of Troy and his adventures.

78–79. **iterum . . . iterum** An example of anaphora.

80. **ubi (omnēs) dīgressī (sunt)** That is, after the banquets.

81. **lūna** The subject of *premit*.
premit Translate "suppress" or "hide."
cadentia sīdera These are not shooting stars but the stars sinking under the horizon as the night passes.

82. **sōla** Refers to Dido.
strātīs relictīs Dative after the compound verb *incubat*. These are the couches abandoned after the banquet, not beds for sleeping.

84. **genitōris imāgine** Ablative of means with *capta*. Dido is "struck by the image of his father" in the appearance of Ascanius.

85. **sī . . . possit** An indirect question following the understood interrogative *poscēns*. "(Asking) if she could."

As It Was CONTINUED

76 incipit effārī mediāque in vōce resistit;
she begins to speak in mid speech she stops

77 nunc eadem lābente diē convīvia quaerit,
now when day (light) is slipping away she seeks the same feast,

78 Īliacōsque iterum dēmēns audīre labōrēs
She crazy demands to hear Trojan works again and

79 exposcit pendetque iterum nārrantis ab ōre.
she hangs by the mouth of the narrator. (hanging on his words)

80 Post ubi dīgressī, lūmenque obscūra vicissim
Afterwards when they have departed, the dark moon hides its light in turn

81 lūna premit suādentque cadentia sīdera somnōs,
and the falling stars persuade sleep,

82 sōla domō maeret vacuā strātīsque relictīs
She alone grieves at the vacant home and reclines upon the

83 incubat. Illum absēns absentem auditque videtque,
deserted couches. She absent hears and sees that absent

84 aut gremiō Ascanium genitōris imāgine capta
she retains Ascanius on her lap having been seized by the image of

85 dētinet, īnfandum sī fallere possit amōrem.
the father, if she is able to deceive the unspeakable love.

Fig. 23
A Fresco from Pompeii Depicting Queen Dido.

Vocabulary

86. coepī, coepisse, coeptum to begin, commence
adsurgō, -ere, adsurrēxī, adsurrēctum to rise
turris, turris, f. tower, turret
iuventūs, iuventūtis, f. youth, young men

87. exerceō, -ēre, -uī, -itum to drive, exercise
prōpugnāculum, -ī, n. rampart, battlement

88. tūtus, -a, -um protected, safe, secure
pendeō, -ēre, pependī to hang, depend
opus, opereris, n. work, labor, deed, task
interrumpō, -ere, -rūpī, -ruptum to interrupt
minae, -ārum, f. (pl.) threat, menace, pinnacle

89. mūrus, -ī, m. (city) wall, battlement
aequō, -āre to equal, match, level, even
māchina, -ae, f. machine, engine, device

Notes

86. iuventūs The subject of both *exercet* (87) and *parant* (88). Note that Vergil uses both a singular and a plural verb with this collective noun.

87. prōpugnācula bellō *Bellō* is a dative of purpose. "Ramparts for war."

88. parant Both *portūs* and *prōpugnācula* (in 87) are direct objects of this verb.
pendent opera interrupta The neuter plural *opera* is the subject of *pendent*. Translate *opera* in the singular. "The work hangs suspended."

88–89. minaeque mūrōrum Literally "threatenings of walls" but translate as "threatening walls."
Minaeque . . . māchina Both of these nouns are in apposition to *opera*, i.e., they are examples of the work suspended.

Stopping for Some Practice   ABLATIVE ABSOLUTES

Translate the following ablative phrases as ablative absolutes using "when," "since," and "although."

Example: *lābente diē* (77)   "when the day(light) was slipping"
                                          "since the day(light) was slipping"
                                          "although the day(light) was slipping"

strātīs relictīs	Aenēā dūctō	sīderibus cāsīs
urbe vagātā	urbe parātā	illō absente vīsō
ferrō actō	labōribus audītīs	Ascāniō detentō

Now find the phrases in the passage (IV. 65–89) on which these ablative phrases are based.

Fig. 24.
A Roman Dining Couch.

As It Was CONTINUED

86 Nōn coeptae adsurgunt turrēs, nōn arma iuventūs *nom*

The towers having been begun do not rise, the youth do not train with

86

87 exercet portūsve aut prōpugnācula bellō *pres*

weapons or not prepare the ports or the protected ramparts for war:

88 tūta parant: pendent opera interrupta minaeque

The huge threats of the walls and interrupted work hangs and

89 mūrōrum ingentēs aequātaque māchina caelō.

The machine having been equal to the sky.

AFTER READING WHAT VERGIL WROTE

Thinking about How the Author Writes   POETIC MODIFIERS

A distinctive feature of Vergil's language, and one which makes his poetry particularly difficult to understand in English, is the way Vergil interchanges adjectives and genitive phrases. Several examples appear in the passage you have just read:

Vergil's poetic expression	prose equivalent
minaeque mūrōrum, "threats of walls"	*minántēs mūrēs*, "threatening walls"
nemora Crēsia, "Cretan groves"	*nemora Crētae*, "groves of Crete"
saltūs Dictaeōs, "Dictaean glades"	*saltūs Dictēs*, "glades of Mt. Dicte"
Sīdoniās opēs, "Sidonian resources"	*opēs Sīdōnis*, "resources of Sidon"

Here are some other examples from earlier passages you have read:

corpus Hectoreum, "the Hectorean body"	*corpus Hectōris*, "the body of Hector"
Tiberīna ostia, "the Tiberian mouth"	*ostia Tiberis*, "the mouth of the Tiber river"

While such expressions sound somewhat strange in English, they were more poetic to ancient Romans.

Now let's try some English examples:

Chicagoan roads	roads of Chicago
Washingtonian airports	airports of Washington
honks of cars	honking cars
whistles of police officers	whistling police officers

This is a lot simpler in English, where nouns can be used as modifiers. So

Chicago roads
Washington airports
car honks
police officer whistles

Thinking about What You Read

1. How does Vergil's comparison of Dido to a wounded deer affect your perception of what is happening to Dido and how she feels?

2. Describe the behavior of Dido as she tries to cope with her love for Aeneas in this passage.

3. How many examples of asyndeton can you find in this passage?

4. To whom is Vergil speaking in lines 65–66? How does he describe the minds of prophets (*vātum mentēs*)? What evidence does he have to say this?

5. What Latin words or phrases can you find in this passage that foreshadow the death of Dido later in Book IV?

Fig. 25.
A Roman Banquet.

Who Can Deceive a Lover?
(*Aeneid* IV. 279–303)

Before You Read What Vergil Wrote

Introduction

At the command of Jupiter, Aeneas begins preparations to sail from Carthage to Italy, but he cannot hide his secret plans from Dido.

Keep This Grammar in Mind   Gerunds and Gerundives

A gerund is a verbal noun. English forms gerunds by adding the suffix "–ing" to the verb.

Verb	Gerund
to love	loving
to warn	warning

Gerunds can be used in any way that nouns are used, including as subjects or direct objects.

Loving someone requires honesty. ("**Loving**" is the subject of the sentence)
Honesty requires **loving** one another. ("**Loving**" is the direct object of the sentence.)

Latin forms gerunds by adding the suffix *–nd* and second declension neuter singular endings to the present active verb stem.

Genitive Singular	*amandī* "of loving"	*monendī* "of warning"
Dative Singular	*amandō* "to loving"	*monendō* "to warning"
Accusative Singluar	*amandum* "loving"	*monendum* "warning"
Ablative Singular	*amandō* "by loving"	*monendō* "by warning"

Unlike English, Latin does not use the gerund in the nominative case. If a nominative verbal noun is needed, Latin uses the infinitive instead. Gerunds are always singular.

When a Latin gerund takes a direct object, the gerund becomes a gerundive, i.e., a verbal adjective. Gerundives are *-us, -a, -um* adjectives which can be used in all genders and numbers. The gerundive and its noun are both placed in the case used grammatically by the gerund.

Example: *monendīs virīs* "by warning the men."

Here are two examples of gerunds and gerundives you will see in this selection from the *Aeneid*:

Gerundive
rēbus . . . novandīs (IV. 290)
"**by making** things new"

Gerund
mollissima fandī / *tempora* (IV. 293–294)
"the easiest times **(of) for speaking**"

WHAT VERGIL ACTUALLY WROTE

Vocabulary

279. **vērō** adv. truly, indeed, but
    a(d)spectus, -ūs, m. sight, appearance
    obmūtēscō, -ere, -tuī to stand speechless
    āmēns, āmentis mad, frenzied, distraught

280. **arrigō, -ere, -rēxī, -rēctum** to erect, stand on
    end
    horror, horrōris, m. shudder(ing), horror,
    alarm
    coma, -ae, f. hair, locks, tresses
    faux, faucis, f. jaws, throat; gulf
    haereō, -ēre, haesī, haesum (with dat.) to cling
    (to)

281. **abeō, -īre, iī (-īvī), -itum** to depart
    dulcis, dulce sweet, dear, fond

282. **attonitus, -a, -um** astounded
    monitus, -ūs, m. advice, warning

283. **ambiō, -īre, -īvī (iī), -itum** to go around with

284. **audeō, -ēre, ausum sum** to dare, venture
    adfātus, -ūs, m. address, speech
    exordium, -(i), n. beginning, commencement
    sūmō, -ere, sūmpsī, sūmptum to take

285. **celer, celeris, celere** swift, speedy, quick
    dīvidō, -ere, -vīsī, -vīsum to divide, distribute
    illūc adv. there, to that place

286. **rapiō, -ere, -uī, -ptum** to seize, snatch
    varius, -a, -um various, different, diverse
    versō, -āre to keep turning, roll, revolve

287. **alternō, -āre** to change, alternate, waver   _changing_
    potior, potius preferable, better   _better_
    sententia, -ae, f. opinion, resolve, view   _opinion_

288. **Mnēstheus, -eī** or **–eos, acc. –ea,** m. Trojan
    leader
    Sergestus, -ī, m. a Trojan leader
    fortis, forte brave, strong, valiant, stout
    Serestus, -ī, m. a Trojan leader

289. **aptō, -āre** to equip, make ready, furnish
    tacitus, -a, -um silent, still, secret
    cōgō, -ere, coēgī, coāctum to muster, compel

Notes

279. **aspectū** Ablative of means. "At the sight" of
    Mercury who has just come to give Aeneas
    Jupiter's orders.
    āmēns Masculine nominative singular.

280. **arrēctae comae** Understand *sunt.*
    horrōre Ablative of means; "in horror."
    faucibus Dative with *haesit;* translate "stuck in
    his throat."

281. **ardet** Takes a complementary infinitive. "To
    burn to" or "to be eager to."
    fugā Ablative of manner; "by flight."

282. **attonitus** Modifies *Aenēās* understood as the
    subject of *ardet.*

283. **quid** Introduces a **rhetorical question**, i.e., a
    question for which no reply is expected.
    agat A deliberative subjunctive. "What can he
    do?"
    quō Agrees with *adfātū.* (284).
    ambīre Complementary infinitive with *audeat*
    (284). "Dare to conciliate with."

284. **adfātū** Ablative of means. Translate with *quō*
    (283). "By what speech."
    exordia This word refers to the beginning of a
    speech.

285–286. Vergil emphasizes Aeneas' uncertainty
    by saying that Aeneas is confused several
    different ways.

286. **rapit . . . versat** Understand *animum* as the
    direct object of both of these verbs.

287. **alternantī** This participle is a substantive
    referring to Aeneas. Dative of reference. "To
    him wavering."
    potior Modifies *sententia.*

289. **aptent** Subjunctive in an indirect command.
    The verb is understood: Aeneas calls his
    lieutenants together "to command them that
    they . . . ."
    tacitī Although this nominative plural
    adjective modifies the three leaders
    understood as the subject of *aptent,* translate
    "silently."

As It Was

279 At vērō Aenēās aspectū obmūtuit āmēns,
But truly mad Aeneas stood speechless at the sight,

280 arrēctaeque horrōre comae et vōx faucibus haesit.
his hairs stood on end in horror and the voice stuck in his throat.

281 Ardet abīre fugā dulcīsque relinquere terrās,
He is eager to depart by sweet flight and to abandon the sweet lands,

282 attonitus tantō monitū imperiōque deōrum.
astonished by the empire and so great advice of the gods

283 Heu quid agat? Quō nunc rēgīnam ambīre furentem
Alas what should he do? By what speech now should he dare to conciliate

284 audeat adfātū? Quae prīma exordia sūmat?
with the raging queen? Which first beginning should he take?

285 Atque animum nunc hūc celerem nunc dīvidit illūc
Also the soul now here swift now divided to that

286 in partīsque rapit variās perque omnia versat.
and seizes the mind in various parts and revolves through all things.

287 Haec alternantī potior sententia vīsa est:
This opinion seems preferable to him swavering:

288 Mnēsthea Sergestumque vocat fortemque Serestum,
He calls Mnestheus and Sergestus and the strong Serestus,

289 classem aptent tacitī sociōsque ad lītora cōgant,
to equip the fleet of ships and compel silently the allies to the shore,

Keep This Vocabulary in Mind

WORDS ABOUT BACCHUS

In this passage Vergil compares Dido to a frenzied worshiper of *Bacchus* (-ī, m.), the god of wine. This god, known in Greek as Dionysus, gets his Latin name from the shout *iō Bacchē*, used by his worshipers. Objects and places connected with this god and his religious rites are described as **bacch**ic. A female follower of Bacchus is usually called a **bacch**ante. In this passage Vergil uses another word for bacchante, *Thyias* (-adis f.). These bacchantes or Thyiads gathered in the countryside, often at night, to worship the god in mystic rites called *orgia* (-ōrum n. pl.) in which Bacchus was thought to take control of the women, who sang and danced wildly. Notice that the English word "orgy," derived from Latin *orgia*, recalls this wild behavior but not the serious religious context of the bacchantes. From the behavior of the bacchantes in these *orgia* Latin created the verb *bacchor* (-ārī, -ātum), which means "to rush wildly, rave." Ancient Romans would frequently think of these *orgia* taking place in Greece, especially in Thebes, where Bacchus was born. For this reason, Vergil refers to *orgia* taking place on Cithaeron, a mountain near Thebes in Greece.

Here is a list of the bacchic vocabulary Vergil uses in this passage:

Bacchus, -ī m. (god of) wine
bacchor, -ārī, -ātum to rush wildly, rave
Cithaerōn, -ōnis m. Greek mountain near Thebes, on which the rites of Bacchus were celebrated
Thyias, -adis f. Thyiad or Bacchante, a woman devotee of the worship of Bacchus

Vocabulary

290. **causa, -ae, f.** cause, reason
novō, -āre to renew, make new, alter, build

291. **dissimulō, -āre** to conceal, dissimulate, pretend otherwise
intereā adv. meanwhile, (in the) meantime
quandō when, since
optimus, -a, -um best, finest

292. **nesciō, -īre, -īvī (-īī)** to not know, be ignorant
rumpō, -ere, rūpī, ruptum to break, burst (forth), utter
spērō, -āre to hope (for, to), expect, suppose

293. **temptō, -āre** to try, attempt, seek, test
aditus, -ūs, m. approach, access
mollis, molle soft, yielding, easy, mild

294. **modus, -ī, m.** manner, limit, method
ōcior, ōcius swifter, quicker; very swift

295. **pāreō, -ēre, -uī, -itum** (with dat.) to obey, yield
iussum, -ī, n. command, behest, order
facessō, -ere, -(īv)ī, -ītum to do, make, fulfill

296. **dolus, -ī, m.** deceit, strategem, fraud
fallō, -ere, fefellī, falsum to deceive, cheat, mock
amāns, amantis, m. (f.) lover

297. **praesentiō, -īre, -sēnsī, -sēnsum** to perceive first, suspect
mōtus, -ūs, m. movement, emotion
excipiō, -ere, -cēpī, -ceptum to receive, catch, understand, reply

298. **tūtus, -a, -um** protected, safe, secure
timeō, -ēre, -uī to fear, dread
impius, -a, -um wicked, accursed, disloyal

299. **dēferō, -ferre, -tulī, -lātum** to carry down, report
armō, -āre to arm, equip, furnish

Notes

291. **dissimulent** Introduces an indirect question.
sēsē = Aeneas. The accusative subject of the infinitive *temptātūrum (esse)* (293) in indirect discourse. Understand a verb of thinking like *putat*. "(He thinks that) he will try . . . ."

292. **nesciat . . . spēret** Both verbs are subjunctive in a dependent clause in indirect discourse.

293. **aditūs** The direct object of *temptātūrum (esse)*.
quae An interrogative adjective introducing an indirect question after *temptātūrum (esse)*. Modifies *tempora* (294). Understand the subjunctive *sint* in this indirect question and translate "what times would be . . . ."

294. **quis** Poetic form of *quibus*, interrogative adjective modifying *rēbus* in another indirect question after *temptātūrum (esse)*.
dexter Translate as "favorable" here.

295. **imperiō** Dative with *pārent*.
laetī Although this nominative plural adjective modifies the three leaders understood as the subject of *pārent*, translate as "happily."

296. **quis** Introduces a rhetorical question.
possit A deliberative subjunctive.

297. **mōtūs . . . futūrōs** These "future movements" refer to Aeneas' future actions.
excēpit prīma "She first understands;" i.e., Dido knows what Aeneas is going to do before he does it.

298. **omnia tūta timēns** *Omnia* is the direct object of *timēns*. "Fearing everything safe." Dido fears not only those things which are not safe but also things which are.
eadem impia Fāma *Fāma* is not "fame" but rumor. Vergil describes *fāma* as *eadem* or "the same;" it is the same Rumor that earlier spread gossip about Dido's relationship with Aeneas (IV. 173–197).
furentī This substantive participle refers to Dido. "To her raging."

299. **dētulit** Introduces indirect discourse. *Fāma* (298) is the subject.

As It Was CONTINUED

290 arma parent et quae rēbus sit causa novandīs

to prepare the arms and to conceal what is the cause by renewing

291 dissimulent; sēsē intereā, quandō optima Dīdō

the matters; meanwhile, he thinks that he himself will try approaches, since

292 nesciat et tantōs rumpī nōn spēret amōrēs,

the best Dido does not know and does not expect so much love to be broken

293 temptātūrum aditūs et quae mollissima fandī

294 tempora, quis rēbus dexter modus. Ōcius omnēs

295 imperiō laetī pārent et iussa facessunt.

296 At rēgīna dolōs—quis fallere possit amantem?—

297 praesēnsit, mōtūsque excēpit prīma futūrōs

298 omnia tūta timēns. Eadem impia Fāma furentī

299 dētulit armārī classem cursumque parārī.

Fig. 26.
Bacchus.

Vocabulary

300. **saeviō, - īre, - īvī (-iī), - ītum** to rage, storm
inops, inopis needy, destitute, bereft (of)
incendō, -ere, -ī, -ēnsum to inflame, burn

301. **bacchor, -ārī, -ātum** to rush wildly, rave
quālis, quāle of what sort, (such) as
commoveō, -ēre, -mōvī, -mōtum to move, stir, shake, agitate
exciō, -īre, -īvī, -itum to arouse, excite, stir

302. **Thyias, Thyiadis,** f. Thyiad or Bacchante, a woman devotee of the worship of Bacchus
stimulō, -āre to spur, goad, prick, incite
trietēricus, -a, -um triennial
Bacchus, -ī, m. (god of) wine

303. **orgia, -ōrum,** n. (pl.) mystic rites, orgies
nocturnus, -a, -um of the night, nocturnal
Cithaerōn, Cithaerōnis, m. Greek mountain near Thebes, on which the rites of Bacchus were celebrated

Notes

300. **inops animī** *Inops* is an adjective which takes a genitive. "Bereft of mind." A simpler translation would be "out of her mind."

301. **excita** Modifies *Thyias* (302), which is feminine nominative singular.
sacrīs This neuter plural substantive is an ablative of means with *excita*. "Excited by sacred objects."

302. **ubi** Translate "when."
audītō . . . Bacchō An ablative absolute. "when Bacchus is heard." Bacchus here refers to the cry *iō Bacchē* shouted by his worshippers.
stimulant The subject is *orgia* (303).
trietērica Modifies *orgia* (303). This word refers to the celebration of these religious rites once every three years.

303. **nocturnus** Modifies the masculine *Cithaerōn*, which has a Greek nominative ending. By "nocturnal Cithaeron" Vergil means that the Bacchic rites take place at night. Translate as "at night" or "nightly."
vocat The subject of this verb is **Cithaerōn**.
clāmōre Cithaerōn With this **alliteration** Vergil creates the sound of Bacchus' worship.

Fig. 27.
Bacchante with a Thyrsus.

As It Was Continued

300 Saevit inops animī tōtamque incēnsa per urbem

he rushed   having been mixed   having been burned

301 bacchātur, quālis commōtis excita sacrīs

                                having been aroused

                    they stimulated   triennial   abl

302 Thyias, ubi audītō stimulant trietērica Bacchō

     having been
         heard

303 orgia nocturnusque vocat clāmōre Cithaerōn.

After Reading What Vergil Wrote

Thinking about How the Author Writes   Vergil's Tragic Muse

This passage is filled with dramatic elements which illustrate Vergil's debt to ancient tragedy. This scene would be quite effective both on the stage and on the screen. This reading contains a number of powerful scenes. Find each of the following scenes in this reading and identify the dramatic and visual words which create the tragic scene. Then put the events in the order in which they occur in the reading.

> Dido sensing something is wrong
> Aeneas hesitating about what he should do
> Aeneas' men eager to depart
> Dido running wildly through the city
> Aeneas reacting to Mercury's message
> Rumor spreading word of Aeneas' deceit
> Aeneas secretly calling his lieutenants for council

Which of these scenes do you think are most effective? Which would you include in a film version of the *Aeneid* and why?

Thinking about What You Read

1. Describe Aeneas' physical appearance as Mercury leaves (279).

2. Why does Vergil describe the *terrās* as *dulcīs* (281)?

3. Why is Aeneas' *animum* described as *celerem* (285)?

4. Why do you think Aeneas finds it so difficult to speak to Dido?

5. What modern equivalent would you suggest for Vergil's bacchante simile to describe Dido wandering madly through the city?

Fig. 28.
A Pompeian Peristyle.

THE DEATH OF DIDO
(*Aeneid* IV. 642–666)

BEFORE YOU READ WHAT VERGIL WROTE

Introduction

Dido climbs a pyre piled high with all the mementos of her relationship with Aeneas and commits suicide.

Keep This Grammar in Mind   Sī CLAUSES OR CONDITIONS

Have you ever heard that "if" is the longest word in the English language? The point of this expression is that "if" implies conditions, possibilities, and probabilities that may or may not take place. Thus in English we express the following conditions:

Simple Conditions (There is a real possibility that these sentences may happen.)
1. Present: If the Trojan ships never touch the shores of Libya, Dido is happy.
2. Past: If the Trojan ships never touched the shores of Libya, Dido was happy.

Future Vivid Conditions (There is a much lower probability that these will happen.)
3. Future More Vivid: If the Trojan ships never touch (will have touched) the shores of Libya, Dido will be happy.
4. Future Less Vivid: If the Trojan ships should never touch the shores of Libya, Dido would be happy.

Contrary-to-Fact Conditions (There is no possibility that these will happen or have happened.)
5. Present: If the Trojan ships were never to touch the shores of Libya, Dido would be happy.
6. Past: If the Trojan ships had never touched the shores of Libya, Dido would have been happy.

Latin uses verb tense and mood to indicate how possible, probable, or impossible a conditional sentence is:

Simple Conditions
1. Present: present indicative tense
   *Sī Dardaniae carīnae lītora Libyae numquam **tangunt**, Dīdō fēlīx **est**.*
2. Past: past indicative tense
   *Sī Dardaniae carīnae lītora Libyae numquam **tetigērunt**, Dīdō fēlīx **erat**.*

Future Vivid Conditions
3. Future More Vivid: future perfect and future tenses
   *Sī Dardaniae carīnae lītora Libyae numquam **tetigerint**, Dīdō fēlīx **erit**.*
4. Future Less Vivid: present subjunctive tense
   *Sī Dardaniae carīnae lītora Libyae numquam **tangant**, Dīdō fēlīx **sit**.*

Contrary-to-Fact Conditions
5. Present: imperfect subjunctive tense
   *Sī Dardaniae carīnae lītora Libyae numquam **tangerent**, Dīdō fēlīx **esset**.*
6. Past: pluperfect subjunctive tense
   *Sī Dardaniae carīnae lītora Libyae numquam **tetigissent**, Dīdō fēlīx **fuisset**.*

Which of these conditions do you think best describes Dido's relationship with Aeneas? Look for Vergil to use such a condition in the passage you are about to read.

WHAT VERGIL ACTUALLY WROTE

Vocabulary

642. **trepidus, -a, -um** trembling, excited
coeptum, -ī, n. undertaking, beginning
efferus, -a, -um wild, savage, mad

643. **sanguineus, -a, -um** bloody, bloodshot
aciēs, -ēī, f. edge, line, eye(sight)
macula, -ae, f. spot, splotch, stain
tremō, -ere, -uī, to tremble, quiver, shake

644. **interfundō, -ere, -fūdī, -fūsum** to pour
among, suffuse
gena, -ae, f. cheek
pallidus, -a, -um pale, wan, pallid

645. **interior, interius** inner, interior
inrumpō, -ere, -rūpī, -ruptum to break into

646. **cōnscendō, -ere, -ī, -ēnsum** to mount, climb
furibundus, -a, -um wild, frenzied
gradus, -ūs, m. step, gait, pace, stride
ēnsis, ēnsis, m. sword, knife
reclūdō, -ere, -sī, -sum to open, unsheathe

647. **Dardan(i)us, -a, -um** Trojan, Dardanian
ūsus, -ūs, m. use, service, employment

Notes

642. **coeptīs** Ablative of cause with *effera*. Refers
to Dido's preparations for her death. "Wild
because of the undertakings."
Dīdō The subject of *inrumpit* (645), *cōnscendit*
(646) and *reclūdit* (646).

643. **aciem** Translate here "eyes."
trementīs This transferred epithet grammatically modifies *maculīs* but refers in sense to
Dīdō (642).

644. **genās** Accusative of respect with *interfūsa*;
"suffused in respect to her cheeks." In
English we would say "with her cheeks
covered."
morte Ablative of cause with *pallida*; "pale
because of death."

645. **domūs** Genitive singular.
līmina This threshold leads into a courtyard in
the middle of Dido's palace.

646. **furibunda** Translate this adjective as an adverb
"wildly."

647. **Dardanium** Modifies *ēnsem*. The sword is
Trojan because it used to belong to Aeneas.
hōs Agrees with the accusative masculine
plural *ūsūs*.
mūnus Acc. neuter sing. in apposition to *ēnsem*
(646). Vergil uses this word to emphasize
the **irony** of Dido's committing suicide with
a sword which Aeneas had given her.
in Translate as "for."

transferred epithet lost in English

As It Was

642 At trepida et coeptīs immānibus effera Dīdō

but *N* *meaningless* *wild* *N*

But trembling and wild because of her huge undertakings, Dido turning her

643 sanguineam volvēns aciem, maculīsque trementīs

bloody eyes, having suffused the cheeks with trembling spots pale

644 interfūsa genās et pallida morte futūrā,

from a future death, she breaks into the inner doorways of the

645 interiōra domūs inrumpit līmina et altōs

house she wildly climbed the lofty steps

646 cōnscendit furibunda gradūs ēnsemque reclūdit

and opens the Trojan sword

647 Dardanium, nōn hōs quaesītum mūnus in ūsūs.

a gift not having been sought for this use.

Keep This Vocabulary in Mind   A ROMAN HOUSE AND FURNITURE

As you read Vergil's description of Dido's death, it is helpful for you to imagine the layout of an upscale Roman house. Romans tended to enclose their open spaces within the walls of their house, while any open space connected with an American home is usually located outside the walls of the actual house. This open space may be surrounded by a fence. While Americans would consider such yards or gardens private property, they would not consider them part of the structure of a house. Romans, on the other hand, usually located this open space in the center of the house with many of the major rooms opening on to this inner courtyard. It is in such an open inner courtyard (*peristyl(i)um*) that Dido builds a funeral pyre on which she commits suicide.

The main public room of a Roman house is the *ātrium*, in which guests were greeted. Many Roman *ātria* had a rectangular basin (*impluvium*) in the floor to catch rainwater from a hole in the ceiling (*compluvium*). The *compluvium* was also a source of natural lighting. The ceiling of an *ātrium* was often very high. Vergil describes the sound of lament after Dido's death going *ad alta ātria*, i.e., to the high atrium of Dido's palace.

> **ātrium, -(i)ī,** n. great hall, atrium
> **cubīle, cubīlis,** n. couch, bed
> **gradus, -ūs,** m. step, gait, pace, stride
> **līmen, līminis,** n. threshold, doorway, entrance; abode; shrine; palace
> **peristyl(i)um, -ī,** n. peristyle, court
> **porticus, -ūs,** f. colonnade, portico
> **strātum, -ī,** n. a covering, blanket; bed, couch; pavement
> **torus, -ī,** m. (banqueting) couch, bed
> **vestibulum, -ī** n. entry, vestibule

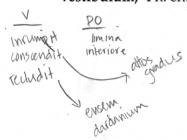

Fig. 29.
Peristyle from the House of the Vettii.

Vocabulary

648. postquam conj. after (that), when
Īliacus, -a, -um Trojan, Ilian
vestis, vestis, f. cloth(ing) garment, robe
nōtus, -a, -um (well) known, familiar
cubīle, cubīlis, n. couch, bed

649. cōnspiciō, -ere, -spexī, -spectum to see, behold
paulum adv. (a) little, slightly, somewhat
moror, -ārī, -ātum to delay, hesitate, hinder

650. incumbō, -ere, -cubuī, -cubitum (with dat.) to recline on
torus, -ī, m. (banqueting) couch, bed
verbum, -ī, n. word, speech, talk

651. dulcis, dulce sweet, dear, fond
exuviae, -ārum, f. (pl.) spoils, relics, mementos
sinō, -ere, sīvī, situm to permit, allow

652. exsolvō, -ere, -ī, solūtum to loose(n), free

653. vīvō, -ere, vīxī, vīctum to live, be alive
peragō, -ere, -ēgī, -āctum to accomplish, finish

654. imāgō, imāginis, f. likeness, image, ghost, soul, form

655. praeclārus, -a, -um very renowned
statuō, -ere, -uī, -ūtum to set (up), found

656. ulcīscor, ulcīscī, ultum sum avenge, punish
inimīcus, -a, -um hostile, enemy, unfriendly
frāter, frātris, m. brother
recipiō, -ere, -cēpī, -ceptum to receive, take

Notes

648. hīc Translate "hereupon" or "then."
Īliacās Modifies *vestīs*, another gift of Aeneas.
nōtum Translate as "familiar."

649. lacrimīs et mente Ablative of means. Literally "with (her) tears and with (her) mind." Make the noun *lacrimīs* an adjective describing *mente* in English. "With a tearful mind." This is **hendiadys**.
morāta Refers to Dido. "Delaying."

650. novissima verba Literally "(her) most recent words." In English we would say "her very last words."

651. exuviae Vocative plural. Dido is speaking to all the mementos of her time with Aeneas. This is **personification**.

652. mē Object of *exsolvite*.
cūrīs Ablative of separation with *exsolvite;* "free me from these cares."

653. vīxī Dido uses the perfect tense to emphasize that her life is over. "I have lived."
quem This relative pronoun refers to *cursum*. "The course which."
cursum "Course (of life)."

654. magna This adjective modifies *imāgō*.
meī Genitive singular personal pronoun with *imāgō*. Translate "my."
sub terrās *Sub* takes the accusative here to show "direction to." Dido is going "down under the earth."
sub terrās ībit Note the **euphemism**.
imāgō Translate here "ghost" or "soul."

656. ulta Perfect participle of the deponent verb *ulcīscor*. "Having avenged."
virum This man is Sychaeus, Dido's first husband, who was killed by her brother Pygmalion. Translate "my husband."
poenās . . . recēpī Translate "I took revenge."

As It Was Continued

648   Hīc, postquam Īliacās vestīs nōtumque cubīle

Then, after she saw the Trojan robe and familiar couch, slightly delay

649   cōnspexit, paulum lacrimīs et mente morāta

she reclined on the couch and she said

650   incubuitque torō dīxitque novissima verba:

her very last words with a tearful mind;

651   "Dulcēs exuviae, dum fāta deusque sinēbat,

"Sweet momentos, while a god & fate were permitting

652   accipite hanc animam mēque hīs exsolvite cūrīs.

accept this soul and free me from these cares.

653   Vīxī et quem dederat cursum fortūna perēgī,

I have lived and I have finished the course which fortune had

654   et nunc magna meī sub terrās ībit imāgō. alliteration

given and now my great soul will go down under the earth.

655   Urbem praeclāram statuī, mea moenia vīdī, alliteration

I founded a very reknowned city, I have seen my walls,

656   ulta virum poenās inimīcō ā frātre recēpī,

I took revenge on my unfriendly brother having avenged my husband

asyndeton

Now It's Your Turn   CONDITIONS AGAIN

Use the word marked in bold to help you fill in the blank with the appropriate English or Latin verb in the following conditions (based upon sentences from *Aeneid* IV. 279–303). Then indicate whether the condition is simple, vivid, or contrary to fact.

1. Aeneas burns to go away by flight if he ____is____ astonished by the gods' order.

   Aenēās **ardet** abīre fugā sī imperiō deōrum attonitus **est**.

   This is a ___Simple___ condition.

2. Aeneas would burn to go away by flight if he __should be ∧__ astonished by the gods' order.

   Aenēās **ardeat** abīre fugā sī imperiō deōrum attonitus __sit__.

   This is a ___Vivid___ condition.

3. Aeneas would have burned to go away by flight if he _had been_ astonished by the gods' order.

   Aenēās **arsisset** abīre fugā sī imperiō deōrum attonitus _fuisset_.

   This is a _Contrary to Fact_ condition.

Vocabulary

657. fēlīx, fēlīcis happy, fortunate, blessed
nimium too (much), excessively
tantum so much, only, merely

658. Dardan(i)us, -a, -um Trojan, Dardanian
tangō, -ere, tetigī, tāctum to touch, reach
carīna, -ae, f. keel; ship, boat

659. imprimō, -ere, -pressī, -pressum to press
(upon), imprint
torus, -ī, m. (banqueting) couch, bed
morior, -ī, mortuum to die, perish
inultus, -a, -um unavenged, unpunished

660. iuvō, -āre, iūvī, iūtum to help, please

661. hauriō, - īre, hausī, haustum to drain, drink
(in)
crūdēlis, crūdēle cruel, harsh, bloody
altum, -ī, n. the deep (sea); heaven

662. Dardan(i)us, -(i)ī m. Trojan, Dardanian
ōmen, ōminis, n. portent, omen, sign

Notes

657. fēlīx Note the **anaphora**.
fēlīx, heu nimium fēlīx With these words
understand the pluperfect subjunctive
fuissem in the conclusion of a contrary-to-
fact condition. "I would have been happy."
tantum Translate this word with *sī*, "if only."

658. nostra Modifies *lītora* (657).
carīnae Note the **synecdoche**.

659. impressa A middle/reflexive participle.
Translate with *ōs* as "Having pressed (her)
mouth."
torō Dative with the compound verb *impressa*.
Translate "on the couch."
moriēmur Future indicative of a deponent
verb. Note the regal plural. "We will die."
inultae The subject of *moriēmur*.

660. moriāmur Present subjunctive of a deponent
verb. "Let us die."
iūvat This verb is used impersonally here,
i.e., its subject is the infinitive *īre*. "It is
pleasing."
sub umbrās *Sub* takes the accusative case here
to indicate direction towards. "Down under
the shades."
īre sub umbrās This expression is a
euphemism for "to die."

661. hauriat A volitive subjunctive. "Let him
drink."
oculīs Ablative of means; "with his eyes."
ignem The fire of her funeral pyre.
crūdēlis Modifies *Dardanus* (662).
altō Translate here "the sea." Dido is imagining
Aeneas on his ship at sea.

662. Dardanus Subject of *hauriat* (661). Refers to
Aeneas. "The Trojan."
ōmina The signs Dido is referring to include
Aeneas' sorrow at leaving her and the
misfortunes his unfaithfulness will bring
him. Dido thus sees her death as an omen of
Aeneas' future suffering.

As It Was Continued

657 fēlīx, heu nimium fēlīx, sī lītora tantum
Happy, I would have been happy, if only the Trojan

658 numquam Dardaniae tetigissent nostra carīnae." *contrary to fact*
ships had never touched our shores"

659 Dīxit, et ōs impressa torō "Moriēmur inultae,
She said, and having pressed her mouth on the couch" We will die unavenge—

660 sed moriāmur" ait. "Sīc, sīc iuvat īre sub umbrās.
but let us die "she said." Thus, thus it is pleasing to go below the shadow—

661 Hauriat hunc oculīs ignem crūdēlis ab altō
Let the cruel Trojan drink this fire with his eyes from the sea

662 Dardanus, et nostrae sēcum ferat ōmina mortis."
and let him bear with himself the omens of (our) deaths"

Hyperbole

Now It's Your Turn

CONDITIONS CONTINUED

Use the word marked in bold to help you fill in the blank with the appropriate English or Latin verb in the following conditions (based upon sentences from *Aeneid* IV. 279–303). Then indicate whether the condition is simple, vivid, or contrary to fact.

1. Mnestheus, Sergestus and brave Serestus __obey__ the command if Aeneas calls them.

   Mnēstheus Sergestusque fortisque Serestus imperiō **parent** *sī Aenēās eōs* **vocat.**

   This is a ___simple___ condition.

2. Mnestheus, Sergestus and brave Serestus _∧ would have obeyed_ the command if Aeneas called them.

   Mnēstheus Sergestusque fortisque Serestus laetī imperiō ___pareant___ sī Aenēās eōs **vocet.**

   This is a ___vivid___ condition.

3. Mnestheus, Sergestus and brave Serestus _∧ had obeyed_ the command if Aeneas had called them.

   Mnēstheus Sergestusque fortisque Serestus laetī imperiō ___parissent___ sī Aenēās eōs **vocāvisset.**

   This is a _Contrary to fact_ condition.

Vocabulary

Notes

663. Dīxerat Note that the action of the pluperfect *dīxerat* ("She had spoken") takes place before the action of the present tense *aspiciunt* (664).

illam Direct object of *aspiciunt* (664).

media inter tālia *Tālia* is a neuter plural substantive modified by the adjective *media*. "Among the middle of such things." Dido speaks, kisses the couch, grabs her sword, and in the middle of such things (i.e. these three actions) the servants watch her collapse.

ferrō Ablative of means; "with the sword."

664. conlābor, -ī, -lāpsum to fall in a heap, faint

a(d)spiciō, -ere, -spexī, -spectum to see, behold

ēnsis, ēnsis, m. sword, knife

cruor, cruōris, m. blood, gore

664. conlāpsam Modifies *illam* (663); "having collapsed."

aspiciunt This verb has three direct objects: *illam* (663), *ēnsem* (664), and *manūs* (665). The subject of *aspiciunt*, however, is *comitēs*.

cruorē This ablative of means should be understood with both *spūmantem* and *sparsās* (665).

665. spūmō, -āre to foam, froth, spray

spargō, -ere, sparsī, sparsum to scatter, sprinkle

665. spūmantem Modifies *ēnsem* (664). Note the chiasmic arrangement of *ēnsem spūmantem sparsāsque manūs*.

666. ātrium, -(i)ī, n. hall, court, atrium

concutiō, -ere, -cussī, -cussum to shake, shatter

bacchor, -ārī, -ātur to rave, rush wildly

666. concussam Modifies *urbem*.

Fāma Translate "Rumor."

As It Was Continued

663 Dīxerat, atque illam media inter tālia ferrō

in the middle of such things

she had spoken, and the friends see that one having colapsed by

664 conlāpsam aspiciunt comitēs, ēnsemque cruōre

the sword, and the companions see the spraying sword and the hand

665 spūmantem sparsāsque manūs. It clāmor ad alta

sprinled with blood. The shout went to the high halls:

666 ātria: concussam bacchātur Fāma per urbem.

the rumor rushes through the city having been shaken. (echoing)

Alliteration
Onomatopoeia

AFTER READING WHAT VERGIL WROTE

Thinking about How the Author Writes   ECHOING / SELF-REFERENCING

In this passage Vergil consciously refers back to earlier passages in the epic and expects his readers to recognize these echoes. Vergil creates these textual echoes by repeating themes and phrases from earlier portions of the epic. Here are a few places where the vocabulary in the passage you have just read echoes earlier parts of Book IV.

References to *Fama* (Rumor)

IV. 666 *concussam bacchātur* **Fāma** *per urbem.*

1.) IV. 173: *Extemplō Libyae magnās it* **Fāma** *per urbēs.*
Rumor of Dido's relationship with Aeneas spreads through the cities of Libya.

2.) IV. 298–299 *Eadem impia* **Fāma** *furentī / dētulit armārī classem cursumque parārī.*
Rumor of Aeneas' preparations for departure reach Dido.

Furens Vocabulary

IV. 642 ***effera*** *Dīdō*

1.) IV. 68–69 *Ūritur īnfēlīx Dīdō tōtāque vagātur / urbe* **furēns.**

2.) IV. 298–299 *Eadem impia Fāma* **furentī** */ dētulit armārī classem cursumque parārī.*

Bacchante Image and Vocabulary

IV. 666 *concussam* **bacchātur** *Fama per urbem.*

1.) IV. 300–301 *Saevit inops animī tōtamque incēnsa per urbem /* **bacchātur.**

Such textual echoes demonstrate the cohesion of the *Aeneid*, which is meant to be read as a whole, not in isolated passages. Perhaps these few examples will inspire you to read extended passages from the *Aeneid*, or even the entire epic, in Latin.

Stopping for Review   REVIEWING FIGURES OF SPEECH

Here is a list of the figures of speech that have been presented throughout this book. Give a definition of each in your own words and find an example of each from the *Aeneid*.

alliteration   hysteron proteron

anaphora   onomatopoeia

anticipation   pleonasm

antithesis   prolepsis or anticipation

asyndeton   simile

apostrophe   synchesis

chiasmus   synecdoche

extended simile   tmesis

hendiadys   transferred epithet

hyperbole

Thinking about What You Read

1. Use details from this passage to describe Dido's physical appearance as she prepares to die.

2. Of what memorable accomplishments does Dido boast in her farewell speech?

3. For what reason(s) do you think Aeneas gave Dido his sword (646)? Why does Vergil add the comment *nōn hōs quaesītum mūnus in ūsūs* (647) in reference to this sword?

4. Explain the difference in meaning between *moriēmur* (659) and *moriāmur* (660). What effect does this repetition have on Dido's speech?

5. Find words and phrases in this passage which illustrate Vergil's tragic Muse discussed in the last reading.

Fig. 30.
An Unsheathed Sword.

APPENDIX

GRAMMATICAL APPENDIX

SECTION 1: DECLENSIONS OF NOUNS

Nouns are the names of persons, places, or things. In Latin, nouns, pronouns, and adjectives are inflected to show their grammatical relations to the other words in the sentence. These inflectional endings are usually equivalent to prepositional phrases in English.

The names of the cases and their functions are as follows:

LATIN CASE	USE IN THE SENTENCE	ENGLISH CASE	EXAMPLE
Nominative	Subject or subj. complement.	Nominative.	puer (*the* or *a boy*)
Genitive	Shows possession and other relationships.	Possessive or the objective, with "of."	puerī (*of the boy*, or *of a boy or boy's*)
Dative	Indirect object and other relationships.	Objective, often with "to" or "for."	puerō (*to* or *for the boy*)
Accusative	Direct object.	Objective.	puerum (*boy*, or *the boy*)
Ablative	Occurs in adverbial phrases, usually with a preposition.	Objective, as object of many prepositions.	puerō (*by the boy, from, with, on, at,* etc.)

There are two additional cases which occur infrequently, and are not usually given with the decensions:

Vocative	Case of address. (The Latin inflectional ending is the same as in the nominative with exceptions noted, p. 191.)	Nominative of address.	puer! (*Boy!*)
Locative	Case of "place at which," with cities, towns, small islands, and **domus** (*home*), **rus** (*country*), and **humus** (*the ground*) only.	Objective, with "at."	Rōmae (*at Rome*)

INFLECTION IN GENERAL

The inflectional ending of a word shows its *number, gender,* and *case.* The general concepts of number and case are similar to their counterparts in English (singular-plural, case structure outlined above). However, *gender* in Latin is often *grammatical* only, and unrelated to *natural* gender. Although there are the same three genders (masculine, feminine, neuter) in Latin as in English, it is not uncommon for a word like nauta (*sailor*), which is naturally male, to appear in a feminine declension (1st declension). Inflected words are composed of two parts: the *base* and the inflected portion. The *base* is that part of the word which remains unchanged, and the base of any noun may be determined by removing the ending of the *genitive singular* form. The base of **terra** is **terr-**; the base of **ager** is **agr-**, and so on.

FIRST AND SECOND DECLENSION NOUNS

The gender of most 1st declension nouns is feminine. That of most 2nd declension nouns is neuter (ending in **-um**) or masculine (ending in **-us** or **-er**).

1st Declension — Fem.

	Sing.	Plur.
Nom.	terra (*land*)	-ae
Gen.	terrae	-ārum
Dat.	terrae	-īs
Acc.	terram	-ās
Abl.	terrā	-īs

2nd Declension — Masc.

	Sing.	Plur.
Nom.	animus (*mind*)	-ī
Gen.	animī	-ōrum
Dat.	animō	-īs
Acc.	animum	-ōs
Abl.	animō	-īs

2nd Declension — Neut.

	Sing.	Plur.
Nom.	caelum (*sky*)	-a
Gen.	caelī	-ōrum
Dat.	caelō	-īs
Acc.	caelum	-a
Abl.	caelō	-īs

2nd Declension Masc. Ending in -er

	Sing.	Plur.	Sing.	Plur.
Nom.	magister (*teacher*)	-ī	puer (*boy*)	-ī
Gen.	magistrī	-ōrum	puerī	-ōrum
Dat.	magistrō	-īs	puerō	-īs
Acc.	magistrum	-ōs	puerum	-ōs
Abl.	magistrō	-īs	puerō	-īs

THIRD DECLENSION NOUNS

The trademark of the 3rd declension is the ending **-is** in the genitive singular. It is added to the base. All genders are represented in the 3rd declension.[1]

	Sing.	*Plur.*		*Sing.*	*Plur.*		*Sing.*	*Plur.*		*Sing*	*Plur.*
Nom.	lux (*light*)	lūcēs		parens (*parent*)	parentēs		nāvis (*ship*)	-ēs		nox (*night*)	noctēs
Gen.	lūcis	-um		parentis	-um		nāvis	-ium		noctis	-ium
Dat.	lūcī	-ibus		parentī	-ibus		nāvī	-ibus		noctī	-ibus
Acc.	lūcem	-ēs		parentem	-ēs		nāvem	-ēs (-īs)		noctem	-ēs (-īs)
Abl.	lūce	-ibus		parente	-ibus		nāve	-ibus		nocte	-ibus

	Sing.	*Plur.*		*Sing.*	*Plur.*		*Sing.*	*Plur.*
Nom.	mare (*sea*)	-ia		genus (*type*)	genera		flūmen (*river*)	flūmina
Gen.	maris	-ium		generis	-um		flūminis	-um
Dat.	marī	-ibus		generī	-ibus		flūminī	-ibus
Acc.	mare	-ia		genus	-a		flūmen	-a
Abl.	marī	-ibus		genere	-ibus		flūmine	-ibus

[1]Nouns ending in **-is** or **-es** that have the same number of syllables in the genitive and the nominative take **-ium** in the genitive plural and, sometimes, **-īs** in the accusative plural.

Nouns whose bases end in double consonants take **-ium** in the genitive plural and, sometimes, **-īs** in the accusative plural.

Neuter nouns ending in **-e, -al,** or **-ar** take **-ī** in the ablative singular, **-ia** in the nominative and accusative plural, and **-ium** in the genitive plural.

IRREGULAR NOUNS OF THE THIRD DECLENSION

A. **Vīs** (*force in sing., strength in plur.*), fem., is declined **vīs, vis, vī, vim, vī,** (plur.) **vīrēs, vīrium, vīribus, vīrēs (-īs), vīribus.**

B. **Puppis, puppis** (*stern, ship*), fem., and **turris, turris** (*tower*), fem., usually have **-im** in the accusative singular, and **-ī** in the ablative singular.

C. The ablative in **-ī** is occasionally used with i-stem nouns like **classis, classis** (*fleet*).

D. **Senex, senis** (*old man*), masc., has **senum** in the genitive plural.

E. The declension of **Iuppiter** (*Jupiter*): **Iuppiter, Iovis, Iovī, Iovem, Iove.**

F. **Hērōs, hērōis, hērōī, hērōa, hērōe** is a Greek masc. noun meaning *hero.*

G. **Īlias, Īliados** (*Iliad*), fem., is declined like hērōs.

FOURTH DECLENSION NOUNS

Most fourth declension nouns are masculine and are formed from the 4th principal part of the verb.

	Masc.			**Fem.**			**Neut.**	
	Sing.	*Plur.*		*Sing.*	*Plur.*		*Sing.*	*Plur.*
Nom.	portus (*port*)	-ūs		domus (*house*)	-ūs		cornū (*horn*)	-ua
Gen.	portūs	-uum		domūs (-ī)	-uum (-ōrum)		cornūs	-uum
Dat.	portuī (-ū)	-ibus		domuī (-ō)	-ibus		cornū	-ibus
Acc.	portum	-ūs		domum	-ōs (-ūs)		cornnū	-ua
Abl.	portū	-ibus		domū (-ō)	-ibus		cornū	-ibus

FIFTH DECLENSION NOUNS

Very few nouns in the fifth declension are declined throughout. Most fifth declension nouns are rarely found in the genitive, dative, and ablative plural.

All fifth declension nouns are feminine except **merīdiēs,** which is masculine, and **diēs,** which is either masculine or feminine in the singular but always masculine in the plural.

	Sing.	*Plur.*		*Sing.*	*Plur.*
Nom.	diēs (*day*)	diēs		rēs (*matter*)	rēs
Gen.	diēī (**diē**)	-ērum		reī	rērum
Dat.	diēī (**diē**)	-ēbus		reī	rēbus
Acc.	diem	-ēs		rem	rēs
Abl.	diē	-ēbus		rē	rēbus

ALTERNATIVE OR SYNCOPATED ENDINGS

Latin nouns (and adjectives) sometimes have alternative or syncopated (i.e., contracted) endings, especially in poetry.

1. **First declension: -um** for **-ārum** in genitive plural. **Rēgīna deum** for **deōrum.** *Queen of the gods.*

2. **Second declension: -um** for **-ōrum** in genitive plural. For example, **superum** (for **superōrum**). *Of the gods.*

3. **Third declension i-stems:**

    A. **Accusative plural, third declension: -īs** can be used instead of **-ēs** in the accusative plural of third declension nouns, adjectives, and participles. For example, **sonantīs scopulōs.** *Sounding rocks.*

    B. **-im** for **-em** in accusative singular with words like **Tiberim, puppim, turrim.** (But Vergil also uses the *-em* ending on other words like **nāvem.**)

    C. **-ī** for **-e** in ablative singular with words like *ignī* and *amnī*

    D. **-um** instead of **-ium** in the genitive plural of third declension i-stem nouns and present active participles such as **volucrum, vātum,** and **venientum.**

DECLENSION OF GREEK NOUNS

Many Greek names are easily declined in Latin. Here are some examples for the first and second Latin declensions. In the third declension all the endings are the same except for the acc. sing, which uses the Greek ending -a. Fourth and fifth declensions do not exist in Greek. Only the singular is given because these are all names.

	First Declension	**Second Declension**	**Third Declension**
Nom.	Cassandra	Dēiphobus	Hector
Gen.	Cassandrae	Dēiphobī	Hectoris
Dat.	Cassandrae	Dēiphobō	Hectorī
Acc.	Casandram	Dēiphobum	Hectora
Abl.	Cassandrā	Dēiphobō	Hectore
Voc.	Cassandra	Dēiphobe	Hector

Even though Greek nouns could easily adopt Latin case endings, occasionally a Greek ending was used in Latin. Roman authors like Vergil were fluent in Greek and knew the names in Greek, so it was natural for them to use the Greek form even in Latin. Below are the most important Greek endings which Vergil uses.

	First Declension	**Second Declension**	**Third Declension**
Nom.		**-os** for **-us**	
		Dēlos for Dēlus	
Acc.	**-ān** or **-ēn** for **-am**		**-in** or **-im** or **-a** for **em**
	Aenēān for Aenēam		Īrim for Īrida
	Achatēn for Achatam		
	Hecatēn for Hecatam		

SECTION 2: SYNTAX OF CASES

NOMINATIVE CASE

1. The subject of a finite verb is nominative. **Aenēās** veniet. *Aeneas will come.*

2. Predicate Nominative (Subject Complement). After the verb *to be* or any form thereof the subject complement replaces an object of the verb. It is in the same case as the subject. Aenēās **vir** Teucrus erat. *Aeneas was a Trojan man.*

GENITIVE CASE

1. Possession. **Phoebī** soror. *Phoebus' sister.* BUT: Rēgīna **mea.** *My queen.* (Possessive adjective)

2. Quality (When a noun is modified). **Tantae mōlis** erat condere. *Founding was of so great an effort.*

3. Subjective. Murmure **montis.** *With the roar of the mountain.* (If the noun "roar" were changed to a verb, *mountain* would become its subject .)

4. Objective. Lacrimae **rērum.** *The tears of things.* (If the noun "tears" were changed to the verb phrase "shed tears about," "things" would become its object.)

5. Partitive: **nymphārum** ūna. *One of the nymphs. Note:* The following adjectives modify their noun directly and are not followed by the genitive:

    omnis — *all of*   summus — *top of*
    tōtus — *whole of*   medius — *middle of*

    Cardinal numerals and quīdam take ex or dē plus the ablative case rather than the partitive genitive. (See "Ablative With Cardinal Numbers" below.)

6. With verbs of reminding, remembering and forgetting. **Huius** meminisse. *To remember this (day). Note:* To remember or forget a *thing* is rendered by meminī plus the accusative case: **Haec** meminisse. *To remember these things.*

7. Appositional Genitive. Used instead of nouns in apposition with words like vōx, nōmen, verbum, rēs, urbs, etc. Ab sede **Lavīnī**. *From the seat of Lavinium.*

8. Verbs of accusing or condemning take the genitive. Damnātī **mortis**. *Convicted of the death.*

9. With miseret, paenitet, piget, pudet, and taedet, the genitive is used as the cause of the feeling. Miserēre **labōrum**. *Pity my labors.*

10. Genitive of indefinite value is expressed by tantī (*of such value*), quantī (*of how great value*), magnī (*of great value*), parvī (*of little value*), and their comparative or superlative genitive forms. Est mihi **tantī**. *It is worthwhile (it is of such value) to me.*

11. Genitive of respect or specification. Dīves **opum**. *Rich in resources.*

DATIVE CASE

1. Indirect object. **Mihī** causās memorā. *Recall to me the reasons.*

2. Indirect object with intransitive and passive verbs: **Comitī**que **onerī**que timentem. *Fearing for (my) companion and my burden.*

3. Indirect Object with Compound Verbs: Some verbs are compounded with ad, ante, con, in, ob, post, prae, prō, sub, super in such a way as to change their meanings and call for a dative object. **Captae** superāvimus **urbī**. *We have survived the captured city.*

4. Dative of Possession (with the verb *to be*, either expressed or understood): Tantaene **animīs caelestibus** īrae (sunt)? *Do heavenly minds have such great anger?* Note how the dative of possession is usually translated into English as the subject of the verb *to have*.

5. Dative of agent is used with some of the perfect passive constructions (and with gerundives) to show the "doer" of the action. Memorandum **mihi**. *I must remember.*

6. Dative of Purpose: Rēgem ventūrum **excidiō** Libyae. *That a king would come for the destruction of Libya.*

7. Dative of Reference: The person or thing affected in the sentence: Hoc rēgnum **gentibus** esse. *That this would be a kingdom for peoples.* *Note:* When the datives of purpose and reference are used together (as in rēgem ventūrum **excidiō** Libyae), they are called the double dative.

8. Dative of Separation: Occasionally, after compounds with ab, dē, ex, ad, the dative occurs instead of the usual ablative. **Mihi** ēripuit mentem. *It snatched my mind from me.*

9. The dative occurs with adjectives of *fitness* (aptus), *nearness* (proximus), *likeness* (similis), *friendliness* (amīcus), and their opposites. Inimīca **mihī**. *Unfriendly to me.* **Deō** similis. *Like a god.*

ACCUSATIVE CASE

1. Direct Object of a transitive verb. **Causās** memorā. *Recall the reasons.*

2. Subject of the infinitive: In indirect statements and after iubeō (*order*), patior (*allow*), and sinō (*permit*), the subject of the infinitive goes into the accusative case. Sīc volvere **Parcās**. (Juno had heard that) *The Fates roll thus.*

3. Predicate accusative or object complement where a second accusative is used after verbs like appellō (*name*), dēligō (*choose*), faciō (*make*). Faciat tē **parentem**. *She would make you the parent.*

4. Accusative of Extent (how long in time or space). Also called accusative of duration of time. Tot **annōs** bella gerō. *I am waging wars for so many years.*

5. Accusative of Place to Which. Note: Vergil uses this accusative with and without a preposition. In **patriam** venit. *He comes into his country.*

6. Accusative with Middle/Passive Verbs. **Sinūs** collēcta. *Having gathered the folds.*

7. Accusative of Exclamation. **Miserum**! *The wretch!*

7. Object of certain prepositions: These prepositions take an accusative object: ad, ante, circum, contrā, inter, intrā, ob, per, post, prope, propter, super, trāns, ultrā. Per **variōs casūs**. *Through various misfortunes.* See prepositions below.

8. Accusative supine after a verb of motion to express purpose. **Servītum** ībō. *I will go to guard.*

ABLATIVE CASE

1. Object of certain prepositions (all those not listed as governing the accusative case). The more common ones are ā/ab, cum, dē, ē/ex, in, prae, prō, sine, sub. See prepositions below.

2. Personal agent, expressed with a passive verb and a person, with ā /ab. Vincor **āb Aeneā** . *I am conquered by Aeneas.*

3. Separation. Nē Dīdō **fīnibus** arcēret. *Lest Dido keep him from her territory.*

4. Place from which. Ab **orīs** vēnit. *He came from the shores.*

5. Ablative with Cardinal Numbers. Duo dē **numerō**. *Two of the number.*

6. Ablative of Cause. **Metū** līquēre. *They left because of fear.*

7. Ablative of Means. Implicuit comam **laevā**. *He seized his hair with his left hand.*

8. Ablatives with Special Verbs. With the deponent verbs ūtor (*use*), fruor (*enjoy*), fungor (*accomplish*), potior (*gain*), and vēscor (*feed on*), the ablative is usually used. **Hīs vocibus** ūsa est. *She used these words.*

8. Albative with opus and ūsus (meaning *need*). Non mille **carinīs** mihi opus est. *I do not need a thousand ships.*

9. Ablative of Accordance: **Spontē suā**. *Of his own accord.*

10. Ablative of place where (usually, but not always, with a preposition like *in*). In **lītore** condunt.*They hide on the shore.* **Terrīs** iactātus et **altō**. *Tossed on lands and on the sea.* If the preposition is omitted with names of towns, *domus, rūs,* and *humus,* the locative case is used (see below).

11. Ablative of Comparison. When quam *(than)* is omitted in comparisons, the ablative is used. **Nōtā** maior imāgō. *An image greater than the one known.*

12. Specification or Respect: This ablative tells in what respect something is done or is true. Parēs **aetāte**. *Equal in respect to age.*

13. Degree of Difference: After comparatives, this ablative shows the extent or degree to which the objects differ. **Multō** tremendum magis. *More frightful by much.*

14. Ablative of manner, telling "how," may omit the usual cum if the noun is modified. **Modīs** pallida **mīrīs**. *Pale in a marvelous manner.* **Magnō** cum **murmure**. *With a great roaring.*

15. Accompaniment. Cum **gente** bella gerō. *I wage wars with the people.*

16. Ablative of means or instrument of an action occurs without a preposition in most cases. **Aere** ruēbant. *The plowed with bronze.*

17. Ablative of time when, without a preposition. **Aestāte novā.** *In the new season.*

18. Ablative Absolute: This construction consists of a noun or pronoun in the ablative case plus a present active or perfect passive participle, or two nouns in the ablative case, or a noun and an adjective, with the participle understood. The construction is usually translated by a clause referring to time *(when)*, cause *(since, because)*, concession *(although)*, condition *(if)*. In any given instance any of the above translations may be appropriate, depending upon the sense of the rest of the context. **Nūmine laesō.** *Because a deity was wounded.*

19. Quality or Description: **Pulchrā orīgine** Caesar. *Caesar of beautiful origin.*

VOCATIVE CASE

The vocative case is used for direct address. Its forms are exactly like those of the nominative case, except for 2nd declension nouns ending in -us or -ius. **O, amīce!** *O, friend!* **O Vergilī!** *O, Vergil.*

LOCATIVE CASE

The locative case is used only to indicate "place where" or "place at which" with names of towns or cities, humus *(soil)*, domus *(home)*, and rūs *(the country)*. In all other cases the ablative of "place where" with the preposition *in* is used. The locative endings are:

	Sing.	Plur.
1st Declension	**-ae**	**-īs**
2nd Declension	**-ī**	**-īs**
3rd Declension	**-ī or -e**	**-ibus**

Rōmae — *in Rome,* **domī** — *at home,* **rūrī** — *in the country*

PREPOSITIONS, PREFIXES

Most of the prepositions in Latin are used to govern the use of the accusative case. About one third of them govern the ablative, and a few govern both cases, depending upon the verb used in the sentence. Many prepositions are also commonly used as prefixes. Attached to the front of a word, they give it a different shade of meaning. Examples are below.

PREPOSITION	CASE	MEANING	COMPOUND	MEANING
ā, ab	Ablative	*away from*	**ab**dūcō	*lead away*
ad	Accusative	*to*	**ad**dūcō	*lead to, influence*
ante	Accusative	*before*	**ante**ferō	*bear before*
apud	Accusative	*at, among*		
circum	Accusative	*around, about*	**circum**ferō	*carry around*
contrā	Accusative	*against*		
cum, con, com	Ablative	*with*	**con**trahō	*draw together*
dē	Ablative	*down from*	**dē**scendō	*climb down*
ē, ex	Ablative	*out from*	**ex**pellō	*drive out*
in	Accusative	*into*	**in**iciō	*hurl into*
in	Ablative	*in (place where)*		
inter	Accusative	*between, among*	**inter**rumpō	*interrupt*
ob	Accusative	*on account of*	**oc**currō	*run to meet*
per	Accusative	*through*	**per**rumpō	*break through*
post	Accusative	*after*	**post**pōnō	*put after*
prae	Ablative	*in front of*	**prae**ficiō	*put in command*
praeter	Accusative	*along by, past*	**praeter**eō	*go past*
prō	Ablative	*in front of*	**prō**dūcō	*lead forth*
propter	Accusative	*on account of*		
re-, red-	Prefix only	*back*	**red**imō	*buy back*
sub	Accusative	*up from under*	**sub**eō	*approach*
sub	Ablative	*under*	**sub**trahō	*draw from under*
super	Accusative	*above*	**super**immineō	*tower over*
trāns	Accusative	*across*	**trāns**eō	*go across*
ultrā	Accusative	*beyond*		

SECTION 3: PRONOUNS

Pronouns, as the name implies, take the place of nouns. At times, they are used as adjectives, to modify nouns. Under those circumstances, they agree with the nouns in gender, number, and case.

PERSONAL PRONOUNS

	1st Person					2nd Person		
	Sing.		*Plur.*			*Sing.*	*Plur.*	
Nom.	ego	*I*	nōs	*we*	tū	*you*	vōs	*you*
Gen.	meī	*of me*	nostrum, nostrī	*of us*	tuī	*of you*	vestrum, vestrī	*of you*
Dat.	mihi	*to me*	nōbīs	*to us*	tibi	*to you*	vōbīs	*to you*
Acc.	mē	*me*	nōs	*us*	tē	*you*	vōs	*you*
Abl.	mē	*by, etc., me*	nōbīs	*by, etc., us*	tē	*by, etc., you*	vōbīs	*by, etc., you*

3rd Person: A demonstrative pronoun is used as the pronoun of the 3rd person.

THE DEMONSTRATIVE PRONOUNS (OR ADJECTIVES)

There are five demonstratives used to point out special objects or persons.

Hic *(this here)* refers to what is near the speaker in place, time, or thought. Sometimes the word may also mean *he, she,* or *it.*

Ille *(that there)* refers to something remote from the speaker. It also means *that famous.*

Is, ea, id are most commonly used for *he, she,* or *it.* They may also mean *this* or *that.*

Iste *(that — nearby* or *that of yours)* is often used comtemptuously.

Īdem means *the same.*

Masc.	*Fem.*	*Neut.*	*Masc.*	*Fem.*	*Neut.*	*Masc.*	*Fem.*	*Neut.*	*Masc.*	*F em.*	*Neut.*
hic	haec	hoc	ille	illa	illud	is	ea	id	iste	ista	istud
huius	huius	huius	illīus	illīus	illīus	ēius	ēius	ēius	istīus	istīus	istīus
huic	huic	huic	illī	illī	illī	eī	eī	eī	istī	istī	istī
hunc	hanc	hoc	illum	illam	illud	eum	eam	id	istum	istam	istud
hōc	hāc	hōc	illō	illā	illō	eō	eā	eō	istō	istā	istō
hī	hae	haec	illī	illae	illa	eī	eae	ea	istī	istae	ista
hōrum	hārum	hōrum	illōrum	illārum	illōrum	eōrum	eārum	eōrum	istōrum	istārum	istōrum
hīs	hīs	hīs	illīs	illīs	illīs	eīs	eīs	eīs	istīs	istīs	istīs
hōs	hās	haec	illōs	illās	illa	eōs	eās	ea	istōs	istās	ista
hīs	hīs	hīs	illīs	illīs	illīs	eīs	eīs	eīs	istīs	istīs	istīs

Masc.	*Fem.*	*Neut.*
īdem	eadem	idem
eīusdem	eīusdem	eīusdem
eīdem	eīdem	eīdem
eundem	eandem	idem
eōdem	eādem	eōdem
eīdem	eaedem	eadem
eōrundem	eārundem	eōrundem
eīsdem	eīsdem	eīsdem
eōsdem	eāsdem	eadem
eīsdem	eīsdem	eīsdem

INDEFINITE PRONOUNS

Quis, aliquis, and **quīdam** are the indefinite pronouns. **Quis** is usually used immediately after sī, nisi, nē, and num. Only the quis and quī of the indefinites may be declined: **quis** is declined like the interrogative below; **quī** is declined like the relative.

INTERROGATIVE PRONOUNS

The interrogative pronoun, as its name implies, introduces a question. **Quis** means *who,* and **quid** means *what.* Declension is like the relative, **quis** for **quī,** **quid** for **quod,** with the plural declined the same.

POSSESSIVE PRONOUNS (OR ADJECTIVES)

1st Person Sing.
meus, -a, -um *my, mine*
(Declined like bonus)

1st Person Plur.
noster, nostra, nostrum
(Declined like pulcher)

2nd Person Sing.
tuus, tua, tuum *your*

2nd Person Plur.
vester, vestra, vestrum

3rd Person Reflexive Possessive
suus, sua, suum *his, her, its, their*

Suus refers to the subject and agrees with the noun modified in gender, number, and case.

REFLEXIVE PRONOUNS

The reflexive pronoun of the third person has a single declension for singular and plural, and all three genders.

Nom.	(none)
Gen.	suī
Dat.	sibi
Acc.	sē
Abl.	sē

Note: The oblique cases of the 1st and 2nd person of the *personal* pronouns are used reflexively. amō **mē**. (*I love myself.*)

THE INTENSIVE PRONOUN IPSE

Ipse is used to emphasize nouns and pronouns of any person and agrees with the pronoun contained in the verb. Aenēās **ipse** haec dīxit. *Aeneas himself said these things.*

Sing.			*Plur.*		
ipse	ipsa	ipsum	ipsī	ipsae	ipsa
ipsīus	ipsīus	ipsīus	ipsōrum	ipsārum	ipsōrum
ipsī	ipsī	ipsī	ipsīs	ipsīs	ipsīs
ipsum	ipsam	ipsum	ipsōs	ipsās	ipsa
ipsō	ipsā	ipsō	ipsīs	ipsīs	ipsīs

RELATIVE PRONOUNS

Quī, quae, quod (*who, which*) is the most commonly used of the relative pronouns (or adjectives).

	Sing.			*Plur.*		
Masc.	*Fem.*	*Neut.*		*Masc.*	*Fem.*	*Neut.*
quī	quae	quod		quī	quae	quae
cuīus	cuīus	cuīus		quōrum	quārum	quōrum
cui	cui	cui		quibus	quibus	quibus
quem	quam	quod		quōs	quās	quae
quō	quā	quō		quibus	quibus	quibus

SECTION 4: ADJECTIVES AND ADVERBS

FIRST AND SECOND DECLENSION ADJECTIVES

Adjectives agree with their nouns in gender, number, and case. Those in the predicate after **sum** (*be*) agree with the subject, as in English. Most masculine adjectives are declined like ager, puer, or dominus; neuter adjectives like caelum; and feminine adjectives like terra.

	Masculine		Feminine		Neuter	
	Sing.	*Plur.*	*Sing.*	*Plur.*	*Sing.*	*Plur.*
Nom.	bon**us**	**-ī**	bon**a**	**-ae**	bon**um**	**-a**
Gen.	bon**ī**	**-ōrum**	bon**ae**	**-ārum**	bon**ī**	**-ōrum**
Dat.	bon**ō**	**-īs**	bon**ae**	**-īs**	bon**ō**	**-īs**
Acc.	bon**um**	**-ōs**	bon**am**	**-ās**	bon**um**	**-a**
Abl.	bon**ō**	**-īs**	bon**ā**	**-īs**	bon**ō**	**-īs**

THIRD DECLENSION ADJECTIVES

Third declension adjectives fall into four distinct categories: (1) *three-termination*, with separate endings for all three genders, like **ācer**; (2) *two-termination*, with the same endings for masculine and feminine, like **omnis**; (3) *one-termination*, with the nominative singular the same in all genders, like **potēns**; and (4) the *comparative* of all adjectives, like **longior**. The forms of **plus** (5) are unique. Present participles are declined like **potēns**.

(1) ācer (*keen*)

	Masc.		Fem.		Neut.	
	Sing.	*Plur.*	*Sing.*	*Plur.*	*Sing.*	*Plur.*
Nom.	ācer	ācrēs	ācris	ācrēs	ācre	ācria
Gen.	ācris	-ium	ācris	-ium	ācris	-ium
Dat.	ācrī	-ibus	ācrī	-ibus	ācrī	-ibus
Acc.	ācrem	-ēs (-īs)	ācrem	-ēs (-īs)	ācre	-ia
Abl.	ācrī	-ibus	ācrī	-ibus	ācrī	-ibus

(2) omnis (*every, all*)

	Masc. & Fem.		Neut.	
	Sing.	*Plur.*	*Sing.*	*Plur.*
Nom.	omnis	-ēs	omne	-ia
Gen.	omnis	-ium	omnis	-ium
Dat.	omnī	-ibus	omnī	-ibus
Acc.	omnem	-ēs (-īs)	omne	-ia
Abl.	omnī	-ibus	omnī	-ibus

(3) potēns (*powerful*)

	Masc. & Fem.		Neut.	
	Sing.	*Plur.*	*Sing.*	*Plur.*
Nom.	potēns	potentēs	potēns	potentia
Gen.	potentis	-ium	potentis	-ium
Dat.	potentī	-ibus	potentī	-ibus
Acc.	potentem	-ēs (-īs)	potēns	-ia
Abl.	potentī (-e)	-ibus	potentī (-e)	-ibus

(4) longior (*longer*)

	Masc. & Fem.		Neut.	
	Sing.	*Plur.*	*Sing.*	*Plur.*
Nom.	longior	longiōrēs	longius	longiōra
Gen.	longiōris	-um	longiōris	-um
Dat.	longiōrī	-ibus	longiōrī	-ibus
Acc.	longiōrem	-ēs (-īs)	longius	-a
Abl.	longiōre	-ibus	longiōre	-ibus

(5) plūs (*more*)

	Masc. & Fem.	Neut.	
	Plur.	*Sing.*	*Plur.*
Nom.	plūrēs	plūs	plūra
Gen.	-ium	plūris	-ium
Dat.	-ibus	plūrī	-ibus
Acc.	-ēs (-īs)	plūs	-a
Abl.	-ibus	plūre	-ibus

THE NINE IRREGULAR ADJECTIVES

There are nine adjectives ("the naughty nine") which are regular in the plural and irregular in the singular. The plurals of these words are declined like **bonus**. With the exceptions noted, the *singulars* of these adjectives are declined like **tōtus**.

alius	*other, another* (neut. — aliud)
ūllus	*any*
ūnus	*one, alone*
neuter	*neither* (gen. — neutrīus)

alter	*the other* (gen. — alterīus)
nūllus	*no, none*
sōlus	*alone, only*
uter	*which of two* (gen. — utrīus)

tōtus (*whole, all*)

	Masc.	Fem.	Neut.
Nom.	tōtus	tōta	tōtum
Gen.	tōtīus	tōtīus	tōtīus
Dat.	tōtī	tōtī	tōtī
Acc.	tōtum	tōtam	tōtum
Abl.	tōtō	tōtā	tōtō

NUMERALS

Of the numerals, only **ūnus**, **duo**, **trēs**, the hundreds, and the plural of **mīlle** are declined.

	ŪNUS			DUO			TRĒS		MĪLLE
	M.	*F.*	*N.*	*M.*	*F.*	*N.*	*M. & F.*	*N.*	*P. only*
Nom.	ūnus	ūna	ūnum	duo	duae	duo	trēs	tria	mīlia
Gen.	ūnīus	ūnīus	ūnīus	duōrum	duārum	duōrum	trium	trium	mīlium
Dat.	ūnī	ūnī	ūnī	duōbus	duābus	duōbus	tribus	tribus	mīlibus
Acc.	ūnum	ūnam	ūnum	duōs	duās	duo	trēs (-īs)	tria	milia
Abl.	ūnō	ūnā	ūnō	duōbus	duābus	duōbus	tribus	tribus	mīlibus

There are four types of numerals: Cardinal Numerals (adjectives) one, two, etc.; Ordinal Numerals (adjectives) first, second, etc.; Distributives (adjectives) one by one, two by two, three each, etc.; Numerical Adverbs (once, twice, etc.).

	CARDINALS	ORDINALS	DISTRIBUTIVES	ADVERBS	NUMERALS
1	ūnus, -a, -um	prīmus, -a, -um	singulī, -ae, -a	semel	I
2	duo, duae, duo	secundus	bīnī	bis	II
3	trēs, tria	tertius	ternī (trinī)	ter	III
4	quattuor	quārtus	quaternī	quater	IV
5	quinque	quintus	quīnī	quinquiens	V
6	sex	sextus	sēnī	sexiens	VI
7	septem	septimus	septēnī	septiens	VII
8	octō	octāvus	octōnī	octiens	VIII
9	novem	nōnus	novēnī	noviens	IX
10	decem	decimus	dēnī	deciens	X
11	undecim	undecimus	undēnī	ndeciens	XI
12	duodecim	duodecimus	duodēnī	duodeciens	XII
13	tredecim	tertius decimus	ternī dēnī	terdeciens	XIII
14	quattuordecim	quārtus decimus	quaternī dēnī	quater deciens	XIV
15	quindecim	quintus decimus	quīnī dēnī	quīndeciens	XV
16	sēdecim	sextus decimus	sēnī dēnī	sēdeciens	XVI
17	septendecim	septimus decimus	septēnī dēnī	septiens deciens	XVII
18	duodēvīgintī	duodēvīcēsimus	duodēvīcēnī	duodēvīciens	XVIII
	(octōdecim)	(octāvus decimus)	(octōnī dēnī)	(octiens deciens)	
19	undēvīgintī	undēvīcēsimus	undēvīcēnī	undēvīciens	XIX
	(novendecim)	(nōnus decimus)	(novēnī dēnī)	(noviens deciens)	
20	vīgintī	vīcēsimus	vīcēnī	vīciens	XX
21	vīgintī ūnus	ūnus et vīcēsimus	vīcēnī singulī	vīciens semel	XXI
30	trīgintā	trīcēsimus	trīcēnī	trīciens	XXX
40	quadrāgintā	quadrāgēsimus	quadrāgēnī	quadrāgiens	XL
50	quinquāgintā	quinquāgēsimus	quinquāgēnī	quīnquāgiens	L
60	sexāgintā	sexāgēsimus	sexāgēnī	sexāgiens	LX
70	septuāgintā	septuāgēsimus	septuāgēnī	septuāgiens	LXX
80	octōgintā	octōgēsimus	octōgēnī	octōgiens	LXXX
90	nōnāgintā	nōnāgēsimus	nōnāgēnī	nōnāgiens	XC
100	centum	centēsimus	centēnī	centiens	C
101	centum ūnus	centēsimus prīmus	centēnī singulī	centiens semel	CI
200	ducentī, -ae, -a	duocentēsimus	ducēnī	ducentiens	CC
300	trecentī	trecentēsimus	trecēnī	trecentiens	CCC
400	quadringentī	quadringentēsimus	quadringēnī	quadringentiens	CCCC
500	quingentī	quingentēsimus	quingēnī	quingentiens	D
1000	mīlle	mīllēsimus	mīllenī	mīlliens	M
2000	duo mīlia	bis mīllēsimus	bīna mīlia	bis mīlliens	MM

COMPARISON OF ADJECTIVES

There are three degrees of comparison in Latin, just as there are in English: *positive, comparative,* and *superlative.* The *comparative* is formed by adding **-ior** for the masculine and feminine, and **-ius** for the neuter to the base of the *positive.* The *superlative* is formed by adding **-issimus, -a, -um** to the base. The *comparative* is declined like **longior** (see Section 3); the *positive* is declined like bonus for 1st and 2nd declension, like omnis for third declension adjectives (see also Section 3). The *superlative* is declined like bonus.

Note: Six adjectives ending in **-lis** (facilis, difficilis, similis, dissimilis, gracilis, humilis) add **-limus** instead of -issimus to the base to form the *superlative:* (facilis, facilior, facillimus)

Note: Adjectives ending in **-er** add **-rimus** instead of -issimus to form the *superlative.*

miser, -a, -um	miserior, miserius	miserrimus, -a, -um
ācer, ācris, ācre	ācrior, ācrius	ācerrimus, -a, -um

Note: Adjectives ending in **-ius** or **-eus** add **magis** to form the comparative and **maximē** to form the superlative: idōneus, magis idōneus, maximē idōneus.

REGULAR FORMS

POSITIVE	COMPARATIVE	SUPERLATIVE
longus, -a, -um	long**ior,** long**ius**	long**issimus, -a, -um**
fortis, forte	fort**ior,** fort**ius**	fort**issimus, -a, -um**

IRREGULAR COMPARISONS

POSITIVE	COMPARATIVE	SUPERLATIVE
bonus *(good)*	melior	optimus
malus *(bad)*	peior	pessimus
magnus *(large)*	maior	maximus
multus *(much)*	plūs	plūrimus
multī *(many)*	plūrēs	plūrimī
parvus *(small)*	minor	minimus

FORMATION AND COMPARISON OF ADVERBS

Positive adverbs are formed regularly by adding **-ē** to the base of adjectives of the 1st and 2nd declensions (longē). Adjectives of the 3rd declension may be changed to adverbs by adding **-iter** to the base (fortiter). Those with a base of **-nt** simply add **-er** (prūdenter). Examples are below.

POSITIVE	COMPARATIVE	SUPERLATIVE
longē	longius	longissimē
fortiter	fortius	fortissimē
miserē	miserius	miserrimē
ācriter	ācrius	ācerrimē
facile	facilius	facillimē
bene	melius	optimē
male	pēius	pessimē
magnopere	magis	maximē
multum	plūs	plūrimum
parum	minus	minimē
diū	diūtius	diūtissimē

ADVERBS OF LOCATION

hīc (*here*)	hinc (*from here*)	hūc (*to here*)	hāc (*by this way*)	ultrō (*beyond*)
ibi (*there*)	inde (*from there*)	eō (*to there*)	eā (*by that way*)	usquam (*anywhere*)
illīc (*there*)	illinc (*from there*)	illūc (*to there*)	illā (*by that way*)	nusquam (*nowhere*)
istīc (*there*)	istinc (*from there*)	istūc (*to there*)	istā (*by that way*)	intrō (*inwardly, from the outside in*)
ubi (*where*)	unde (*from where*)	quō (*to where*)	quā (*by what way*)	extrō (*outwardly, from the inside out*)

ADVERBS OF TIME

cum (*when*)	hodiē (*today*)	iamdudum (*now for a long time*)	numquam (*never*)	quandō (*when?*)	umquam (*ever*)
deinde (*next*)	iam (*already*)	mox (*soon*)	prīdem (*long ago*)	saepe (*often*)	ut (*when*)
dum (*while*)	iam diū (*long ago*)	nōndum (*not yet*)	prīmum (*first*)	semper (*always*)	

INTERROGATIVE ADVERBS

-ne, an enclitic, expects the answer "*maybe.*"
> Ingemuit**ne** flētū nostrō? (*Did he groan because of my weeping?*)

Num expects the answer "*no.*"
> **Num** flētū ingemuit nostrō? (*He didn't groan because of my weeping, did he?*)

Nōnne expects the answer "*yes.*" Note: Vergil does not use this type of question.
> **Nōnne** flētū ingemuit nostrō? (*He did groan because of my weeping, didn't he?*)

An, -ne, anne, utrum, num, introducing indirect questions, all mean "*whether.*"
> **An** Phoebī soror? **An** nymphārum sanguinis ūna? ([I do not know] *whether you are the sister of Phoebus or one of the nymphs.*)

NEGATIVE ADVERBS (PARTICLES)

nōn (*not*), nē, in a prohibition (*not*)	neque . . . neque, nec . . . nec (*neither . . . nor*)
haud (*not*), nē, in a purpose clause (*lest*)	nē . . . quidem, with the emphasized word between (*not even*)
minimē (*not at all*), nē, after verb of fearing (*that*)	nōn sōlum . . . sed etiam (*not only . . . but also*)
nec, neque (*and not*), nēve, neu (*and not*)	nē quis, nē quid (*so that no one, so that nothing*)

RELATIVE ADVERBS

Relative adverbs introduce certain clauses:
> ubi (*where, when*) Haec **ubi** dicta dedit. *When he said these words.*
> quō (*to where*) In arma feror, **quō** tristis Erīnys vocat. *I am called into arms to where the sad Fury calls.*
> unde (*from which place*) **Unde** omnia Trōia vidērī solita est. *From which place all Troy was accustomed to be seen.*
> cum (*when, since, although*) Flammās **cum** rēgia puppis extulerat. *When the regal ship had raised the flames.*
> quārē (*why, therefore*) **Quārē** agite, Ō tectīs, iuvenēs, succēdite nostrīs. *Therefore, youths, enter our home.*

ADVERBS OF DEGREE

quam (*how*)	paene (*almost*)
cūr, quārē (*why*)	tam (*so*)
ergō, itaque, igitur (*therefore*)	ut, utī (*how*)
ita, sīc (*thus, so*)	

SECTION 5: VERBS INDICATIVE AND IMPERATIVE

REGULAR VERBS

In Latin the verb is especially important. It causes the subject either to act or to be acted upon. It expresses mood, voice, tense, person, and number. It includes four participles, the gerund, and the supine.

The present, imperfect, and the future indicative tenses, active and passive, are formed from the *present stem*, obtained by removing the -re from the present infinitive. The three perfect indicative active tenses are formed from the *perfect stem*, obtained by removing the -ī from the third principal part. The three perfect indicative passive tenses are formed from the fourth principal part, the entire *perfect passive participle*.

FIRST CONJUGATION

PRINCIPAL PARTS OF PARŌ

parō	Pres. Ind., Act., lst Sing.	*I prepare*
parāre	Pres. Inf. Act.	*to prepare*
parāvī	Perf. Ind. Act., 1st Sing.	*I have prepared, I prepared*
parātus	Perf. Pass. Part.	*having been prepared*

INDICATIVE ACTIVE

Present
parō *I prepare*
parās *you prepare*
parat *he prepares*
parāmus *we prepare*
parātis *you.prepare*
parant *they prepare*

Perfect
parāvī *I have prepared*
parāvistī *you have prepared*
parāvit *he has prepared*
parāvimus *we have prepared*
parāvistis *you have prepared*
parāvērunt *they have prepared*

Imperfect
parābam *I was preparing*
parābās *you were preparing*
parābat *he was preparing*
parābāmus *we were preparing*
parābātis *you were preparing*
parābant *they were preparing*

Pluperfect
parāveram *I had prepared*
parāverās *you had prepared*
parāverat *he had prepared*
parāverāmus *we had prepard*
parāverātis *you had prepare*
parāverant *they had prepare*

Future
parābō *I shall prepare*
parābis *you will prepare*
parābit *he will prepare*
parābimus *we will prepare*
parābitis *you will prepare*
parābunt *they will prepare*

Future Perfect
parāverō *I shall have prepared*
parāveris *you will have prepared*
parāverit *he will have prepared*
parāverimus *we will have prepared*
parāveritis *you will have prepared*
parāverint *they will have prepared*

INDICATIVE PASSIVE

Present
paror *I am (being) prepared*
parāris *you are prepared*
parātur *he is prepared*
parāmur *we are prepared*
parāminī *you are prepared*
parantur *they are prepared*

Perfect
parātus, -a, -um **sum** *I have been prepared*
parātus, -a, -um **es** *you have been prepared*
parātus, -a, -um **est** *he has been prepared*
parātī, -ae, -a **sumus** *we have been prepared*
parātī, -ae, -a **estis** *you have been prepared*
parātī, -ae, -a **sunt** *they have been prepared*

Imperfect
parābar *I was being prepared*
parābāris *you were prepare*
parābātur *he was prepared*
parābāmur *we were prepared*
parābāminī *you were prepared*
parābantur *they were prepared*

Pluperfect
parātus, -a, -um **eram** *I had been prepared*
parātus, -a, -um **erās** *you had been prepared*
parātus, -a, -um **erat** *he had been prepared*
parātī, -ae, -a **erāmus** *we had been prepared*
parātī, -ae, -a **erātis** *you had been prepared*
parātī, -ae, -a **erant** *they had been prepared*

Future
parābor *I shall be prepared*
parāberis *you will be prepared*
parābitur *he will be prepared*
parābimur *we shall be prepared*
parābiminī *you will be prepared*
parābuntur *they will be prepared*

Future Perfect
parātus, -a, -um **erō** *I shall have been prepared*
parātus, -a, -um **eris** *you will have been prepared*
parātus, -a, -um **erit** *he will have been prepared*
parātī, -ae, -a **erimus** *we shall have been prepared*
parātī, -ae, -a **eritis** *you will have been prepared*
parātī, -ae, -a **erunt** *they will have been prepared*

IMPERATIVE ACTIVE

PRESENT
Sing.: parā   *prepare*
Plur.: parāte   *prepare*

IMPERATIVE PASSIVE

PRESENT
Sing.: parāre   *be prepared*
Plur.: parāminī   *be prepared*

SECOND CONJUGATION

PRINCIPAL PARTS OF HABEŌ
habeō   *I have*   **habēre**   *to have*   **habuī**   *I have had*   **habitus**   *having been held*

INDICATIVE ACTIVE

Present	*Perfect*
habeō	habuī
habēs	habuistī
habet	habuit
habēmus	habuimus
habētis	habuistis
habent	habuērunt

Imperfect	*Pluperfect*
habēbam	habueram
habēbās	habuerās
habēbat	habuerat
habēbāmus	habuerāmus
habēbātis	habuerātis
habēbant	habuerant

Future	*Future Perfect*
habēbō	habuerō
habēbis	habueris
habēbit	habuerit
habēbimus	habuerimus
habēbitis	habueritis
habēbunt	habuerint

INDICATIVE PASSIVE

Present	*Perfect*
habeor	habitus, -a, -um **sum**
habēris	habitus, -a, -um **es**
habētur	habitus, -a, -um **est**
habēmur	habitī, -ae, -a **sumus**
habēminī	habitī, -ae, -a **estis**
habentur	habitī, -ae, -a **sunt**

Imperfect	*Pluperfect*
habēbar	habitus, -a, -um **eram**
habēbāris	habitus, -a, -um **erās**
habēbātur	habitus, -a, -um **erat**
habēbāmur	habitī, -ae, -a **erāmus**
habēbāminī	habitī, -ae, -a **erātis**
habēbantur	habitī, -ae, -a **erant**

Future	*Future Perfect*
habēbor	habitus, -a, -um **erō**
habēberis	habitus, -a, -um **eris**
habēbitur	habitus, -a, -um **erit**
habēbimur	habitī, -ae, -a **erimus**
habēbiminī	habitī, -ae, -a **eritis**
habēbuntur	habitī, -ae, -a **erunt**

IMPERATIVE ACTIVE
PRESENT
Sing.: habē
Plur.: habēte

IMPERATIVE PASSIVE
PRESENT
Sing.: habēre
Plur.: habēminī

THIRD CONJUGATION

PRINCIPAL PARTS OF DŪCŌ
dūcō   *I lead*   **dūcere**   *to lead*   **dūxī**   *I have led*   **ductus**   *having been led*

The future active of the third conjugation is formed by adding -am, -ēs, -et, etc. to the present stem minus **-e**. To form the passive, -ar, -ēris, -ētur, etc. are added to the present stem minus **-e.**

INDICATIVE ACTIVE

Present	*Perfect*
dūcō	dūxī
dūcis	dūxistī
dūcit	dūxit
dūcimus	dūximus
dūcitis	dūxistis
dūcunt	dūxērunt

Imperfect	*Pluperfect*
dūcēbam	dūxeram
dūcēbās	dūxerās
dūcēbat	dūxerat
dūcēbāmus	dūxerāmus
dūcēbātis	dūxerātis
dūcēbant	dūxerant

Future	*Future Perfect*
dūcam	dūxerō
dūcēs	dūxeris
dūcet	dūxerit
dūcēmus	dūxerimus
dūcētis	dūxeritis
dūcent	dūxerint

INDICATIVE PASSIVE

Present	*Perfect*
dūcor	ductus, -a, -um **sum**
dūceris	ductus, -a, -um **es**
dūcitur	ductus, -a, -um **est**
dūcimur	ductī, -ae, -a **sumus**
dūciminī	ductī, -ae, -a **estis**
dūcuntur	ductī, -ae, -a **sunt**

Imperfect	*Pluperfect*
dūcēbar	ductus, -a, -um **eram**
dūcēbāris	ductus, -a, -um **erās**
dūcēbātur	ductus, -a, -um **erat**
dūcēbāmur	ductī, -ae, -a **erāmus**
dūcēbāminī	ductī, -ae, -a **erātis**
dūcēbantur	ductī, -ae, -a **erant**

Future	*Future Perfect*
dūcar	ductus, -a, -um **erō**
dūcēris	ductus, -a, -um **eris**
dūcētur	ductus, -a, -um **erit**
dūcēmur	ductī, -ae, -a **erimus**
dūcēminī	ductī, -ae, -a **eritis**
dūcentur	ductī, -ae, -a **erunt**

IMPERATIVE ACTIVE
Sing.: dūc[1]
Plur.: dūcite

IMPERATIVE PASSIVE
Sing.: dūcere
Plur.: dūciminī

[1]There are four verbs whose imperative omits the final "e" in the singular: dīc, dūc, fer, fac.

THE -IO VERBS OF THE 3RD CONJUGATION

PRINCIPAL PARTS OF CAPIŌ

capiō	*I seize*
capere	*to seize*
cēpī	*I have seized*
captus	*having been seized*

INDICATIVE

The six tenses of the indicative active are conjugated like audiō (4th conjugation) except that the -i of capiō is short throughout the present tense.

In the indicative passive, the second person singular, present passive, differs from its parallel in audiō: caperis, audīris.

IMPERATIVE ACTIVE	IMPERATIVE PASSIVE
Sing.: cape	*Sing.:* capere
Plur.: capite	*Plur.:* capiminī

FOURTH CONJUGATION

PRINCIPAL PARTS OF AUDIŌ

audiō	*I hear*
audīre	*to hear*
audīvī	*I have heard*
audītus	*having been heard*

INDICATIVE ACTIVE

Present	Perfect
audiō	audīvī
audīs	audīvistī
audit	audīvit
audīmus	audīvimus
audītis	audīvistis
audiunt	audīvērunt

Imperfect	Pluperfect
audiēbam	audīveram
audiēbās	audīverās
audiēbat	audīverat
audiēbāmus	audīverāmus
audiēbātis	audīverātis
audiēbant	audīverant

Future	Future Perfect
audiam	audīverō
audiēs	audīveris
audiet	audīverit
audiēmus	audīverimus
audiētis	audīveritis
audient	audīverint

INDICATIVE PASSIVE

Present	Perfect
audior	audītus, -a, -um **sum**
audīris	audītus, -a, -um **es**
audītur	audītus, -a, -um **est**
audīmur	audītī, -ae, -a **sumus**
audīminī	audītī, -ae, -a **estis**
audiuntur	audītī, -ae, -a **sunt**

Imperfect	Pluperfect
audiēbar	audītus, -a, -um **eram**
audiēbāris	audītus, -a, -um **erās**
audiēbātur	audītus, -a, -um **erat**
audiēbāmur	audītī, -ae, -a **erāmus**
audiēbāminī	audītī, -ae, -a **erātis**
audiēbantur	audītī, -ae, -a **erant**

Future	Future Perfect
audiar	audītus, -a, -um **erō**
audiēris	audītus, -a, -um **eris**
audiētur	audītus, -a, -um **erit**
audiēmur	audītī, -ae, -a **erimus**
audiēminī	audītī, -ae, -a **eritis**
audientur	audītī, -ae, -a **erunt**

IMPERATIVE ACTIVE	IMPERATIVE PASSIVE
Sing.: audī	*Sing.:* audīre
Plur.: audīte	*Plur.:* audīminī

ALTERNATIVE AND SYNCOPATED VERB FORMS

Latin verbs have the following syncopated forms in poetry:

1. **Perfect active indicative, third person plural: -ēre** can be used instead of **-ērunt** in the perfect active indicative, third person plural. For example, **tenuēre** for **tenuērunt**. Be careful not to confuse such syncopated perfect endings with the endings of present infinitives in the second conjugation, i.e, **tenuēre** ('they held') and **tenēre** ("to hold").

2. **All verbs formed from the 3rd principle part:** The syllables –vi and –ve in the perfect tenses can be omitted. For example, **audierat** for **audīverat** and **amāsse** for **amāvisse**.

3. **Second person singular passive verbs that end in -ris.** The passive ending **-ris** is syncopated by using the ending *-re* in-stead. For example, **amābāre** for **amābāris** "you were loved."

INDICATIVE MOOD

1. The historical present is used to make the past more vivid: Aenēās rem **narrat**. *Aeneas told the story.*

2. **Iam** with any expression of time, plus the present, equals the English perfect: **Iam** diū in Libyā **est**. *He has been in Libya for a long time.* **Iam** plus the imperfect equals the English pluperfect: Iam rēgīna multōs annōs **regnābat**. *The queen had been reigning for many years.*

3. **Dum** (*while*) plus the present equals the English past. **Dum stupet**, rēgīna incessit. *While he stood amazed, the queen came.*

4. **Quamquam** and **etsī** (*although*) take any tense of the indicative: **Quamquam** animus meminisse horret. *Although his mind shuddered to remember.*

5. **Postquam** (*after*), **ubi** (*when*), **simul atque** (*as soon as*), plus the Latin perfect, equal English pluperfect: Haec **ubi** dicta **dedit**, dēseruit. *When he had said these things, he deserted.*

6. Causal clauses introduced by **quod** or **quoniam** employ the indicative: **Superat quoniam** Fortūna, sequāmur. *Since Fortune conquers, let us follow.*

7. Temporal clauses introduced by **cum** and showing true time are in the indicative: Tālia fātus erat **coepit cum** tālia vātēs. *He has said such things when the prophet began to say the following.*

8. Relative clauses are usually in the indicative: Vinum **quod** bonus in cadis **onerāverat** Acestēs. *The wine which good Acestes had loaded in the jars.* (For relative clauses in the subjunctive, see below.)

DEPONENT VERBS (PASSIVE IN FORM; ACTIVE IN MEANING)

There are deponent verbs in all four conjugations. All are regularly passive in form. Exceptions are the future infinitive and the present and future participles, which are active in form.

THE IRREGULAR VERB SUM

PRINCIPAL PARTS

sum *I am*   **esse** *to be*   **fuī** *I have been*   **futūrus** *being about to be*

INDICATIVE

Present	Perfect	Imperfect	Pluperfect	Future	Future Perfect
sum	fuī	eram	fueram	erō	fuerō
es	fuistī	erās	fuerās	eris	fueris
est	fuit	erat	fuerat	erit	fuerit
sumus	fuimus	erāmus	fuerāmus	erimus	fuerimus
estis	fuistis	erātis	fuerātis	eritis	fueritis
sunt	fuērunt	erant	fuerant	erunt	fuerint

IMPERATIVE ACTIVE

Sing.: es   *be (you)*
Plur.: este   *be (you all)*

THE IRREGULAR VERB POSSUM

PRINCIPAL PARTS

possum *I am able*   **posse** *to be able*   **potuī** *I have been able*

INDICATIVE

Present	Perfect	Imperfect	Pluperfect	Future	Future Perfect
possum	potuī	poteram	potueram	poterō	potuerō
potes	potuistī	poterās	potuerās	poteris	potueris
potest	potuit	poterat	potuerat	poterit	potuerit
possumus	potuimus	poterāmus	potuerāmus	poterimus	potuerimus
potestis	potuistis	poterātis	potuerātis	poteritis	potueritis
possunt	potuērunt	poterant	potuerant	poterunt	potuerint

THE IRREGULAR VERB FERŌ

PRINCIPAL PARTS

ferō *I bear* **ferre** *to bear* **tulī** *I have borne* **lātus** *having been borne*

INDICATIVE ACTIVE

Present	Perfect	Imperfect	Pluperfect	Future	Future Perfect
ferō	tulī	ferēbam	tuleram	feram	tulerō
fers	tulistī	ferēbās	tulerās	ferēs	tuleris
fert	tulit	ferēbat	tulerat	feret	tulerit
ferimus	tulimus	etc.	etc.	etc.	etc.
fertis	tulistis				
ferunt	tulērunt				

INDICATIVE PASSIVE

Present	Perfect	Imperfect	Pluperfect	Future	Future Perfect
feror	lātus, -a, -um **sum**	ferēbar	lātus, -a, -um **eram**	ferar	lātus, -a, -um **erō**
ferris	lātus, -a, -um **es**	ferēbāris	lātus, -a, -um **erās**	ferēris	lātus, -a, -um **eris**
fertur	lātus, -a, -um **est**	ferēbātur	lātus, -a, -um **erat**	ferētur	lātus, -a, -um **erit**
ferimur	etc.	etc.	etc.	etc.	etc.
feriminī					
feruntur					

IMPERATIVE ACTIVE	IMPERATIVE PASSIVE
Sing.: fer	*Sing.:* ferre
Plur.: ferte	*Plur.:* feriminī

THE IRREGULAR VERB EŌ[1]

PRINCIPAL PARTS

eō *I go* **īre** *to go* **iī (īvī)** *I have gone* **itum (est)** *it has been gone*

INDICATIVE

Present	Perfect	Imperfect	Pluperfect	Future	Future Perfect
eō	iī	ībam	ieram	ībō	ierō
īs	iistī	ībās	ierās	ībis	ieris
it	iit	ībat	ierat	ībit	ierit
īmus	iimus	ībāmus	ierāmus	ībimus	ierimus
ītis	iistis	ībātis	ierātis	ībitis	ieritis
eunt	iērunt	ībant	ierant	ībunt	ierint

IMPERATIVE	PARTICIPLES
Present	*Present:* iēns (euntis)
Sing.: ī	*Future:* itūrus, -a, -um
Plur.: īte	*Gerundive:* eundus

[1]Adeō, ineō, and transeō are transitive and may therefore be conjugated in the passive. Queō and nequeō are conjugated like eō.

THE IRREGULAR VERBS VOLŌ, NŌLŌ, AND MĀLŌ

Nōlō is made from nē-volō, while mālō is curtailed from magis-volō.

Note: With the exception of the present tense, the forms of nōlō and mālō are similar to volō. For forms not given below, see volō, which is complete. Mālō and volō do not have imperative forms. Mālō is also deficient in participles.

PRINCIPAL PARTS

volō *I wish* **velle** *to wish* **voluī** *I have wished*

INDICATIVE

Present	Perfect	Imperfect	Pluperfect	Future	Future Perfect
volō	voluī	volēbam	volueram	volam	voluerō
vīs	voluistī	volēbās	voluerās	volēs	volueris
vult	voluit	volēbat	voluerat	volet	voluerit
volumus	voluimus	volēbāmus	voluerāmus	volēmus	voluerimus
vultis	voluistis	volēbātis	voluerātis	volētis	volueritis
volunt	voluērunt	volēbant	voluerant	volent	voluerint

PRINCIPAL PARTS
mālō *I prefer*   **mālle** *to prefer*   **māluī** *I have prefered*

INDICATIVE
Present
mālō
māvīs
māvult
mālumus
māvultis
mālunt

IMPERATIVE
(none)

PRINCIPAL PARTS
nōlō *I do not wish*   **nōlle** *to be unwilling*   **nōluī** *I have been unwilling*

INDICATIVE
Present
nōlō
nōn vīs
nōn vult
nōlumus
nōn vultis
nōlunt

IMPERATIVE[1]
Sing.: nōlī
Plur.: nōlīte

[1]These forms, plus a complementary infinitive, express a negative command, but not in Vergil.

The Irregular Verb Fīō

Note: Fīō is the irregular passive of faciō. Even though it is conjugated actively in the present, future, imperfect, it always has passive meaning.

PRINCIPAL PARTS
fīō *I am made*   **fierī** *to be made*   **factus** *having been made*

INDICATIVE

Present	*Perfect*	*Imperfect*	*Pluperfect*	*Future*	*Future Perfect*
fīō	factus, -a, -um **sum**	fīēbam	factus, -a, -um **eram**	fīam	factus, -a, -um **erō**
fīs	*etc.*	fīēbās	*etc.*	fīēs	*etc.*
fit		fīēbat		fīet	
fīmus		fīēbāmus		fīēmus	
fītis		fīēbātis		fīētis	
fīunt		fīēbant		fīent	

Section 6: Infinitives and Indirect Statements

First Conjugation

INFINITIVES

Active		Passive	
Present: parāre	*to prepare*	*Present:* parārī	*to be prepared*
Perfect: parāvisse	*to have prepared*	*Perfect:* parātus esse	*to have been prepared*
Future: parātūrus esse	*to be about to prepare*	*Future:* parātum īrī (rare)	*to be about to be prepared*

Second Conjugation

INFINITIVES

Active	Passive
Present: habēre	*Present:* habērī
Perfect: habuisse	*Perfect:* habitus esse
Future: habitūrus esse	*Future:* habitum īrī

THIRD CONJUGATION

INFINITIVES

ACTIVE		PASSIVE	
Pres.:	dūcere	*Pres.:*	dūcī[1]
Perf.:	dūxisse	*Perf.:*	ductus esse
Fut.:	ductūrus esse	*Fut.:*	ductum īrī

[1]To form the present passive infinitive, replace the -ere of the active form with -ī.

THIRD -IO CONJUGATION

INFINITIVES

ACTIVE		PASSIVE	
Pres.:	capere	*Pres.:*	capī
Perf.:	cēpisse	*Perf.:*	captus esse
Fut.:	captūrus esse	*Fut.:*	captum īrī

FOURTH CONJUGATION

INFINITIVES[2]

ACTIVE		PASSIVE	
Pres.:	audīre	*Pres.:*	audīrī
Perf.:	audīvisse	*Perf.:*	audītus esse
Fut.:	audītūrus esse	*Fut.:*	audītum īrī

[2]The present passive infinitive of the 1st, 2nd, and 4th conjugations is formed by replacing the final -e of the present active infinitive with an -ī.

IRREGULAR VERBS

SUM: INFINITIVES		POSSUM: INFINITIVES		EO: INFINITIVES		FERO: INFINITIVES—ACTIVE		INFINITIVES—PASSIVE	
Pres.:	esse	*Pres.:*	posse	*Pres.:*	īre	*Pres.:*	ferre	*Pres.:*	ferrī
Perf.:	fuisse	*Perf.:*	potuisse	*Perf.:*	iisse	*Perf.:*	tulisse	*Perf.:*	lātus esse
Fut.:	futūrus esse			*Fut.:*	itūrus esse	*Fut.:*	lātūrus esse	*Fut.:*	lātum īrī

VOLO: INFINITIVES		NOLO: INFINITIVES		MALO: INFINITIVES		FIO: INFINITIVES	
Pres.:	velle	*Pres.:*	nōlle	*Pres.:*	mālle	*Pres.:*	fierī
Perf.:	voluisse	*Perf.:*	nōluisse	*Perf.:*	māluisse	*Perf.:*	factus esse
				Fut.:	factum īrī		

DEPONENT VERBS

Present:	farī	*to say*
Perfect:	fātus esse	*to have said*
Future:	fātūrus esse	*to be about to say*

SYNTAX OF THE INFINITIVE

1. In indirect statement when the statement made by a speaker is reported by someone, the subject is in the accusative case, the verb becomes an infinitive, and any subordinate verb becomes subjunctive. In deciding upon the tense of any subordinate verb, the sequence of tenses is followed. In deciding upon the tense of the infinitive, the problem may be resolved by returning the sentence to direct statement, and then using the same tense of the infinitive.

   Dīcit sē **venīre.** *He says that he is coming.* (direct: *I am coming.*)
   Dīxit sē **venīre.** *He said that he was coming.* (direct: *I am coming.*)
   Dīcit sē **vēnisse.** *He says that he has come.* (direct: *I have come.*)
   Dīxit sē **vēnisse.** *He said that he had come.* (direct: *I have come.*)
   Dīcit sē **ventūrum esse.** *He says that he will come.* (direct: *I shall come.*)
   Dīxit sē **ventūrum esse.** *He said that he would come.* (direct: *I shall come.*)

   Subordinate clauses occurring within an indirect statement are often conditions. In such cases, the "if clause" is in the subjunctive and the "conclusion" is an infinitive construction. Dīxit sī īret, nēminem secūtūrum **esse.** *He said that if he should go, no one should follow.*

2. Complementary Infinitive. An infinitive without a subject is used to complete the action of certain verbs:

possum — *I am able*	statuō — *I determine*
volō — *I wish*	cōnor — *I try*
nōlō — *I do not wish*	temptō — *I try*
mālō — *I prefer*	audeō — *I dare*
cupiō — *I desire*	dēbeō — *I ought*
patior — *I allow*	constituō — *I decide*
dubitō — *I hesitate*	parō — *I prepare*
incipiō — *I begin*	dēsistō — *I cease*
	videor — *I seem*

Quae mē aequora **possunt accipere**? *What seas can accept me?*

3. Objective Infinitive. Many verbs which ordinarily would take a complementary infinitive take an objective infinitive when the subject of the verb is different from the subject of the infinitive. Calchās **attollere** mōlem **iussit**. *Calchas ordered (them) to raise a structure.*

4. Subjective Infinitive. Fās est **parcere** gentī. *It is divine will to spare the people.*

5. Historical Infinitive. The infinitive, with a nominative subject, is sometimes used to express past time more vividly. Tum sīc **adfārī**. *Then she spoke thus.*

6. Exclamatory infinitive. This infinitive is used, with an accusative subject, as the main verb in the sentence. Mēne inceptō **dēsistere**? *That I desist from my undertaking?*

Section 7: Participles

First Conjugation

PARTICIPLES

Present Active:	parāns, parantis	*preparing*
Perfect Passive:	parātus, -a, -um	*(having been) prepared*
Future Active:	parātūrus, -a, -um	*(being) about to prepare*

Second Conjugation

PARTICIPLES

Present Active:	habēns, habentis	*having*
Perfect Passive:	habitus, -a, -um	*(having been) held*
Future Active:	habitūrus, -a, -um	*(being) about to hold*

Third Conjugation

PARTICIPLES

Present Active:	dūcēns, dūcentis
Perfect Passive:	ductus, -a, -um
Future Active:	ductūrus, -a, -um

Third -io Conjugation

PARTICIPLES

Present Active:	capiēns, capientis
Perfect Passive:	captus, -a, -um
Future Active:	captūrus, -a, -um

Fourth Conjugation

PARTICIPLES

Present Active:	audiēns, audientis
Perfect Passive:	audītus, -a, -um
Future Active:	audītūrus, -a, -um

Irregular Verbs

Sum:
PARTICIPLES
Fut.: futūrus, -a, -um

Possum:
PARTICIPLES
Pres.: potēns (*Gen.* potentis)

Eō:
PARTICIPLES
Pres.: iēns (euntis)
Fut.: itūrus, -a, -um
Gerundive: eundus

Ferō:
PARTICIPLES—ACTIVE
Pres.: ferēns
Fut.: lātūrus, -a, -um

PARTICIPLES—PASSIVE
Perf.: lātus, -a, -um
Ger.: ferendus, -a, -um

Volō:
PARTICIPLES
Pres.: volēns
(*Gen.:* volentis)

Nolō:
PARTICIPLES
nōlēns
nōlentis (*Gen.*)

Fiō:
PARTICIPLES
Pres.: (none)
Perf.: factus
Gerundive: faciendus

Deponent Verbs

fāns	*saying* (1st conjug.)
fātus	*having said*
fātūrus	*being about to say*

Syntax of Participles

1. Participles are verbals which perform as adjectives. **Moritūra** crūdēlī fūnere Dīdō. *Dido about to die by a cruel death.*

2. The future active participle can express purpose. Fertur **moritūrus** in hostīs. *He is carried off against the enemy in order to die.*

3. Sometimes the present active participle can express purpose. Ībant **ōrantēs** veniam. *They went in order to pray for pardon.*

4. Participles are used with nous and pronouns in the ablative case to express a subordinate clause indicating "when," "since," "although," etc. This construction is called an ablative absolute. **Nūmine laesō** *Because a deity was wounded.*

5. The future active participle combined with sum (first periphrastic conjugation) is a way of expressing futurity, even in past time. Ducem **monitūrus eram**. *I was about to advise the general.*

SECTION 8: GERUNDS, GERUNDIVES, AND SUPINES

FIRST CONJUGATION

GERUND

Nominative:	parāre	*preparing*
Genitive:	parandī	*of preparing*
Dative:	parandō	*for preparing*
Accusative:	parand**um**	*preparing*
Ablative:	parandō	*by preparing*

GERUNDIVE

parandus, -a, -um   *worthy to be prepared*

SUPINE

Acc.	parā**tum**	*to prepare*
Abl.	parātū	*to prepare*

SECOND CONJUGATION

GERUND

Nom.:	habēre
Gen.:	habendī
Dat.:	habendō
Acc.:	habend**um**
Abl.:	habendō

GERUNDIVE

monendus, -a, -um

SUPINE

Acc.	moni**tum**
Abl.	monitū

THIRD CONJUGATION

GERUND

Nom.:	dūcere
Gen.:	dūcendī
Dat.:	dūcendō
Acc.:	dūcend**um**
Abl.:	dūcendō

GERUNDIVE

dūcendus, -a, -um

SUPINE

Acc.	duc**tum**
Abl.	ductū

THIRD -IO CONJUGATION

GERUND

Nominative:	capere
Genitive:	capiendī
Dative:	capiendō
Accusative:	capiend**um**
Ablative:	cupiendō

GERUNDIVE

capiendus, -a, -um

SUPINE

Acc.	cap**tum**
Abl.	captū

FOURTH CONJUGATION

GERUND

Nom.:	audīre
Gen.:	audiendī
Dat.:	audiendō
Acc.:	audiend**um**
Abl.:	audiendō

GERUNDIVE

audiendus, -a, -um

SUPINE

Acc.	audī**tum**
Abl.	audītū

IRREGULAR VERBS

Eō

GERUND

Nominative:	īre
Genitive:	eundī
Dative:	eundō
Accusative:	eund**um**
Ablative:	eundō

SUPINE

it**um**	*to go*
itū	*to go*

Ferō

GERUND

Nom.:	ferre
Gen.:	ferendī
Dat.:	ferendō
Acc.:	ferend**um**
Abl.:	ferendō

SUPINE

lā**tum**	
lātū	

SYNTAX OF GERUNDS, GERUNDIVES, AND SUPINES

1. The gerund is a verbal noun which is declinable only in the singular. The gerund, as a verb, may take an object. **Voluptas vīvendī.** *Desire for living.* Note: There is no nominative form of the gerund. The subjective infinitive is used instead. (See Section 6.)

2. Future passive participles (sometimes called gerundives) express necessity or obligation. **Dicta haud dubitanda.** *Words by no means to be doubted.*

3. The future passive participle used with some form of sum is called the second periphrastic conjugation. Puella **est amanda**. *The girl ought to be loved.*

4. The accusative gerund or gerundive is used in Vergil to express purpose. Cum mihi sē **videndam** obtulit. *When she presented herself to be seen.*

5. The accusative supine (ending in **-um**) is used to express purpose with verbs of motion. **Vēnātum** Aenēās ūnāque Dīdō īre parant. *Aeneas and Dido prepare to go to hunt together.*

6. The ablative supine (ending in **-ū**) is used with certain adjectives to indicate respect. Mīrābile **dictū**. *Marvelous to say.*

SECTION 9: SUBJUNCTIVE VERBS

No meanings are given for the subjunctive because of the great variety of its uses. Each use calls for its own, special translation.

FIRST CONJUGATION

SUBJUNCTIVE ACTIVE

Present	*Perfect*
parem	parāverim
parēs	parāverīs
paret	parāverit
parēmus	parāverīmus
parētis	parāverītus
parent	parāverint

Imperfect	*Pluperfect*
parārem	parāvissem
parārēs	parāvissēs
parāret	parāvisset
parārēmus	parāvissēmus
parārētis	parāvissētis
parārent	parāvissent

SUBJUNCTIVE PASSIVE

Present	*Perfect*
parer	parātus, -a, -um **sim**
parēris	parātus, -a, -um **sīs**
parētur	parātus, -a, -um **sit**
parēmur	parātī, -ae, -a **sīmus**
parēminī	parātī, -ae, -a **sītis**
parentur	parātī, -ae, -a **sint**

Imperfect	*Pluperfect*
parārer	parātus, -a, -um **essem**
parārēris	parātus, -a, -um **essēs**
parārētur	parātus, -a, -um **esset**
parārēmur	parātī, -ae, -a **essēmus**
parārēminī	parātī, -ae, -a **essētis**
parārentur	parātī, -ae, -a **essent**

SECOND CONJUGATION

SUBJUNCTIVE ACTIVE

Present	*Perfect*
habeam	habuerim
habeās	habuerīs
habeat	habuerit
habeāmus	habuerīmus
habeātis	habuerītis
habeant	habuerint

Imperfect	*Pluperfect*
habērem	habuissem
habērēs	habuissēs
habēret	habuisset
habērēmus	habuissēmus
habērētis	habuissētis
habērent	habuissent

SUBJUNCTIVE PASSIVE

Present	*Perfect*
habear	habitus, -a, -um **sim**
habeāris	habitus, -a, -um **sīs**
habeātur	habitus, -a, -um **sit**
habeāmur	habitī, -ae, -a **sīmus**
habeāminī	habitī, -ae, -a **sītis**
habeantur	habitī, -ae, -a **sint**

Imperfect	*Pluperfect*
habērer	habitus, -a, -um **essem**
habērēris	habitus, -a, -um **essēs**
habērētur	habitus, -a, -um **esset**
habērēmur	habitī, -ae, -a **essēmus**
habērēminī	habitī, -ae, -a **essētis**
habērentur	habitī, -ae, -a **essent**

THIRD CONJUGATION

SUBJUNCTIVE ACTIVE

Present	*Perfect*
dūcam	dūxerim
dūcās	dūxerīs
dūcat	dūxerit
dūcāmus	dūxerīmus
dūcātis	dūxerītis
dūcant	dūxerint

Imperfect	*Pluperfect*
dūcerem	dūxissem
dūcerēs	dūxissēs
dūceret	dūxisset
dūcerēmus	dūxissēmus
dūcerētis	dūxissētis
dūcerent	dūxissent

SUBJUNCTIVE PASSIVE

Present	*Perfect*
dūcar	ductus, -a, -um **sim**
dūcāris	ductus, -a, -um **sīs**
dūcātur	ductus, -a, -um **sit**
dūcāmur	ductī, -ae, -a **sīmus**
dūcāminī	ductī, -ae, -a **sītis**
dūcantur	ductī, -ae, -a **sint**

Imperfect	*Pluperfect*
dūcerer	ductus, -a, -um **essem**
dūcerēris	ductus, -a, -um **essēs**
dūcerētur	ductus, -a, -um **esset**
dūcerēmur	ductī, -ae, -a **essēmus**
dūcerēminī	ductī, -ae, -a **essētis**
dūcerentur	ductī, -ae, -a **essent**

THIRD -IO CONJUGATION

SUBJUNCTIVE

The subjunctive tenses of capiō, both active and passive, are formed following the model of *audiō* part, capere, while audiō performs the same way. For example:

ACTIVE		**PASSIVE**	
caperem	audīrem	caperer	audīrer
etc.	*etc.*	*etc.*	*etc.*

FOURTH CONJUGATION

SUBJUNCTIVE ACTIVE

Present	Perfect
audiam	audīverim
audiās	audīverīs
audiat	audīverit
audiāmus	audīverīmus
audiātis	audīverītis
audiant	audīverint

Imperfect	Pluperfect
audīrem	audīvissem
audīrēs	audīvissēs
audīret	audīvisset
audīrēmus	audīvissēmus
audīrētis	audīvissētis
audīrent	audīvissent

SUBJUNCTIVE PASSIVE

Present	Perfect
audiar	audītus, -a, -um **sim**
audiāris	audītus, -a, -um **sīs**
audiātur	audītus, -a, -um **sit**
audiāmur	audītī, -ae, -a **sīmus**
audiāminī	audītī, -ae, -a **sītis**
audiantur	audītī, -ae, -a **sint**

Imperfect	Pluperfect
audīrer	audītus, -a, -um **essem**
audīrēris	audītus, -a, -um **essēs**
audīrētur	audītus, -a, -um **esset**
audīrēmur	audītī, -ae, -a **essēmus**
audīrēminī	audītī, -ae, -a **essētis**
audīrentur	audītī, -ae, -a **essent**

IRREGULAR VERBS

Sum
SUBJUNCTIVE

Present	Perfect
sim	fuerim
sīs	fuerīs
sit	fuerit
sīmus	fuerīmus
sītis	fuerītis
sint	fuerint

Imperf.	Pluperf.
essem	fuissem
essēs	fuissēs
esset	fuisset
essēmus	fuissēmus
essētis	fuissētis
essent	fuissent

Possum
SUBJUNCTIVE

Present	Perfect
possim	potuerim
possīs	potuerīs
possit	potuerit
possīmus	potuerīmus
possītis	potuerītis
possint	potuerint

Imperf.	Pluperf.
possem	potuissem
possēs	potuissēs
posset	potuisset
possēmus	potuissēmus
possētis	potuissētis
possent	potuissent

Eō
SUBJUNCTIVE

Present	Perfect
eam	ierim
eās	ierīs
eat	ierit
eāmus	ierīmus
eātis	ierītis
eant	ierint

Imperf.	Pluperf.
īrem	iissem (īssem)
īrēs	iissēs
īret	iisset
īrēmus	iissēmus
īrētis	iissētis
īrent	iissent

Volō
SUBJUNCTIVE

Present	Perfect
velim	voluerim
velīs	voluerīs
velit	voluerit
velīmus	voluerīmus
velītis	voluerītis
velint	voluerint

Imperfect	Pluperfect
vellem	voluissem
vellēs	voluissēs
vellet	voluisset
vellēmus	voluissēmus
vellētis	voluissētis
vellent	voluissent

Ferō
SUBJUNCTIVE ACTIVE

Present	Perfect
feram	tulerim
ferās	tulerīs
ferat	tulī
etc.	etc.

Imperf.	Pluperf.
ferrem	tulissem
ferrēs	tulissēs
ferret	tulisset
etc.	etc.

SUBJUNCTIVE PASSIVE

Present	Perfect
ferar	lātus, -a, -um **sim**
ferāris	lātus, -a, -um **sīs**
ferātur	lātus, -a, -um **sit**
etc.	etc.

Imperf.	Pluperfect
ferrer	lātus, -a, -um **essem**
ferrēris	lātus, -a, -um **essēs**
ferrētur	lātus, -a, -um **esset**
etc.	etc.

Nolō
SUBJUNCTIVE

Present
nōlim
nōlīs
nōlit
nōlīmus
nōlītis
nōlint

Malō
SUBJUNCTIVE

Present
mālim
mālīs
mālit
mālīmus
mālītis
mālint

Fiō
SUBJUNCTIVE

Present	Perfect	Imperfect	Pluperfect
fīam	factus, -a, -um **sim**	fierem	factus, -a, -um **essem**
fīās	etc.	fierēs	etc.
fīat		fieret	
fīāmus		fierēmus	
fīātis		fierētis	
fīant		fierent	

Most compounds of faciō become -ficiō, while factus becomes -fectus. They are conjugated like capiō. *But* the passive of satisfaciō is satisfīō.

Subjunctive Mood—Independent Uses

1. **The volitive subjunctive**: The volitive subjunctive (sometimes called hortatory and sometimes jussive) indicates a weak command or encouragement. In the first and third persons, singular and plural, the volitive subjunctive is translated into English with the word "let." In the second person singular and plural, the English word "may" is used.

Sīmus fēlīcēs.	*Let us be favorable.*
Doceās eōs.	*May you teach them.*

2. **The optative subjunctive**: The optative subjunctive is a sentence which expresses a wish. The present subjunctive translates with the word "may."

Sīs fēlīx.	*May you be favorable.*
Mē doceās.	*May you teach me.*

3. **The deliberative subjunctive**: The deliberative subjunctive is a question in which something is being considered or deliberated. The present subjunctive is translated into English with phrases like "Am I to . . . ?", "Are you to . . . ?", etc.

Simne fēlīx?	*Am I to be favorable?*
Doceāmne tē?	*Am I to teach you?*

4. **The potential subjunctive**: The potential subjunctive is a sentence which expresses the opinion of the speaker as an opinion. The present subjunctive translates with "should, would" or in potential questions with "can."

Velim tē fēlīcem esse.	*I should like for you to be favorable.*
Velim tē docēre.	*I would like for you to teach.*

Subjunctive Mood—Dependent Uses

1. Any subordinate clause introduced by an interrogative word is an indirect question. It ordinarily depends upon a verb of *knowing, telling, seeing, hearing,* or any expression of uncertainty. The verb of the indirect question goes in the subjunctive. The tense of the subjunctive clause depends upon whether the action of the indicative verb in the main clause is continuing or complete. There are two sequences of tenses (depending upon the two possible times of the main verb):

    A. **Primary** (main verb in present time):

    Scit quid **faciam.** *He knows what I am doing.*
    Scit quid **factūrus sim.**[1] *He knows what I shall do.*
    Scit quid **fēcerim.** *He knows what I did.*

    B. **Secondary** (main verb in past time):

    Scīvit quid **facerem.** *He knew what I was doing.*
    Scīvit quid **factūrus essem.**[1] *He knew what I was going to do.*
    Scīvit quid **fēcissem.** *He knew what I had done.*

2. Purpose Clauses — Adverbial. The purpose clause, usually introduced by ut or nē, modifies the verb. Propriam dicābō **ut** tēcum annōs **exigat**. *I will call her your very own so that she will complete her years with you.* Sometimes Vergil introduces such a clause with a different conjunction: Passus **dum conderet** urbem. *Having suffered to found a city.*

3. Purpose Clauses — Relative. The purpose clause, introduced by a relative prounoun or adjective, is adjectival. Prōgeniem dūcī audierat **quae verteret** arcēs. *She had heard that a race was being produced to destroy the citadel.*

4. Purpose Clauses — Substantive. The clause, usually introduced by ut or nē, is the object of a verb of urging, allowing, willing, desiring, etc. Non **ōrō ut** Latiō **careat**. *I do not pray that he be deprived of Latium.*

5. Result Clauses — Adverbial. **Tantae**ne animīs caelestibus īrae **ut** rēgīna deum tot volvere cāsūs virum **impulerit?** *The celesitial minds have such great anger that the queen of the gods drove the man to undergo so many misfortunes.*

6. Result Clauses — Substantive. Accidit **ut** arma virumque **canam**. *It happens that I sing of arms and a man.*

7. After verbs of fearing. **Vereor** quō sē Iūnōnī **vertant** hospitia. *I fear where the hospitality of Juno turns.* Note: After verbs of fearing, **nē** replaces **ut,** and **ut** becomes negative "that not."

8. **Cum** Clauses (when **cum** means *when, since,* or *although*). **Cum** tē gremiō **accipiet** laetissima Dīdō. *When Dido very gladly accepts you in her lap.*

9. After **Dum** (meaning *until*). Dēlituī **dum** vēla **darent**. *I hid until they would set sail.*

10. Expressions of doubt and hindering: **Dubiī** seu vīvere **crēdant**. *Doubtful whether they believed them to be alive.*

11. Relative Clause of Description — Pietās **quae** tālia **cūret**. *Duty of the sort which might care for such things.*

[1]Since in this instance a future form of the subjunctive is needed, the present and imperfect forms of the verb **sum** are used, along with the future participle, to take the place of the missing form.

SECTION 10: CONDITIONS

SIMPLE CONDITIONS

1. Present: present indicative tense

Sī Dardaniae carīnae lītora Libyae numquam **tangunt**, Dīdō fēlīx **est**.
If the Trojan ships never touch the shores of Libya, Dido is happy.

2. Past: past indicative tense

Sī Dardaniae carīnae lītora Libyae numquam **tetigērunt**, Dīdō fēlīx **erat**.
If the Trojan ships never touched the shores of Libya, Dido was happy.

FUTURE VIVID CONDITIONS

3. Future More Vivid: future perfect and future tenses

Sī Dardaniae carīnae lītora Libyae numquam **tetigerint**, Dīdō fēlīx **erit**.
If the Trojan ships never touch (will have touched) the shores of Libya, Dido will be happy.

4. Future Less Vivid: present subjunctive tense

Sī Dardaniae carīnae lītora Libyae numquam **tangent**, Dīdō fēlīx **sit**.
If the Trojan ships should never touch the shores of Libya, Dido would be happy.

CONTRARY-TO-FACT CONDITIONS

5. Present: imperfect subjunctive tense

Sī Dardaniae carīnae lītora Libyae numquam **tangerent**, Dīdō fēlīx **esset**.
If the Trojan ships were never to touch the shores of Libya, Dido would be happy.

6. Past: pluperfect subjunctive tense

Sī Dardaniae carīnae lītora Libyae numquam **tetigissent**, Dīdō fēlīx **fuisset**.
If the Trojan ships had never touched the shores of Libya, Dido would have been happy.

SECTION 11: VOICE

The voice of a verb indicates whether the subject is acting (active voice) or being acted upon (passive voice). Greek has a third voice (middle) used to indicate that the subject is acting upon itself. English and Latin usually express the middle voice by the use of reflexive pronouns. Vergil sometimes uses passive verb forms as a middle/reflexive. Passive verbs do not normally take a direct object. A Latin verb in the passive voice **with** a direct object is usually being used as a reflexive/ middle voice verb.

Sinūs **collēcta** (est) fluentēs. *She gathered (for herself) the flowing folds (of her garments).*

SECTION 12: INFORMATION ON METER

QUANTITY

The quantity of a syllable in the term used to denote the relative amount of time employed in pronouncing it. About twice as much time should be used in pronouncing a long syllable as a short one.

A syllable is said to be long by *nature*, when it contains a long vowel or a diphthong. It is said to be long by *position* when its vowel is followed by two or more consonants which are separated in pronunciation, or by either of the double consonants x or z, or by j, which was regularly doubled in pronunciation. **H** never helps to make a syllable long, and **qu** counts as a single consonant. Thus the first syllable of **adhūc,** *thus far,* and of **aqua,** *water,* is short.

Except under the metrical accent, a final syllable ending in a short vowel regularly remains short before a word beginning with two consonants or a double consonant.

If a consonant followed by **l** or **r** comes after a short vowel, the syllable containing the short vowel is said to be *common,* i.e., it may be either long or short, according to the pleasure of the one using it.

Note: This is due to the fact that the **l** and **r** blend so easily with the preceding consonant that the combination takes scarcely more time than a single consonant. When the l or r is separated in pronunciation from the preceding consonant, as may be done in all cases, more time is required in pronunciation and the preceding syllable is treated as long.

Observe that the *vowel* in a long syllable may be either long or short, and is to be pronounced accordingly. Thus in **errō,** *wander;* **captō,** *seize;* **vertō,** *turn;* **nox,** *night;* the first *vowel* in each case is short, and must be so pronounced, according to 4, but the syllable is long, and must occupy more time in pronunciation.

A vowel is regularly short before another vowel, or **h,** as **aes-tu-ō,** *boil;* **de-us,** *god;* **tra-hō,** *draw.*
a. This rule does not apply to Greek words in Latin, such as **a-er,** *air;* **I-xī-ōn,** *Ixion* (a proper name).

A vowel is regularly short before **nt** or **nd.** Observe that the *syllable* is this case is long.

A vowel is regularly short before any final consonant except **s.**
a. Some monosyllables ending in **l, r, n,** and **c,** have a long vowel as **sōl,** *sun;* **pār,** *equal;* **nōn,** *not;* **sīc,** *so.*

A vowel is regularly long before **ns, nf, nx,** and **nct.**

Diphthongs and vowels derived from diphthongs or contracted from other vowels are regularly long.

VERSIFICATION

THE DACTYLIC HEXAMETER

One of the most common meters of Latin poetry is the **dactylic hexameter**. It was commonly employed by the Greeks and Romans in epic (narrative) poetry, such as the *Iliad* and the *Odyssey* of Homer, the *Aeneid* of Vergil, and the *Metamorphoses* of Ovid. It is occasionally used in English, as in Longfellow's *Evangeline*. Some of the most beautiful Latin hexameters ever written are those of Vergil and Ovid.

There are six feet in a hexameter (Gr. **hex,** *six;* **metron,** *measure*) verse or line. The first five feet are either dactyls (Gr. **dactylos,** *finger*), i.e., one long syllable followed by two shorts (— ∪ ∪), or spondees, i.e., two longs (— —). The sixth foot is always treated as a spondee (— —).

The final syllable of a hexameter verse may be either long or short (**syllaba anceps**); but for practical purposes in scansion it may be considered long and thus marked.

The Metrical Scheme of a verse is thus:

$$\text{—́ ∪∪ | —́ ∪∪ | —́ ∪∪ | —́ ∪∪ | —́ ∪∪ | —́ ∪}$$

i.e., the first syllable of each foot must be long. It is also given slightly more stress than the other half of the foot. This stress is called the metrical accent.

    a. A short syllable is often lengthened under the metrical accent or before a pause.

The fifth foot of the hexameter is almost always a dactyl. When a spondee is used in this place, it gives the verse a slower movement then usual. Such a verse is then called spondaic.

For metrical purposes each syllable of a Latin verse is considered either long or short, a long syllable occupying approximately twice as much time as short. For this reason a spondaic foot (— —) is considered the metrical equivalent of a dactylic food. (— ∪ ∪).

Observe that only vowels long by nature are marked in the Latin words in this book.

Elision. Whenever a word ends with a vowel, diphthong, or **m**, and the following words begin with a vowel or **h**, the first vowel or diphthong is regularly elided. Elision is not a total omission, but rather a light and hurried half-pronunciation, somewhat similar to grace notes in music.

Hiatus. Occasionally a word ending in a vowel, diphthong, or m is followed by a word beginning with a vowel or **h** and elision does not take place. This is called hiatus.

Semi-hiatus. Sometimes when a word ends in a long vowel or a diphthong and the next word begins with a vowel or **h**, the long final vowel or diphthong is shortened. This is called semi-hiatus.

The vowels **i** and **u** are sometimes used as consonants (**j, v**), as **abiete** (pronounce **abjete**), **genua** (pronounce **genva**).

Hypermeter. Sometimes the final syllable at the end of a verse is elided before a vowel at the beginning of the following verse. This is called synapheia, and the verse whose final syllable is elided is called a hypermeter or a hypermetric verse.

Synizesis. Two successive vowels which do not ordinarily form a diphthong are sometimes pronounced as one syllable for the sake of the meter. This sort of contraction of two syllables into one within a word is called synizesis.

SCANSION

Observe the scansion of the following passage:

Arma virumque canō, Troiae quī prīmus ab ōrīs

Ītaliam fātō profugus Lāvīnaque vēnit

lītora, multum‿ille‿et terrīs iactātus et altō

vī superum saevae memorem Iūnōnis ob īram,

multa quoque‿et bellō passus, dum conderet urbem

īnferretque deōs Latiō; genus unde Latīnum

Albānīque patrēs atque‿altae moenia Rōmae.

In marking the scansion the sign (—) is used to indicate a long *syllable* and the sign (∪) for a short *syllable*. The feet are separated from each other by the perpendicular line (|), the metrical accent is indicated by a (´) over the first syllable of each foot, and elision is indicated by a (‿) connecting the elided vowel with the vowel following.

Hints on the Metrical Reading of Latin Poetry

In reading Latin poetry orally, the words should be kept distinct and no break made between the separate feet, unless there is a pause in sense.

Careful attention should be paid to the meaning of the passage, and the various pauses in sense should be indicated by the voice. Of course the voice should not be allowed to drop at the end of a verse unless there is a distinct pause in sense.

Remember that the rhythm of Latin verse is based primarily upon the regular succession of long and short syllables, that of English primarily on the succession of accented and unaccented syllables.

To obtain facility in reading Latin verse, a considerable amount of it should be memorized, special attention being paid to the quantity, i.e., approximately twice as much time should be given to each long syllable as to a short one.

Caesúra. Whenever a word ends within a foot the break is called caesura. If this coincides with a pause in the verse, it is called the principal caesura, or sometimes simply the caesura of the verse.

A single verse may have more than one caesura, each marked by a pause in sense. The principal caesuras are: (1) After the first long syllable of the third foot; (2) After the first long syllable of the fourth foot.

SECTION 13: FIGURES OF SYNTAX AND RHETORIC

Alliterátion is the repetition of the same letter or sound, as the sound of **v** in **tum vīctū revocant vīrīs,** *then they recall their strength with food.*

Anacolóuthon or want of sequence occurs when the scheme of a sentence is changed in its course.

Anáphora is the repetition of a word or words at the beginning of successive clauses, as **mīrantur dōna Aenēae, mīrantur Iūlum,** *they marvel at the gifts of Aeneas, they marvel at Iulus.*

Anástrophe is an inversion of the usual order of words, as **tē propter,** *on account of you.*

Antíthesis is an opposition or contrast of words or ideas, as **speciē blanda, reapse repudianda,** *charming in appearance, in reality to be rejected.*

Aposiopésis is a breaking off before the close of the sentence, as **quōs ego – sed mōtōs praestat compōnere flūctūs,** *whom I – but it is better to calm the angry waves.*

Apóstrophe is a sudden break from the previous method of discourse and an addressing, in the second person, of some person or object, absent or present, as **Ō patria, Ō dīvum domus,** *O fatherland, O home of the gods!* (In this case the speaker is in Carthage, many miles from his native land, and is making an apostrophe to Troy which had been destroyed by the Greeks.)

Asýndeton is the omission of conjunctions, as **ancora dē prōrā iacitur; stant lītore puppēs,** *the anchor is cast from the prow; the sterns rest on the beach.*

Brachýlogy (breviloquéntia) is the failure to repeat an element which is to be supplied in a more or less modified form, as **tam fēlīx essēs quam formōsissima (es) vellem,** *would that you were as fortunate as (you are) fair.*

Chiásmus is the arrangement of corresponding pairs of words in opposite order, as **Īlionēa petit dextrā laevāque Serestum,** *he sought Ilioneus with his right (hand) and with his left Serestus,* where **Īlionēa** and **Serestum** form one pair and **dextrā laevāque** form the other pair.

Ellípsis is the omission of one or more words which are obviously understood but must be supplied to make the expression grammatically complete, as **Aeolus haec contrā,** *Aeolus thus (spoke) in reply.* The words most commonly omitted are **agō, dīcō, faciō, loquor,** and **sum.**

Enállage is a shift from one form to another, as **vōs** (pl.), **Ō Calliopē** (sg.), **precor,** *I entreat you, O Calliope.*

Eúphemism is the substitution of an agreeable or nonoffensive word or expression for one that is harsh, indelicate, or otherwise unpleasant, as **sī quid eī acciderit,** *if anything should happen to him* (i.e., if he should die).

Eúphony is the effect produced by words or sounds so combined and uttered as to please the ear.

Hendíadys is the expression of an idea by means of two nouns connected by a conjunction instead of by a noun and a limiting adjective, or by one noun limited by another, as **vī et armīs,** *by force of arms;* **vulgus et multitūdō,** *the common herd.*

Hypállage is an interchange in the relations of words, as **dare classibus Austrōs,** *to give the winds to the fleet* (instead of *to give the fleet to the winds*).

Hypérbaton or **Trajéction** is the violent displacement of words, **as per omnīs tē deōs ōrō,** *by all the gods I beg you.*

Hypérbole is rhetorical exaggeration, as **praeruptus aquae mōns,** *a sheer mountain of water,* referring to a great wave of the sea.

Hýsteron Próteron is a reversal of the natural order, as **moriāmur et in media arma ruāmus,** *let us die and rush into the midst of arms.*

Irony is a sort of humor, ridicule, or light sarcasm which states an apparent fact with the manifest intention of expressing its opposite, as **scilicet is superīs labor est, ea cūra quiētōs sollicitat,** *of course this is work for the gods, this care vexes them in their serenity!*

Lítotes or **Understatement** is the use of an expression by which more is meant than meets the ear. This is especially common with the negative. **Nōn indecōrō pulvere sordidī,** *soiled with not unbecoming* (i.e., *glorious*) *dust.*

Métaphor is an implied comparison, as **illa, Troiae et patriae commūnis Erīnys,** *she (Helen), the common curse of Troy and of her land.*

Metónymy is the substitution of one word for another which it suggests, as **Cerēs,** *goddess of grain,* for *grain.*

Onomatopoéia is the use of words of which the sound suggests the sense, as **magnō cum murmure montis,** *with a mighty rumbling of the mountain.*

Oxymóron is the use of words apparently contradictory of each other, as **cum tacent clāmant,** *when they are silent they cry out.*

Paraleípsis or **Preterítion** is an apparent omission by which a speaker artfully pretends to pass by what he really emphasizes, as **nōn dīcō tē pecūniās accēpisse; rapīnās tuās omnīs omittō,** *I do not say that you accepted sums of money; I omit all your acts of rapine;* **praetereō quod nōn mānsit,** *I pass over the fact that he did not remain.*

Personification is an attribution of the element of personality to an impersonal thing, as **aspīrat fortūna labōrī,** *fortune favors our struggle;* **fuge crūdēlīs terrās, fuge lītus avārum,** *flee the cruel lands, flee the greedy shore.*

Pléonasm is the use of superfluous words, as **sīc ōre locūta est,** *thus she spoke with her mouth.*

Polysýndeton is the use of unnecessary conjunctions, as **ūnā Eurusque Notusque ruunt crēberque procellīs Āfricus,** *both the East wind and the South wind and the Southwester rush forth together.*

Prolépsis or **Anticipation** is the use of a word, usually a modifer, before it is logically appropriate, as **summersās obrue puppīs,** *overwhelm the sunken ships,* i.e., *sink and overwhelm the ships.*

Símile is a figure of speech which likens or asserts an explicit comparison between two different things in one or more of their aspects, as **pār levibus ventīs volucrīque simillima somnō,** *like unto the light winds and most resembling winged sleep;* **velutī cum coörta est sēditiō,** *just as when a riot has arisen.*

Sýnchesis is an interlocked order of words, as **saevae memorem Iūnōnis īram,** *fell Juno's unforgetting hate.*

Synécdoche is the use of a part for the whole, or the reverse, as **tēctum,** *roof,* for **domus,** *house;* **puppis,** *stern,* for **nāvis,** *ship;* **mūcrō,** *point,* for **gladius,** *sword.*

Sýnesis is a construction according to sense and not according to grammatical form, as **pars veniunt,** *part come.*

Tmésis is the separation of the parts of a compound word by one or more intervening words, as **quae mē cumque vocant terrae** (for **quaecumque terrae mē vocant),** *whatever the lands that call me.*

A **Transferred Epithet** is an epithet which has been transferred from the word to which it strictly belongs to another word connected with it in thought, as **vēlivolum mare,** *the sail-flying sea,* where *sail-flying* is properly applied to ships which sail the sea rather than to the sea itself.

Zeugma is the junction of two words with a modifying or governing word which strictly applies to only one of them, as **Danaōs et laxat claustra,** *he looses the barriers and (sets free) the Greeks.*

INDEX

GRAMMATICAL AND VOCABULARY SECTIONS

VERGIL TEXTS & ANCILLAE

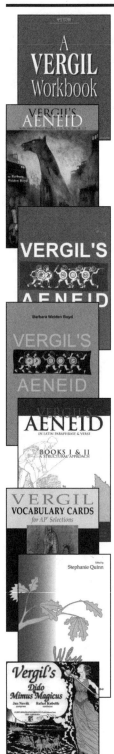

VERGIL WORKBOOK
Barbara Weiden Boyd &
Katherine Bradley

Student Text: xiv + 226 pp (2006) Paperback,
ISBN 978-0-86516-644-1
Teacher's Manual: (2007) Paperback,
ISBN 978-0-86516-656-1

VERGIL'S AENEID
Selections from Books 1, 2, 4,
6, 10, and 12
Barbara Weiden Boyd

2nd Edition Student Text: xxxviii + 410 pp
(2004)
Paperback, ISBN 978-0-86516-584-7
Hardbound, ISBN 978-0-86516-583-0
1st Edition Teacher's Guide: 176 pp (2002)
Paperback, ISBN 978-0-86516-481-9

VERGIL'S AENEID Books I–VI
Clyde Pharr

Illus., xvii + 518 pp. + fold-out
(1964, Reprint 1998)
Paperback, ISBN 978-0-86516-421-5
Hardbound, ISBN 978-0-86516-433-8

VERGIL'S AENEID
10 & 12: Pallas & Turnus
Barbara Weiden Boyd

Student Text: xii + 44 pp. (1998)
Paperback, ISBN 0-86516-415-0
Teacher's Guide: vi + 13 pp. (1998)
Paperback, ISBN 0-86516-428-2

VERGIL'S AENEID
Books I and II
Waldo E. Sweet

Transitional Book
164 pp. (1960, Reprint 1983) Paperback,
ISBN 978-0-86516-023-1

VOCABULARY CARDS
for AP* Vergil Selections
Dennis DeYoung

(2005) 8½" x 11" perforated pages, Paperback,
ISBN 978-0-86516-610-3

WHY VERGIL?
A Collection of Interpretations
Stephanie Quinn, ed.

(2000)
Paperback, ISBN 978-0-86516-418-5
Hardbound, ISBN 978-0-86516-435-2

VERGIL'S DIDO &
MIMUS MAGICUS
Composed by Jan Novák

Limited Edition CD (1997) 40-page libretto
in Latin, English, and German,
ISBN 978-0-86516-346-1

THE LABORS OF AENEAS
What A Pain It Was to Found the
Roman Race
Rose Williams

vi + 108 pp (2003) 6" x 9" Paperback,
ISBN 978-0-86516-556-4

SERVIUS' COMMENTARY
on Book Four of Vergil's Aeneid
An Annotated Translation
Christopher M. McDonough,
Richard E. Prior, and
Mark Stansbury

xviii + 170 pp. (2003) 6" x 9" Paperback,
ISBN 978-0-86516-514-4

VERGIL'S AENEID
Hero • War • Humanity
G. B. Cobbold

xviii + 366 pp., 91 illustrations + 1 map (2005)
5" x 7¾" Paperback, ISBN 978-0-86516-596-0

VERGIL'S AENEID 8 & 11
Italy and Rome
Barbara Weiden Boyd

ix + 96 pp (2006) 6" x 9" Paperback,
ISBN 978-0-86516-580-9

PARSED VERGIL
Completely Scanned-Parsed Vergil's
Aeneid Book I With Interlinear and
Marginal Translations
Archibald A. Maclardy

viii + 344 pp (1899, 1901, reprinted 2005)
6" x 9 Paperback ISBN 978-0-86516-630-1

VERGIL FOR BEGINNERS
A Dual Approach to Early
Vergil Study
Rose Williams

Student Text: x + 86 pp (2006) 6" x 9"
Paperback ISBN 978-0-86516-628-8
Teacher's Guide: vi + 22 pp (2007) 6" x 9"
Paperback ISBN 978-0-86516-629-5

LATIN ALOUD
Audio AP* Selections from Vergil,
Catullus, Ovid, Cicero, and Horace
Robert Sonkowsky

MP3 files on CD (2007) UPC 8-29218-00007-3

VERGIL SELECTIONS
Robert Sonkowsky

Cassette (1985) #23685

**Visit our web site
www.BOLCHAZY.com for complete
descriptions of these
Vergil Texts and Ancillaries.**

BOLCHAZY-CARDUCCI PUBLISHERS, INC.
www.BOLCHAZY.com